THE SKY IS FALLING

UNDERSTANDING AND COPING
WITH PHOBIAS, PANIC, AND
OBSESSIVE-COMPULSIVE
DISORDERS

BY RAEANN DUMONT
WITH A FOREWORD BY
AARON T. BECK

W·W· NORTON & COMPANY
NEW YORK   LONDON

The text of this book is composed in 11/13.5 Berkeley Old Style Book with the display set in Bembo Semibold.
Composition and manufacturing by the Haddon Craftsmen, Inc.
Book design by Margaret M. Wagner

Library of Congress Cataloging-in-Publication Data
Dumont, Raeann.
     The sky is falling : understanding and coping with phobias, panic, and obsessive-compulsive disorders / by Raeann Dumont, with a foreword by Aaron T. Beck.
          p.   cm.
     Includes bibliographical references and index.
     ISBN 0–393–03848–3
     1. Phobias—Popular works.   2. Obsessive-compulsive disorder—Popular works.   3. Panic disorders—Popular works.   I. Title.
     RC535.D85   1996
     616.85'22—dc20   95–30992

ISBN 0-393-31603-3 pbk.

W. W. Norton & Company, Inc., 500 Fifth Avenue, New York, N.Y. 10110
W. W. Norton & Company Ltd., 10 Coptic Street, London WC1A 1PU

1 2 3 4 5 6 7 8 9 0

Contents

FOREWORD   9

ACKNOWLEDGMENTS   11

INTRODUCTION   13

PART I ANXIETY AND MAGIC THINKING

CHAPTER ONE · PATTY CAN'T GO TO THE SUPERMARKET;
JERRY CAN'T LEAVE THE SUBWAY STATION   19

CHAPTER TWO · MY EARLY EXPERIENCE WITH OBSESSIVE-
COMPULSIVE DISORDER (OCD) AND THE REDISCOVERY OF
IT DECADES LATER AS A THERAPIST   31

CHAPTER THREE · STEP ON A CRACK, BREAK YOUR MOTHER'S
BACK: THE FORMATION OF MAGIC THINKING   39

CHAPTER FOUR · WHEN MAGIC THINKING BECOMES A
MALADY: DEFINING PHOBIAS AND OCD   49

PART II TALES OF MAGIC THINKING

INTRODUCTION   55

CHAPTER FIVE · NORA: A STORY OF AGORAPHOBIA   58

CHAPTER SIX · JERRY COULDN'T LEAVE A SUBWAY STATION WITHOUT PICKING UP LITTER   82

CHAPTER SEVEN · JANET, THE BUMP LADY   98

CHAPTER EIGHT · NORM: HIS BRIDGE PHOBIA LED HIM INTO ALCOHOLISM, MESSED UP HIS MARRIAGE, AND ALIENATED HIS KIDS   114

CHAPTER NINE · STEVIE, THE BOY WHO WOULDN'T EAT   132

CHAPTER TEN · GRACIE, THE WOMAN WHO SPENT EIGHT HOURS A DAY BATHING   144

CHAPTER ELEVEN · DAVID FEARED HE COULDN'T HOLD ON TO HIS JOB BECAUSE HE SO DREADED GIVING SALES PRESENTATIONS   161

CHAPTER TWELVE · MR. MORE, THE MAN WHO COULDN'T THROW ANYTHING AWAY   176

CHAPTER THIRTEEN · SAM, THE SNAKE MAN   196

CHAPTER FOURTEEN · JOHANNA, FRANK, LARA, AL: SHORT-TERM SUCCESS STORIES   211

PART III HOW TO CHANGE YOUR OWN MAGIC THINKING

INTRODUCTION   229

CHAPTER FIFTEEN · HOW TO GET BETTER   233

CHAPTER SIXTEEN · HOW TO BE AN EFFECTIVE SUPPORTING
PERSON FOR THE MAGIC THINKER IN YOUR LIFE   266

CHAPTER SEVENTEEN · WHAT ABOUT MEDICATION?   280

APPENDIXES

APPENDIX 1 · GLOSSARY   291

APPENDIX 2 · SELF-HELP WORKSHEETS   295

RESOURCE GUIDE   303

INDEX   307

FOREWORD

FEW professionals know as much as Raeann Dumont about the day-to-day lives, thoughts, feelings, and struggles of people who suffer from phobias and obsessive-compulsive disorders. Only a few people have spent their careers conducting therapy with such clients in the very situations that provoke their anxiety. Of the few therapists who have made this choice, not many have committed themselves to applying the principles of cognitive therapy in these contexts. Raeann Dumont is the rare person who has done both, and she must be regarded as an extraordinary resource to both laypersons and professionals. Her book gives clients and those who care about them a chance to benefit from her unusual range of experience, her insight, ingenuity, and expertise.

The Sky Is Falling is a unique description of how clients think in the situations that produce anxiety, how they think about their lives in ways that keep them from getting better, and how they can work on changing their thinking and reclaiming their lives, which have been lost to fears, rituals, and patterns of avoidance. The book is based firmly on the ideas of cognitive therapy, which Ms. Dumont studied at the Center for Cognitive Therapy in Philadelphia. Ideas are presented clearly and simply, with a good sampling of the author's good-natured humor thrown in. Clients, family members, and other helpers will find *The Sky Is Falling* both enjoyable and useful, a source of direction and hope.

The appearance of *The Sky Is Falling* is well timed. Cognitive therapy has received increasing acceptance as an effective approach to the treatment of depression and other emotional disorders. Studies have shown that anxiety problems such as panic disorders, phobias, post-traumatic disorders, and obsessive-compulsive disorders respond well to cognitive-behavioral interventions.

Many readers have been helped by books that have presented cognitive therapy to a popular audience. Yet the public has been made aware of anxiety disorders largely through presentations that emphasize the role of medication. The publication of *The Sky Is Falling* expands that awareness by offering another valuable perspective on the treatment of phobias and obsessive-compulsive disorders. It is a marvelous book.

AARON T. BECK, M.D.
University Professor of Psychiatry
University of Pennsylvania

ACKNOWLEDGMENTS

The works, thoughts, spirit, and energies of numerous people contributed to the making of this book. Many of the ideas and premises presented herein originated with sources encountered long, long ago (Henny-Penny being a good case in point) which may or may not have been related to anxiety disorders. In too many cases I may have absorbed and adapted the concept and ungraciously forgotten the source. For this I apologize, because I am acutely aware of how indebted a book, a theory, and even a thought is to the work of others that preceded it. There are, however, some people whose contributions have been so influential that they must be noted.

The first of these is Dr. Manuel Zane, M.D., whose pioneering work with anxiety disorders changed the thinking of the psychiatric community. He ushered in the concept of a support person to help the phobic person encounter the context of the phobia. With his generosity of spirit and time he trained me and many others to work with respect and understanding of the disabling fears the phobic person suffers. Martin N. Seif, Ph.D., always offered support and a guiding hand at the Roosevelt Hospital Phobia Clinic when the work was very new and we had little to direct us. Aaron T. Beck, M.D., kindly invited me to participate in his Anxiety Seminars at the Center for Cognitive Therapy at the University of Pennsylvania, where I was exposed to new ways of conceptualizing the thoughts and beliefs that make us who we are. Dr. Beck's teachings on thinking about thinking have had a major influence on my work.

On the many occasions when I felt out of my depth at the Center for Cognitive Therapy, Dr. Ruth L. Greenberg's friendship, encouragement, and support saved the day. Her skill and advice contributed greatly to getting this book published. Herbert Fensterheim, Ph.D., freely shared information and offered encouragement when things looked bleak. Teresa Davis, Ph.D., and I spent many valuable hours together, pushing ideas and thoughts back and forth until they finally took a form that could be communicated simply and clearly to the lay person and still illustrate how complicated and profound treating anxiety disorders can be. Virginia Smith was the guiding force in organizing the material, making it more reader-friendly and preparing it for the appropriate marketing niche. Douglas and Theresa Nicholas have been consistently helpful and supportive with everything; specifically in relation to this book their recommendations on the choice of words, verb forms, and dots and/or dashes have improved its readability. The people at W. W. Norton deserve special accolades for producing a book that I am incredibly pleased to have my name on. My editor Jill Bialosky's careful and incisive editing turned a very nice manuscript into a very fine book, but then, I may be prejudiced.

Last, although not last in my mind or heart, are the many phobic and obsessive-compulsive people I've worked with over the years. All the people who cannot, or would not want to be, mentioned by name are the ones to whom really I owe this book. You allowed me access into your homes and thoughts and were willing to take that incredible leap of faith into my version of reality. To all of you, I owe this book, and I thank you for what you have taught me.

INTRODUCTION

Do you remember Henny Penny? She was the hen from the folktale who woke up one morning feeling out of sorts. While she was pecking around the barnyard having breakfast, an acorn dropped on her head. "The sky is falling, the sky is falling, the sky is falling!" she yelled all over town, causing terror and confusion in the community. The story came to a sad end when Foxy Loxy, knowing it was only an acorn that had fallen, took unfair advantage of the chaos and ate Henny Penny and her hysterical friends for lunch.

Instead of reminding herself that she'd been out late the night before fluffing feathers with the rooster and pecking a bit too much at the fermented corn, Henny Penny translated her unpleasant feelings into a universal condition and an omen of impending disaster. When she felt the acorn on her head, she leaped to the worst conclusion—that the sky was falling. It seemed reasonable to her. I would guess that she had been thinking all morning that something terrible was about to happen. Being hit with an acorn served to confirm her dire premonition.

Henny Penny did what a lot of us do—she formed a conclusion without the benefit of rational thought. This is what I call "magic thinking." You know what magic thinking is—it's knocking on wood after mentioning a bit of good fortune or running out to buy a lottery ticket because numbers 577 appeared to you in a dream. It's saying to yourself, "I feel lucky today," and betting your rent money on a long shot. Magic thinking is believing that the plane you are about to board will crash in spite of the statistical fact that you are hundreds of times safer on a plane than in your own car. Magic thinking is the abandonment of facts, probability, and the laws of cause and effect. Magic thinking is triggered when our fears and anxieties are so extreme they interfere with reality.

The maladies of magic thinking are abundant and diverse. They run the gamut from walking three blocks out of the way in order to avoid crossing the path of a black cat, to compulsive gambling, to crippling phobias and obsessive-compulsive disorders. This book focuses on the last two maladies.

Millions of lives are blighted by irrational fears. The National Institutes of Health estimates that as many as 12 million adults may be afflicted with panic disorder in the course of their lifetimes; another 5 million people suffer from obsessive-compulsive disorders. These maladies are debilitating and can be so severe that they render the victim unable to live a normal life.

Since 1975 I've worked with hundreds of people suffering with anxiety, phobias, and obsessive-compulsive disorders (OCD) and have found that they all share a common characteristic. That characteristic is a propensity for magic thinking.

The Boy Who Couldn't Stop Washing was a groundbreaking book. Prior to its publication in 1989 most people had no idea of the anguish experienced by people who suffer from OCD. With sensitivity and caring, the author, Judith L. Rapoport, described the bizarre rituals her patients felt compelled to perform. The book was an instant success, and it brought to the public's attention a previously neglected population. Although Dr. Rapoport mentions the efficacy of behavior therapy, the main focus of her book was medication. My many clients who read *The Boy Who Couldn't Stop Washing* were glad to have finally found an authoritative depiction of their problem, but were often disappointed that most of Dr. Rapoport's case examples found help through medication.

Current thinking on the treatment of phobias and obsessive-compulsive disorders is a combination of cognitive/behavioral therapy in conjunction with medication. In the course of my work with obsessive-compulsive people, I found that many were unable or unwilling to use medication. Since there is already an abundance of information available on drug treatment, I decided to make the principles of cognitive/behavioral therapy the focus of my book so that the people suffering from phobias and OCD can understand the thinking that creates the problem and free themselves of their debilitating fears and rituals.

The objective of this book is to help readers overcome fears and obsessions by recognizing magic thinking and by learning how to reality test inaccurate beliefs and replace them with principles that will allow them to live securely in the real world of facts and probability.

In the first part of this book I describe how I learned from my phobic and OCD clients that it's possible to experience two different events at the same time. I explore the development of personal belief systems and how we establish "reality" for ourselves, and explain how magic thinking evolves out of faulty cause-and-effect understanding, using my own experience as a young victim of OCD.

In the second section I introduce some of the very fascinating people I've worked with. To illustrate the diversity of the maladies of magic thinking, I've chosen to present a wide variety of phobic and obsessive-compulsive disorders.

The third part of the book is all about how to overcome the maladies of magic thinking. You will find complete directions on how to plan your own treatment program with charts and diaries, and examples of how to use the charts. Another chapter is for those who live with an obsessive-compulsive or phobic person. It will help you to understand and work with the magic thinker in your life. The final chapter is a brief overview of currently used medication. In the back of this book is a glossary. Look through the glossary before you read the rest of the book to be sure that you understand how I'm using the words and terms. You will also find a resource guide for obtaining help and more information.

Phobias and OCD have finally been recognized as a prevalent problem, and outcome studies are reporting that the vast majority of victims *do* get better with proper treatment. I believe that the techniques presented in the program offered in this book will provide significant help to those of you who suffer from magic thinking.

PART I

ANXIETY AND MAGIC THINKING

CHAPTER ONE

PATTY CAN'T GO TO THE SUPERMARKET; JERRY CAN'T LEAVE THE SUBWAY STATION

FROM her window Patty could see the lights of the store. For the hundredth time she looked out the window. Across the street was a beauty parlor, a shoe store, a bakery; and finally, at the corner, a supermarket. It couldn't be more than two hundred feet to the corner, then another forty feet to cross the street. At Patty's pace it would only require a little more than 120 steps to get to the store. Most of that day she had spent pacing the apartment, roaming through her rooms in a fog of anxiety; if she didn't go to the store soon it would be too late; she had to go.

She reviewed her plan again. First, ninety-six to a hundred paces to the corner, staying close to the buildings. Then a dash across the street; finally the last few paces to the doors. Patty felt her panic rising—she couldn't remember the layout of the inside of the store. She closed her eyes, rubbed her forehead, and said to herself, "Remember, remember, where is the frozen food section—think, where is it?" Her temples throbbed with the effort of her concentration; her hands and legs were shaking; her heart was beating wildly—she could not remember any aspect of the store's interior. "This is impossible," she said to herself. "I'm drawing a total blank." She took several slow, deep breaths to calm herself. "I'll just do the best I can," she thought. After several minutes of deep breathing she looked at her watch and said, "I have to go, and I have to go now."

Patty checked her bag to make sure that she had a flashlight, a small can of apple juice, a whistle, and plenty of one-dollar bills. She pulled on her coat, put a piece of wide tape over the bolt of the lock to make sure that it couldn't lock behind her, and left the apartment. Quickly she slipped down the stairs rather than wait in the hallway for the elevator; she hurried through the lobby, but when she reached the street she froze.

Patty felt like she was going to die. Her heart was beating so hard and fast it shook her whole body; her head was throbbing, and her legs felt like rubber bands, threatening to give way at any moment. She leaned against the building, closed her eyes, took three deep breaths, and told herself, "I must. I have no choice, I can't wait. I must go across the street." When there was a break in the traffic, she bolted across the street in the middle of the block and ran to the corner, stumbling along the way. "That's bad luck," she thought. Immediately her symptoms intensified. When she got to the entrance of the supermarket she gulped in air but still felt as though she were suffocating. The bright lights and signs and labels in the store were blinding. She hesitated for a moment to steady herself, then lurched through the store like a crazy person. She grabbed a loaf of bread, instant coffee, cheese, and a jar of peanut butter. When she got to the checkout counter three people were ahead of her. Oblivious to their glares, she squeezed past them, left twelve one-dollar bills on the end of the counter, mumbled, "Keep the change," and fled the store.

On her return to the apartment she dropped the groceries on the floor and collapsed onto the couch in a spasm of trembling and sobbing. "I can't go on like this," she said.

Meanwhile, in another part of town Jerry was still struggling to get out of the subway station. He had left work resolving to go directly home. The night before two hours had passed before he was able to leave the station; he had no intention of repeating that disaster. He had been in the last car of the train, a bad position for him because that meant that he had to walk the entire length of the platform before he could exit the station.

"I won't look," he told himself as the train pulled away. "I'll keep my eyes up and directly ahead of me." But then, as though pulled by a magnet, his eyes jerked down and to the right and fell on a pencil lying on the platform. "Oh God," he thought. "How can people be so careless? Someone could slip on this and really hurt themselves." He quickly picked up the pencil and scanned the platform for other potential dangers. In short order he found an empty Pepsi bottle, several plastic bags, many pieces of paper, and an old sweatshirt; he put all of these in the large canvas bag he always carried for that purpose. "Maybe there was something at the far end of the platform that I missed," he thought. He retraced his steps to the end of the platform, picking up more debris and depositing it in his bag as he went along. By the time he had scoured the platform again and was ready to leave, another train had come in and unloaded another mass of people.

This time Jerry found a newspaper, several candy-bar wrappers, and numerous unidentifiable items, all of which he picked up and deposited into the bag. Then another train came in with even more people, and again Jerry had to scour the platform. Because it was the tail end of the rush hour, trains arrived at the station about every five minutes, and every time a train came in he had to start again from the end of the platform and clean up every bit of trash. By seven o'clock Jerry had dumped several bags full of trash into the litter basket. Now the trains were coming in less frequently, so he stationed himself at the far end of the platform. As soon as a train pulled out he again rushed along the platform following the departing passengers, picking up any newly dropped garbage. Thankfully, he was able to get through the turnstile before the next train came. He busied himself picking up the rubble around the token booth and up the steps. At the street corner he again emptied his canvas bag and checked his watch. "Well," he said grimly. "At least I'm getting a little faster."

WHEN I first heard Patty's story, I said to myself, "Typical agoraphobic." In Jerry's case I said "Obsessive-compulsive disorder." Of course, that was the easy part. Despite negative attitudes toward labels and their apparent limitations, their use is helpful in describing the gross, or obvious, features of maladaptive behavior. (Patty and Jerry's behavior was "maladaptive" because it didn't realistically enhance or secure their survival.) Labels help define a disorder and place it on the curve of human behavior. They provide guidelines for understanding the problem or condition and a rudimentary point from which to start therapy.

I was trained to do in vivo therapy by Dr. Manuel Zane of the White Plains Phobia Clinic in White Plains, New York. He called it "Contextual Therapy" because it is conducted in context of the problem. For instance, if a person is phobic of elevators, we worked in elevators. Most psychiatric literature refers to this method of therapy as "in vivo" (meaning "in life") or "supported exposure." All the terms mean basically the same thing. The person with the problem is required to encounter the feared object or situation with the therapist at his or her side.

First I would have my client establish a hierarchy of things or situations that were anxiety-producing; then together we would work out a plan for exposure to the least anxiety-producing item on the list. The idea was that I, as the therapist, could demonstrate that there really was no objective danger in any of these things or situations, and help the fearful person to confront each of the items on the list and to see that nothing terrible happened. When we had worked all the way through the list, the person would see the folly of these fears and no longer be fearful. In vivo therapy for people suffering with phobias and OCD is the "treatment of choice," and most of the time it works. Some of the time it even works the way I expect it to, but more often it takes unexpected twists and turns, dazzling leaps forward, and despairing retreats.

In the early 1970s when Dr. Zane was training people to do his Contextual Therapy, he preferred to work with people who were not schooled as psychiatrists or psychologists, because he felt that the medical establishment was biased against his type of "interactive" therapy. At that time I was teaching first aid and cardiopulmonary resuscitation at a college in New York. I met Dr. Zane through a colleague. He thought that I would be a beneficial addition to his group because the symptoms of a panic attack can feel similar to those of a heart attack. He felt it would be good for me to teach CPR to the other therapists in training so that they could reassure their clients that what they were experiencing was a panic attack, not a heart attack. We could also point out to the clients that we were prepared to resuscitate them if necessary (of course, it never was).

Although in vivo therapy for phobias and OCD has been recognized as an essential part of treatment, a sad fact of life is that even now, with enlightened attitudes about phobias and OCD, less than 15 percent of people applying for treatment receive the "treatment of choice." In vivo therapy is difficult to schedule (it's not a good idea to be stuck in a tunnel in rush-hour traffic with a claustrophobic client); it's taxing; and most of all it is totally unpredictable. For these reasons most in vivo therapy is done by nonlicensed professionals working in conjunction with clinics or psychiatrists.

While working in vivo with people suffering with phobias and obsessive-compulsive disorders (OCD), I would listen to their accounts of torment and anxiety so intently that my head would ache. I kept telling myself, "I'm missing something here. I still can't figure out why Patty is so afraid of going to the supermarket, or why, if Jerry really doesn't want to pick up all that junk in the subway station, he still does it."

I had plenty of reference books that defined and described the conditions. I had therapy manuals with recommended therapeutic procedures and supervisors to advise me and direct my interventions with my phobic and obsessive-compulsive clients. Finally, I had the clients themselves to tell me about the disorders as they experienced them, but although my brain understood the difficulty they experienced and appreciated their plight, in my heart I knew that there was a serious deficiency in my understanding of the real problem. This gnawing sense of deficiency kept me wondering and thinking.

Each of the unanticipated developments in the therapy process caused me to wonder anew, "What am I missing here? Why is this happening? Why can't I understand what's driving this fear?"

INNER SCENES

My view of myself in the therapy relationship was that of a conduit. I was invited into the lives of people who were locked into senseless, limiting, and destructive ways of behavior. Together we identified the behavior that needed changing, and I took them by the hand (literally, in many cases) and led them to a free and eminently sensible life.

Unfortunately there were several things I overlooked in this theory of therapy. One was the internal events that took place inside the client simultaneously with our in vivo exposure. While I accompanied my client into the feared situation and listened to a detailed account of her view of the situation and her physical sensations, she was also experiencing an inner scene of chaos and disaster that I was totally unaware of. With Patty the supermarket was only the top tenth of her iceberg of terror. What I couldn't see was the catastrophic inner scene going on in her mind. I didn't know enough about OCD to be aware of possible inner scenes, and the clients I worked with were reluctant to tell me about them, either because the scenes were too scary to describe, or they feared they sounded too crazy, or, even more amazing, they weren't aware of the scenes, which took place on a subliminal level. An inner scene produced all of the thoughts and sensations of a real crisis, but nothing tangible to describe.

As best I remember, there was no brilliant moment of discovery. (Retrospectively, I realized that Dr. Zane had been telling me about it all along; he described it as an inner chaos and disorganization of thoughts.) My understanding only gradually widened as I learned more about my clients.

Understanding inner scenes did not necessarily make my work any easier. My first questions were still: What's the behavior and how do we change it? Is there an inner scene? What is the inner scene? How and to what degree is the inner scene affecting the behavior? Where did the inner scene come from? and what keeps it going? Put in the context of my work: Why, while we stand here calmly discussing getting into the elevator and going to the fifth floor, is Jill experiencing scenes of suffocation and death? Why, after touching the bottom of his shoe twenty times, is Tom still convinced that he will die of contamination?

One person I worked with described his inner scenes as being like videotapes in his mind that turned on automatically; once they were on he got helplessly caught up in them. One of his inner scenes was of the commuter train he was riding falling off the tracks and plunging into the icy river below. His scene was accompanied by the physical sensations of falling, chills and shivering, and terror appropriate to an unwilling dip into an icy river.

It is important to note that not all inner scenes are of a calamitous nature. While I was pondering the mystery of inner scenes, I experienced my own on a stiflingly hot, crowded, noisy subway in New York. I was miserable. My feet were getting stepped on; my shoulder was aching from carrying a heavy bag of books; my ribs were periodically jabbed by a sharp, aggressive elbow; I felt suffocated by the smell and heat. Suddenly I was transported to an overcrowded commuter train headed north out of Tokyo toward Matsushima—a trip I had made ten years before.

It must have been the physical similarities that stimulated the memory pathways. The conditions in the Japanese train ten years ago had been equally uncomfortable. But instead of being crabby and irritable then, I was glad to be escaping the August heat of Tokyo, and I was excitedly looking forward to spending three days in a Buddhist hostel near the ocean. Now, instead of feeling victimized by the crowded subway, in total defiance of my current reality I relived the pleasant excitement of the trip to Matsushima. With this singular experience I started to become more aware of my own inner scenes and to ask other people about theirs, especially when I thought their mood didn't match what seemed to me the obvious circumstances.

The source of my inner scene on the train was an experience that I had actually had, and the conditions and physical sensations were similar enough to arouse the memory; but where could my client's inner scene of being on a train falling into the river have come from? My client had never experienced anything even remotely similar to that scene. All his scenes (at least all the ones he reported to me) were of horrible, violent death. The image of the train plunging into the river forced itself onto my client, and he was unable to escape from it. The chaos of his inner scene dominated his mind; it became, at that moment, his only reality. My inner scene made an intolerable situation less so; his inner scene made a neutral situation terrifying.

Is it possible, I asked myself, that all my phobic and obsessive-compulsive clients are responding to an inner scene? Where do these catastrophic inner scenes come from? Why are the hosts of these catastrophic scenes so helpless to control them?

While I was engaged in pondering these questions, a colleague recommended that I read the recently published *Cognitive Therapy and the Emotional Disorders,* by Aaron T. Beck. I experienced a moment of "Eureka" when I read:

> Psychological problems are not necessarily the product of mysterious, impenetrable forces but may result from commonplace processes such as faulty learning, making incorrect inferences on the basis of inadequate or incorrect information, and not distinguishing adequately between imagination and reality. Moreover, thinking can be unrealistic because it is derived from erroneous premises; behavior can be self-defeating because it is based on unreasonable attitudes.

Thus, psychological problems can be mastered by sharpening discriminations, correcting misconceptions, and learning more adaptive attitudes.

This is the kind of basic, commonsense principle that makes us feel that we really knew it all along, but just didn't know how to explain it as well. It demystifies the phobic and obsessive response; it explains why people can be intelligent and highly functioning in most aspects of their life, but fall into quivering confusion in their phobic situation.

The client who was convinced that he would die of contamination by touching the bottom of his shoe suffered from "faulty learning," and "making incorrect inferences on the basis of inadequate or incorrect information." The man who had a panic attack on the commuter train was not "distinguishing adequately between imagination and reality."

This approach gave me a precise way of thinking about a problem and a specific course to pursue. Together, my client and I must uncover the frightening images and learn to distinguish between imagination and reality, or understand the inadequate or incorrect learning on which the incorrect inferences are based.

The guidebook used by therapists is the *Diagnostic and Statistical Manual-IV*. For short we call it the "DSM Four." It gives names, numbers, and descriptions of every imaginable emotional disorder. When we get together at conferences or meetings, we might describe someone we work with as having "G.A.D. and Axis II galore." That's a short way of saying that the person suffers from Generalized Anxiety Disorder and also has other serious problems that complicate therapy. On insurance forms and other documents that require a diagnosis we use a numbering system prescribed by the DSM Four to describe the condition. The *Diagnostic and Statistical Manual* is a work in constant progress; it is continually being reassessed and revised to keep up with new findings and to hone the descriptions and conditions of each of the disorders to an ever finer point. It probably never will be able to convey adequately the subtle variations and nuances exhibited by the diverse individuals we work with, but it serves as a useful guidebook to what might otherwise be confusing terrain.

The DSM Four lists Obsessive-Compulsive Disorder (OCD) with the Anxiety Disorders, and Obsessive-Compulsive Personality Disorder (a person who is perfectionistic, preoccupied with details, inflexible, hoards useless things, and is frequently a workaholic) with Personality Disorders. There is tremendous overlap with phobias, obsessive-compulsive disorders, and obsessive-compulsive personality disorders. In many cases it would be extremely difficult to draw a fine line where phobic behavior ends and obsessive-compulsive behavior begins.

In this book I will be focusing on "distorted views of reality" and "magic thinking," which are the essential ingredients of phobias and OCD. (They are also the essential ingredients of many other emotional problems, but these are the two I specialize in.) I use the terms "phobic" and "obsessive-compulsive," although in reading the case histories you will see that most people's lives aren't nearly so neat and tidy that a single label can describe their suffering. A major problem that causes difficulty in normal life functioning creates a damaging ripple effect, which will spread to all areas of life.

Consider the case of Norm (Chapter 8), who suddenly developed a phobia of driving over bridges. To ease his anxiety, he began having a few stiff drinks with breakfast to aid in driving over the bridge between his home and his office. When that ceased to work, despite an increase of alcohol, he quit his job. In time his wife couldn't stand him; his kids thought he was a jerk; and he became depressed. He increased his drinking to relieve his depression, guilt, and anxiety. By the time I saw him in therapy, his marriage was a mess, he was suicidally depressed, alcoholic, and still phobic of driving over bridges. Helping Norm to understand his distorted view of reality concerning his fear of bridges had a curative ripple effect in terms of dealing with his depression and family matters.

Almost two thousand years ago Epictetus said, "Men are not moved by things but the views which they take of them," a truly wonderful and profound statement. But why is it that we view things one way and not another? Why do we mess up our lives so badly just because we view situations or things in a negative or distorted manner? And of course, more important, what do we do about it?

I do not subscribe to the "secondary gain" philosophy, which claims that some people like being irrational or difficult because of the questionable rewards of special attention or services their condition gains for them. I really believe that everyone would prefer to be healthy, wholesome, and whole, if only they knew how.

It is my hope that this book will provoke a hard and careful look at reality—my clients', my own, and yours—and provide a way to develop a new, more constructive perspective for dealing with magic thinking.

CHAPTER TWO

MY EARLY EXPERIENCE WITH OBSESSIVE-COMPULSIVE DISORDER (OCD) AND THE REDISCOVERY OF IT DECADES LATER AS A THERAPIST

WHEN I was four years old I contracted a terrible case of impetigo that started on the upper right corner of my mouth and quickly spread to my entire lower face. Aside from making me look scrofulous, it was unbearably painful. If I talked, ate, smiled, or touched my face, it hurt. To me at that time, it was just about as bad a thing as could happen, but the panicky reactions I received from the adults in my life suggested that it could get a lot worse. It could spread over my entire face; it could get in my eyes and make me blind; it could leave scars all over my face. The impetigo didn't get worse or do any of those things I feared. The doctor gave my mother a salve that she put on the raw skin after washing off the blisters. Twice a day for a month I screamed and cried while my mother scraped off the white scabs and mopped the underlying ooze from my face so that she could pat on the salve.

The doctor told my mother that I probably got the impetigo from putting dirty things such as toys or unwashed fruits in my mouth, so from that day forward she washed everything I came in contact with—everything. She washed my pencils and my crayons; she washed my dolls and my doll's tea set (just in case); she washed my foods. If the grocer offered me a strawberry while we were out shopping, I wasn't allowed to accept it (she told him I was allergic—a word of marvelous convenience). And most of all she washed me. When I came in from playing outside, after I used the toilet, after playing with the dog, or just because I was standing around and hadn't been washed for a while, my mother scrubbed me from the tips of my fingers to my elbows. The subsequent occasional outbreaks of impetigo (never as severe as the first, due to my mother's readiness with the magic salve) caused her to intensify her efforts.

The cause and effect were etched indelibly in my mind: Something dirty in my mouth equals the pain and suffering of impetigo. I don't really know if this was an accurate cause-and-effect equation. After every onset of impetigo I could always recall some incident that might explain it (putting my fingers to my mouth before washing them or eating unexamined grapes at a friend's house).

When I was six or seven there was a dreadful polio epidemic. People who grew up after the development of the Salk vaccine can't imagine the terror associated with polio. Images of its devastation were everywhere—kids with withered arms, pictures of iron lungs, a famous man in a wheelchair, and the March of Dimes poster kid with his iron-bound legs. People were advised to avoid crowds, so they kept their kids at home all summer. Birthday parties were cancelled, camps and public swimming pools were closed. The prevailing feeling was that of being under siege. My hand-washing was intensified. Outside were unseen germs ready to wreak havoc on my person, and my defense was to wash.

I suffered considerable social embarrassment because of my hand-washing. "Sissy (a name bestowed on me, I believe, because of my position of little sister, not my cowardice in the face of danger) has to go home and wash." Dirty Donnie, a playmate forced on me by virtue of the fact that his parents were friends of my parents, would pee in his pants while we were playing and he would not only not rush home to wash up and change into clean clothes, but would torment me with threats of contaminating me with his urine until I could bear the fear no longer and had to run home to wash. With malice in my heart I waited for Donnie to die of his dirtiness, or at least show signs of weakening, but he never did.

As I got older, I noticed the grubbiest sorts of kids eating their sandwiches with hands so dirty they discolored the bread—and nothing bad happened to them. I saw people in their gardens pick tomatoes, brush the soil off the skin, and eat them—and nothing bad happened to them. I saw numerous violations of the "clean hands equals safety; dirty hands equals disaster" rule, and nothing bad happened to any of the violators. Gradually I began to question the veracity of the rule.

But the problem was more complicated than merely seeing the error and changing it as you would the transposed numbers in an incorrectly balanced checkbook. When my hands were dirty, or I thought they were, they had a special feel about them. They felt huge and as though they were vibrating. I tended to hold them away from myself. Along with the sensation in my hands came a gripping feeling in my stomach. My thoughts were, "I can't feel right until I wash my hands. I must feel right immediately or something bad will happen." The issue shifted from the dirt on the hands to the feeling in the stomach and the vibrating feelings I felt in my hands. So though I could tell myself that my hands weren't really dirty, they just had a little newsprint on them, I still felt the need to wash them.

There was a delay in the relaying of the message. My head was saying, "Not dirty—no danger," but my stomach was still saying, "Danger, danger, do something quick!"

I had outgrown my tendency for impetigo, and the Salk vaccine made us safe from polio, but I continued to wash my hands into my early teens. My mother, forgetting her contribution through her unrelenting scrubbing of me, watched me washing my hands one day and said, "I think that's a 'Lady Macbeth complex'; you must feel guilty about something." God knows, as a healthy, relatively normal adolescent I felt I had everything to be guilty about. But after she said it, the hand-washing became a screaming indictment of a person who does wicked things. The solution to the problem became an even bigger problem, and I found myself between a rock and a hard place. I had to either stop responding to the urgent demands of my stomach or wear the flaming banner of a defective person.

After years of conscientious effort my head now rules, but occasionally I will still get that feeling in my stomach when I am not able to wash my hands after handling something dirty or slimy. My preference to wash my hands before eating and after using the bathroom persists, and I don't really intend to change it unless the alternative is starvation or eternal constipation.

Although my mother had made me self-conscious about how often I washed, I don't think my behavior was ever really identified as a problem. Certainly I had never heard the term "obsessive-compulsive disorder." In those days the physicians treating disorders of childhood considered OCD just slightly more common than the Abominable Snowman.

Decades after my experience with OCD, a client I was working with came to me for help with a condition prediagnosed as "mysophobic" (a phobia of dirt or dust). I had had several years of experience working with phobias such as agoraphobia, claustrophobia, and phobias of bridges, tunnels, cats, and bugs. But mysophobia was different, though I couldn't quite put my finger on why or how.

The techniques of working with mysophobic clients were the same as with my "regular phobic" people. But these clients were less willing to give information; they would suddenly go silent and cut me out during exposure exercises; they would experience very high levels of anxiety without any apparent phobic stimuli. During one of my supervision sessions I spoke with Dr. Zane about my confusion. "Yes," he said, "they are different because the context of the phobia is in their mind." Unfortunately, it took me several more months of experience to understand what Dr. Zane was saying.

One day I was working with one of the mysophobic people, and we were talking about an exposure task that involved taking a shoe out of a paper bag. She jumped up and said, "I can't, I just can't. I have to wash," and headed for the washroom.

"But you haven't touched it yet," I said. And suddenly from the dark recesses of my mind came the memory of my own huge, vibrating hands and that gripping feeling in my stomach that could only be relieved by washing. I instantly understood what Dr. Zane meant when he said "the context of the phobia is in their mind," and the difference that had seemed so elusive became crystal clear.

With a "regular phobic" person the phobic stimuli are "out there" (the bridge, the cat, the unsafe place); occasionally there is a physical sensation such as a rapid heartbeat or dizziness. But those suffering from what I finally recognized as an obsessive-compulsive disorder fear their own thoughts. The thoughts are always of impending death or disaster. They may be brilliantly clear catastrophic images. Always, they seem to be uncontrollable. They interject themselves into the mind of the sufferer and overtake the cognitive functions. They cannot be dismissed; they cannot be reasoned with; they leave the person feeling utterly helpless to do anything except perform the senseless ritual that will neutralize the devastating thoughts.

A phobic person can have some sense of control by avoiding situations that create anxiety, but a person suffering from OCD can never be successfully avoidant, because the potential for devastating thoughts is always lurking there in the shadows of the mind, waiting for a quiet or undefended moment to take over.

An agoraphobic woman can raise the children, keep house, and maintain normal social contacts. Although she might be severely limited by the agoraphobia, she could still have a semblance of normality in her life. In contrast, OCD victims are often totally consumed by their rituals. They may spend eight or twelve hours a day washing, or repeat the same action (dressing and undressing; going up and down stairs) over and over again, fearing that it wasn't done right the previous times, until the rituals become their whole life. My phobic clients could easily tell me what they feared. ("I'm afraid to drive through the tunnel because I might get stuck and suffocate or go crazy." Or "I'm afraid to leave the house because I might get sick, or lost, and not be able to get home in time to save myself.") As long as they are not in the phobic situation the fearful thoughts can not arouse their anxiety. But OCD clients found the thoughts themselves so fearful, unacceptable, and anxiety-producing that they strongly resisted acknowledgment of them. Because the content of their thoughts is usually horrific ("I thought of stabbing my child"; "I thought of having sex with the devil."), the person forms a negative judgment of himself for having such disturbing thoughts ("I must be a murderer if I could think such a thing"; "I am a disgusting person for having such thoughts.").

In vivo exposure to the phobic object or situation is the

backbone of my work with phobic people. The purpose is to help the person control the anxiety without leaving the phobic setting. I use a similar approach with my OCD clients by encouraging them to touch something they deemed dirty or dangerous and then help them resist magic thinking, performing their ritual, or saying their litany.

On one occasion I was helping a woman in her home to expose herself to areas of possible "contamination" caused by workmen who had recently painted her apartment. She suddenly became very upset and said, "I have to wash. I touched the radiator; now I'm poisoned."

"But you can't have touched the radiator," I said. "We're standing eight feet away from it."

"I'm poisoned, I can feel the poison all over me," she said.

Nothing I could say or do altered her conviction that she was poisoned. She spent the next three hours in the shower scrubbing herself. I tried to figure out what had happened. How could she possibly have thought that she had touched the radiator when she was nowhere near it? How could she have been so convinced that whatever was on the radiator was so toxic, when obviously the painters must have touched it, and it's probably used in every apartment in the building?

Why did the streets hold such terror for Patty, although she could see from her window that people went about their daily business without anything terrible happening to them?

Why had I been so convinced that Dirty Donnie's urine would poison me when it clearly had no deleterious effect on him? How do we come to our convictions? How do we know what we know? How do we decide what is "real"? Why are things "real" for some people and not for others?

The issue of what is real, and how we can test, or demonstrate, or prove a "reality" seemed to be crucial in understanding the enigma of phobias and OCD.

Over the years I continued to gather information (mostly from my clients; at that time there wasn't much published material on phobias and OCD) and worked at compiling developmental profiles on the people who suffered from these conditions.

Although mine was a relatively mild and uncomplicated obsessive-compulsive disorder, the underlying pattern is the same as that of Howard Hughes, who feared contamination, and the many OCD and/or phobic clients I've worked with.

The erroneous premises that contribute to phobic fears and obsessive-compulsive disorders are these:

1. A personal belief system of the self and of how the world works based on faulty information.
2. An environment or aspect of the environment that is perceived as threatening.
3. Real-life experiences that are assessed on the basis of the faulty information, thereby seeming to confirm the belief system.
4. A solution based on magic thinking or avoidance.

CHAPTER THREE

STEP ON A CRACK, BREAK YOUR MOTHER'S BACK: THE FORMATION OF MAGIC THINKING

MELODY, our neighbor's seven-year-old daughter, is walking down the street just ahead of me. She's looking down at the sidewalk and changing her gait from time to time with funny little hops. I catch up with her and ask her what she's doing.

"I can't step on the cracks," she says.

"Why not?" I ask.

She looks at me as if I've just come from outer space and says, "Step on a crack and break your mother's back."

"Oh," I say, feigning surprise, "do all children have to avoid stepping on cracks?"

"I guess so," she answers.

"Do you know of any mothers whose backs have been broken?"

By this time Melody has clearly lost interest in the subject and doesn't care to pursue it any longer; she sets off in another direction, and answers over her shoulder, "No, but it could happen."

We can safely say that Melody's cause-and-effect reasoning is certainly false. More likely, though, it never occurred to her to question the causation between stepping on a crack and breaking her mother's back, because so much of what happens in her life seems like magic. When she walks into her bedroom, she flips a little switch and the lamp on her night table across the room turns on. At her age, she wouldn't be able to explain that causation any more than she could the possibility of her mother's back being broken by her child stepping on a crack. Superstitions develop when we attempt to control an unknown universe filled with terrors.

A year ago Melody's grandmother became ill and began to waste away. It was a mysterious and frightening time for Melody. One day she asked her mother if her grandmother was going to die. Angrily, her mother said, "Don't say that," as though saying it could make it happen. Melody didn't say it again; she even tried to stop herself from thinking it, but often the thought would just pop into her head. When her grandmother died, Melody felt responsible because of her thoughts (thinking or talking about Grandma dying equals Grandma dying). Now a part of her "reality" is that thoughts or words can be a powerful magic that makes things happen.

Melody has probably developed her private system of counter-magic: saying or performing specific rituals to cancel out bad thoughts. If she should have an angry or hurtful thought about her mother and become fearful that something bad might happen because of the bad thought, she counters it with good magic that will undo the bad magic. Melody knows the counter-magic works because in spite of angry thoughts toward her mother, nothing bad has happened to her. The continuance of Melody's belief is dependent on the continuance of the coincidences. As long as she continues with the ritual and nothing bad happens to her mother, the belief in the ritual will be confirmed. Because Melody's environment is mostly secure and healthy, in time she will probably realize that she's been walking to school for weeks without avoiding the cracks in the sidewalk and her mother's back is fine.

She will also learn that wishes (good or bad) very rarely come true. Her evaluation of her experiences will create a more objective "reality" that will allow her to make predictions about future events and to feel secure in her world without depending on ritual.

Have you ever knocked on wood after mentioning good fortune? Thrown salt over your shoulder? Changed plans so that an event would not take place on Friday the thirteenth? Torn the closet apart looking for your lucky hat so you would be prepared for an important golf game? If so, you are a magic thinker—part of the grand army of tradition that wards off bad luck or evil by performing a ritual or subscribing to a superstition.

Webster's *Third New International Dictionary* defines a ritual as "any practice done or regularly repeated in a set, precise manner so as to satisfy one's sense of fitness and often felt to have a symbolic or quasi-symbolic significance." A superstition is "a belief, conception, act or practice resulting from ignorance, unreasoning fear of the unknown or mysterious . . . trust in magic or chance, or a false conception of causation . . . " How does magic thinking relate to phobias and obsessive-compulsive disorders—to rituals and superstitions?

Einstein once said, "It is the theory that determines what we can observe." Because we believe something to be true, we see only the facts that confirm our belief. Take the Iowa farmer who walked three times around his house and barn, snapping his fingers, every night before retiring. After many years of observing this strange ritual his neighbor finally asked him why he did that. "It's an old Indian technique to keep the tigers away," explained the farmer. "But there aren't any tigers within thousands of miles of here," said the startled neighbor. "I know," replied the farmer with a smile. "Effective, isn't it?"

Because a belief system is created without conscious intent or awareness, it appears to exist as a universal reality. Melody and the farmer were both caught in intellectual traps. They had developed faulty cause-and-effect understanding and a closed system of beliefs and habits that prevented contradictory information from being recognized.

WHAT IS REALITY?

How do we know what we know? When we accept something as a fact, how do we know that it is factual? What makes us believe that our "reality" is the real "reality"? If I were to point to the sky on a sunny day and ask a hundred English-speaking people if they knew what color it is, the vast majority would not doubt that the sky is blue. We know by consensus because all of us English-speaking people have agreed to call that particular wavelength of light blue. But our way of knowing the world and who we are in it is not based on consensus or hard, immutable facts. We start forming our beliefs the moment we are born as an effort to understand and control experiences through our awareness of cause and effect.

Our personal belief systems are based on our experiences and our evaluation of those experiences. From the moment of our birth (and probably even before) we are information processors. We catch on very early in life that some things make us feel bad and some things make us feel good. Naturally, most of us would rather feel good, and we repeat the actions that give us pleasure and avoid those that make us feel bad. We may discover that crying gets us dry bottoms and a warm bottle, so crying seems to be a solution to discomforts in life. However, the "outside" reality may be that every four hours our caretaker changes diapers and gives us a bottle, while the infant thinks that she is causing things to happen because the things that happen coincide with crying. This is an example of an erroneous cause-and-effect belief based on the limited reality of an infant. All of us, in every stage of life, have a limited reality.

Our personal belief system has been constructed by observing coincidences (crying equals dry bottom and a warm bottle; pulling the cat's tail equals a scratched hand). By observing coincidences and evaluating experiences we develop a belief of cause and effect and create a sense of control or understanding of the world. The continuance of a belief is dependent on the continuance of the coincidences. If the expected coincidence repeatedly fails to occur, the belief will be questioned. Evaluation of our experiences creates a "reality" that allows us to make predictions about future events.

There are many problems with this kind of theory-building, however. The most obvious is the circular character of "the theory determines what we can observe" . . . but the theory is based on what we observe. Another problem is our erratic memory retrieval system. Events are not always remembered accurately or in the proper sequence. During periods of trauma or intense arousal, memory tracks are laid down more indelibly than during less dramatic periods. If we have experienced a traumatic event, we will remember it more fully; the sounds, the smells, the colors will be more vivid. And everything in our memory that was associated with the trauma becomes bigger than life—bad, dangerous, and to be avoided at all costs.

Few of us make it through childhood without experiencing trauma: getting lost or separated from our mother while shopping; a serious illness or a stay in the hospital; loss of important people through death, divorce, or moving to a new city.

So it is safe to say that most of us have an imperfect belief system. But if our lives have been basically stable we are able to muddle along, safeguarding ourselves by knocking on wood or throwing salt over our shoulder.

DEVELOPMENT OF A MALADY OF MAGIC THINKING

What happens when a person's life is not secure or healthy? What happens when a child gets contradictory messages from his parents? When the parents say "I love you," but their behavior is hateful or hostile? When a child loses the people she loves through death or divorce, or when her parents are emotionally disturbed or themselves have distorted cause-and-effect beliefs?

This person may grow up doubting her own reality. She may view the world as a dangerous place if she frequently sees her parents out of control or excessively fearful. She may feel that she needs a sense of control over her environment in order to feel safe. How does she get control of her environment? She resorts to the world's oldest solution—magic and ritual. If a child comes in contact with a possible contaminant, if she has unacceptable urges, if she thinks unacceptable thoughts, she may believe that magic or ritual will undo the damage and make the world safe again.

DOUBTING REALITY

A person with the malady of magic thinking questions her own experiences. She might think: How do I know that I put milk in the baby's bottle and not ammonia? Although there is no ammonia in the house and the bottle smells like milk. Or a person may become terrified and say, "If I get into that elevator it will get stuck and I'll suffocate or go crazy," although he has been watching the elevator go up and down for twenty minutes without any evidence of problems, and he knows perfectly well that people don't suffocate in elevators.

COGNITIVE DISTORTIONS

Like Henny Penny magic thinkers engage in a vast repertoire of mistaken conclusions based on the following cognitive distortions:

1. *Catastrophizing*: The worst will always happen—I won't just be uncomfortable, I'll faint, die, or go crazy.
2. *Overgeneralizing*: Because I felt horrible once I'll always feel horrible—I made a mistake, I never do anything right.
3. *Emotional Reasoning*: I must be going to faint because I think that I'm going to faint. I think that I look like a jerk, therefore I am a jerk.
4. *Either/Or Thinking*: Either I'm perfect or I'm terrible. Either I feel good or I'm such a mess I can't function.
5. *Ignoring the Positive*: Just because I didn't faint, die, or go crazy the last twenty times doesn't mean that I won't this time.

THE POWER OF THOUGHTS

An important part of the magic thinker's belief system is the belief that a thought can make things happen. Melody believed that thinking about her grandmother dying would cause her to die. Most of us grow up wishing on stars, wishing on four-leaf clovers, wishing when we blow out the candles on our birthday cake. We've been encouraged to believe that our wishes or thoughts can either make things happen or prevent them from happening. An OCD sufferer says to herself, "Because I think I put ammonia in the baby's bottle, the baby will die," or a phobic person might believe that because he thinks he might get stuck in the elevator, he will get stuck.

When we abandon cause-and-effect thinking, life gets very complicated because, as we discovered earlier, there is "good magic" and "bad magic." If we think a bad thought, we believe it will cause something bad to happen. And we learn that we can undo the bad with good magic (saying a litany or performing a ritual). The anxiety that the magic thinking creates is controlled by the rituals and avoidance, but the rituals and avoidance lead to phobias and OCD.

CONTAGION OF PROPERTIES

To further complicate the problem, some magic thinkers believe that contamination or harmful properties spread. The woman who thought she put ammonia in her baby's bottle would likely throw out the bottle and scrub all the surfaces the bottle might have touched. A person with agoraphobia who suffered a panic attack in the supermarket would fear not only returning to the supermarket, but the street approaching the supermarket and the parking lot as well.

NEED FOR CERTAINTY

Another aspect of magic thinking is a need for absolute certainty. A magic thinker does not consider probabilities; if there is any possibility of disaster, the situation is viewed as though disaster were inevitable. The thoughts of imminent disaster create the same sensations one might experience in the face of an actual disaster.

UNREALISTIC SENSE OF RESPONSIBILITY

Many obsessive-compulsive (OC) victims suffer from an overblown sense of responsibility. They believe that every act or neglect to act on their part can have worldwide consequences. One person I worked with lived with the crushing guilt that she was responsible for the assassination of President Kennedy because she had told a friend that she didn't like Kennedy. Another felt responsible for the deaths during the 1989 California earthquake.

"I should have warned them," he said.

"Did you know that it was about to occur?" I asked.

"No," he answered. "But I should have."

Another felt impelled to pick up every piece of broken glass and litter for fear of being held responsible for someone getting injured. Another thought that if she were to throw her pantyhose out in Manhattan it would cause a murder. And another couldn't leave his shoes misaligned in the closet because it might cause harm to his daughter who was away at college. When visiting friends or relatives, some OCs insist on rearranging kitchens and unplugging lamps and appliances in order to prevent a fire. This is rarely considered an endearing trait.

AVOIDANCE AND RITUAL

An important part of the malady of magic thinking is the belief that the physical sensations of anxiety are dangerous. Even though the person may have experienced them thousands of times without dying or going crazy, every experience of anxiety is regarded as an imminent threat to physical or psychological well-being that must be avoided or extinguished immediately.

Phobic people tend to avoid anxiety-producing situations. The agoraphobic woman will get friends or relatives to do her shopping. The man who is phobic of elevators will claim that he walks up ten flights of stairs for the exercise.

The OC relieves the physical sensations of anxiety and the sense of helplessness by performing a ritual, but because the person questions his own reality he may not be certain (and he *must* be certain) that he has performed the ritual correctly, so he has to repeat it. He may have to repeat it several times before he is certain that it has been done correctly and he is safe from the danger. The need to repeat the rituals may become so overwhelming that the person spends most of his day in the bathroom washing or hours driving back and forth along the road checking to see if he has accidentally hit someone. The ritual becomes an unwieldy monster. Where once the ritual had been the solution, it now becomes a part of the problem, and the obsessive-compulsive person begins to avoid situations that may require the performance of rituals. He is in a no-win situation: He either has to give up the rituals and suffer the anxiety and uncertainty or continue them and be forced to accept his lack of control and his irrationality.

Often the obsessive-compulsive person will say that she knows the rituals are illogical, but she is so overwhelmed by the fears, the physical sensations, and the sense of urgency that she isn't able to resist the compulsion. The rituals relieve the immediate distress but leave the person feeling helpless, depressed, and hostile—and the cycle continues. The hostile feelings will produce unacceptable thoughts, which require rituals to undo the bad magic, which leave the person feeling helpless, depressed, and hostile. . . .

CHAPTER FOUR

WHEN MAGIC THINKING BECOMES A MALADY: DEFINING PHOBIAS AND OCD

IT IS HARD being a person. Life doesn't always go the way we would like it to. From our first days we suffer frustrations and disappointments. We often don't get fed when we are hungry, aren't soothed when distressed, or aren't cared for in a way that keeps us physically comfortable. We frequently find ourselves in situations where the rules of behavior are unclear or contradictory and therefore put us at risk of criticism or humiliation. We may see our dearest dreams shattered, our aspirations go unfulfilled. In the course of our lives most of us suffer serious losses and injury or illness. Our environment can be unpredictable; the people we love and work with can be difficult. Still, in spite of all the complexities and adversities of living, most of us manage to muddle through—some of us muddle through more effectively than others—but it is more the wonder that we do as well as we do.

We are taught in subtle, and sometimes not so subtle, ways that wishing or believing will make things happen; that we can control our lives, and sometimes the universe, with our thoughts or beliefs. It is comforting to think that in a world of chaos we have control. It is no wonder that most of us engage in some degree of magic thinking. But at what point does it become a malady?

Magic thinking becomes dangerous when it causes difficulties or limitations that do not emanate from the reality of the situation; when it becomes more than just a quick knock on wood or a brief stroking of a rabbit's foot. If magic thinking causes a person to spend hours a day purging bad magic, or creates intense fear of situations that are realistically not dangerous, or renders him incapable of functioning normally, it is a malady. At that point magic thinking no longer comforts us or gives us a sense of control in a chaotic world; it reduces us to fearful, slavish creatures endlessly battling phantoms.

We are focusing specifically on the magic thinking maladies more popularly known as phobias and obsessive-compulsive disorders, so let's define those terms.

A phobia is "an exaggerated and often disabling fear usually inexplicable to the subject, having occasionally a logical but usually an illogical or symbolic object . . . " (Webster's Third New International Dictionary). Encountering the fear-producing object or situation causes distressing physical sensations (rapid heartbeat, dizziness, weakness, tremors, a sense of unreality) in the phobic person, which impels her to escape from the current situation and assiduously avoid any future encounter with it.

Obsessions are recurrent ideas, thoughts, or images that intrusively pop into the mind and seem to have a life of their own. They are repetitive, like a broken record that repeats the same few bars of a song over and over and over again. Often the thoughts are scary: "What if I lose control and kill someone?" or senseless: "How do I know I'm a man and not a Martian?".

Compulsions are the response to obsessions, the "counter-magic" to make things safe again. They manifest themselves as rituals of washing, cleaning, or repetitive checking that must be done in a very specific manner, or in the form of a litany that must be said exactly right a specific number of times.

COMMON FEATURES OF PHOBIAS AND OBSESSIVE-COMPULSIVE DISORDERS

Obsessive-compulsive disorders include a wide variety of problems—everything from hand-washing to compulsively picking up tiny bits of lint, to avoidance of driving for fear of inadvertently killing someone. Phobias may involve blood, insects, animals, public transportation, public speaking, open spaces, closed spaces, being alone, or leaving an area deemed as safe. But most phobic and obsessive-compulsive people share common features:

1. They may feel a need for absolute certainty. They cannot tolerate ambivalence or not knowing. The laws of probability have no relevance. If there is one chance in 5 million that any given plane may crash, they will refuse to fly, certain that the plane they are on will be the one fatal flight. If there is one chance in 10 million that they might contract venereal disease from a public lavatory, they will refuse to use any public lavatory.
2. They may have a sense of uncontrolled thoughts. Disturbing thoughts and/or images pop into their heads, and they are unable to get rid of them. They may have long periods of rumination where the same thought rolls around and around in their mind and allows them no peace. Many decisions seem monumental (Should I wear my black socks or my navy socks?) and difficult beyond all reason.

3. They suffer from intense fears, usually of some form of contamination (by dirt, germs, toxic chemicals, or drugged food) or objects or situations (cats, bridges, elevators) that stimulate unacceptable thoughts or urges and/or an overwhelming sense of impending danger. Because of the fears phobic or OC people avoid many situations and activities.
4. They experience disturbing physical sensations (rapid heartbeat, feelings of suffocating, chest pressure, nausea, unreality accompanying the thought of danger).
5. Obsessive-compulsive persons perform rituals and/or recite litanies. These are often elaborate and time-consuming and are dominant factors in the sufferers' lives. Often the sufferers recognize that the rituals are senseless, but they are unable to resist the compulsion to perform them. Phobic people may avoid so many situations that they become housebound, or they may live with constant, unrelenting anxiety, or they may relieve their anxiety with alcohol, which may cause additional problems.

If any of the above relate to you and are causing problems in dealing with day-to-day situations, you may have a malady of magic thinking. This book is meant for you. It will give you practical information and support. Read through the book quickly to give yourself a good overview of the problem, then go back to the case example that best describes your problem to see how it can be worked out. Use the charts and the self-help worksheets to establish your own work sessions.

If none of the statements refer to you but to an important person in your life, pay special attention to chapter 16. It will help you to understand magic thinking and it describe techniques on how to be supportive and positive without getting caught in the snare of the malady of magic thinking.

PART II

TALES OF MAGIC THINKING

INTRODUCTION

OVER the years I've worked with many hundreds of people. Every one has been interesting and unique. The majority of the people I've worked with have seen me perhaps ten or twenty times, and in that comparatively brief period gained enough understanding of the many ways to view reality and the pitfalls of magic thinking to enable them to reassess their reactions to formerly feared objects or situations and plan suitable formats for change. Others I have worked with over a very long period of time—in some cases, many years.

The cases presented in the following section were chosen because they describe a wide range of problems, and each one of them presents a different focus. Most of the stories are of people I saw over a long period of time. I selected them in order to illustrate the multitudinous complications that can develop as a result of using magic thinking as a solution to the chaos created by a distorted view of reality.

A commonly asked question is, "Where did my phobia or

compulsion come from? Is it chemical; is it genetic; did it come from childhood abuse?" Originally I thought that knowing the answer to this question was crucial to the success of the therapy. But I have come to the conclusion that not only is it not crucial to the success of the therapy, but frequently it is unknowable. In some of the cases I report here we can see life stresses that precipitated the original panic attack that probably led to the phobic or OC condition. In others the problems seemed to start so early that we might guess that they were chemical or genetic. In still others there doesn't seem to be any explanation for the problem.

One of the reasons for this unknowability is that clients don't always give complete or accurate information. They may withhold or alter information because they may be ashamed of a past incident; or because they fear that they may sound too crazy; or because they just don't remember very well. Another reason is that we are extremely complicated creatures, and the sources of most human ills (cancer, heart disease, and so on) are still mysteries—so to expect definitive answers for the cause of emotional problems is not always realistic. But the good news is that it is not necessary to know the origin of the problem to be able to effectively treat it.

Because most of the cases presented involve people I have worked with over a long period of time, and the results were not always unqualified successes, you may wonder if it always takes so long to control phobias and obsessive-compulsive disorders, or whether anyone ever gets cured. First of all, it doesn't always take long. The cases I've chosen represent the most seriously affected people I have worked with, people who have either had their problem for a very long time or who have no reliable support systems.

The issue of being completely cured is a difficult one. We live in an anxiety-producing world, and the thought of being "cured" of anxiety is neither desirable nor realistic—anxiety is our safety-alert system; we don't want to be "cured" of it. However, we don't want to be imprisoned by it, either. By identifying magic thinking and countering it with reality, phobias, panic attacks, and OCD can be conquered, and people can live normal lives. One caveat I do offer people is to think of their problem as an allergy. Often when we experience more stress than usual, are premenstrual, or fighting a cold or the flu, the symptoms of our problem may be more difficult to manage—but that does not mean that we can't live a full and normal life.

Before I accompany my clients into their anxiety-producing situations, I always explain about anxiety. The first thing clients have to know is that although the sensations feel awful, they are not dangerous. We begin our sessions with the least anxiety-producing situations; and we use an anxiety scale (10 being the worst anxiety they have ever experienced, 0 being no anxiety) so that my clients can communicate to me exactly how they are feeling during our sessions. At this time I also discuss the use and purpose of the worksheets and keeping a diary.

All the episodes and conversations reported actually occurred, but to protect the anonymity of my clients, names, places, and identifying details have been changed.

CHAPTER FIVE

NORA: A STORY OF AGORAPHOBIA

ONE EVENING Nora rushed home from her job as a secretary to fix dinner for her family, hurriedly ate, washed the dishes, and ran for the bus so she could get to the hospital to see her mother before visiting hours were over.

Nora, a thirty-three-year-old mother of a nine-year-old son and a daughter six years old, was under a lot of stress. Her husband had been unemployed for several months; he had always been a heavy drinker and somewhat abusive, but during his period of unemployment he had gotten worse. Both her children were having trouble in school. Her son had been caught stealing, and her daughter appeared to have a learning disorder. Then Nora's mother, who was her major support person, became ill and required hospitalization.

It was a cold February evening. When Nora got off the bus and started walking up the hill toward the hospital, she was overcome by frightening physical sensations. She felt a weird feeling of unreality, as though her head were not connected to her body. When she looked up the hill at the hospital, it seemed so far away, as if she was looking through the wrong end of a telescope. She felt wave after wave of panic. Her heart was pounding in her chest and she couldn't breathe. She caught a taxi and went back home and right to bed.

The next day Nora was feeling better but still shaken by the experience; she went to work as usual. That evening she had a meeting with her daughter's teacher and was unable to visit her mother in the hospital. By the next day her mother was home again.

About two weeks after her aborted trip to the hospital Nora was in the supermarket with both children. Her daughter was whining and begging for everything she saw in the candy racks. Nora was still upset about the stealing incident in school, so she was trying to keep a close eye on her son, when suddenly she started to get that feeling again. This time it started with a pounding in her head and was quickly followed by a strangling feeling, then the sense of unreality and rapidly beating heart. She thought, "Oh my God, I'm going to die right here in the middle of the supermarket with both kids pulling at me." She grabbed the children by the hands and ran out of the super-market, leaving the loaded basket in the aisle.

By the time Nora got home, she was shaking and crying un-controllably. She called her mother and asked to take her to a doctor. The doctor took Nora's blood pressure, did an EKG, took a sample of blood to send to a lab for testing, and listened to a description of the two "attacks" Nora had experienced. He told Nora that he could find nothing physically wrong with her. Instead of being relieved, Nora grew even more upset. She knew that something was wrong with her—it wasn't "normal" to be having these attacks. If her problem couldn't be identi-fied it couldn't be cured.

During the following weeks Nora moved around with a

sense of extreme fragility. She felt that if she wasn't careful she could bring on another attack. And it did happen again. This time Nora was in the supermarket without the children, standing in line with her purchases when she felt her heart start to beat faster; again the suffocating feeling and the dizziness came over her. At first she was self-conscious and embarrassed, thinking that the other people in line knew that something was wrong with her. She tried her best to stay in line, but the sensations grew more intense until finally she felt she couldn't stand it any longer. She left the grocery basket in line, pushed her way past the people in front of her, and ran home.

IN its extreme form, agoraphobia can be one of the most crippling of the maladies of magic thinking. An agoraphobic credits places and people with magical safe or unsafe qualities. The north side of the street may be safe, the south side unsafe; the corner store safe, the supermarket unsafe; an aunt may be safe, a mother unsafe. An underlying belief of an agoraphobic is "I am vulnerable, the world is a dangerous place, and I need someone to take care of me."

"Agoraphobia" has become an umbrella term to describe an entire spectrum of behaviors. The sufferer may be totally unable to leave the house and fearful of being alone. In less severe cases the agoraphobic may be only marginally limited; he may never go to the city alone or may fear department stores.

At first agoraphobia may seem strange or outlandish. You may ask, "How can an intelligent, competent person be afraid to leave his house?" But we establish our basic beliefs by evaluating our experiences. Much of our evaluation is based on what we anticipate the outcome to be; not surprisingly, if we expect an outcome to be unpleasant or painful, we will try to avoid it. Problems arise when our evaluation process is faulty and we attribute dangerous properties to objects or situations that, in fact, are not dangerous. This happens because we too frequently attribute our problems to "something out there" rather than to what is going on inside us. Like Nora, if we experience a panic attack in a supermarket, we would be more likely to blame the supermarket for our discomfort than the content of our thinking. Having evaluated the supermarket as a dangerous place, we will anticipate further bad experiences in supermarkets and make every effort to avoid them. When we look carefully at the way phobias develop, we can see that they make their own kind of sense.

THIS last episode in the supermarket left no doubt in Nora's mind that there was something seriously wrong with her. She called a new doctor for an emergency appointment. After a careful examination he too said that there was nothing physically wrong with her. He suggested that it was just her nerves and gave her a prescription for a tranquilizer. With misgivings she started taking the tranquilizers, and for a few weeks she seemed to feel a little less shaky—until one day, on her way home from work one evening, she had another attack.

This attack was like the proverbial straw that broke the camel's back. Nora had done everything possible to get rid of the attacks, but nothing worked. To her that meant one of two things: either she had some obscure disease that no one could diagnose, or she was going insane. Either way, it was just a matter of time before the final, terrible end. For a while she continued going to work, but then she started having attacks regularly on the way home. By the time Nora reached the house she would be so exhausted and distraught that she went right to bed.

Her husband was still without a job, and her family was totally dependent on her income. Although she was clearly getting worse, neither she nor her husband wanted her to leave her job. In order to take some of the pressure off her, Nora's husband assumed many of the household duties and arranged to pick her up after work. This system worked fine until her husband got a job and was no longer able to pick her up. When Nora had to go home alone, the attacks began again with a vengeance.

After discussing the problem with the doctor who prescribed the tranquilizers, Nora decided to take a leave of absence from her job. The first several weeks at home were blissful. She spent a lot of time resting. She tackled some heavy cleaning jobs that hadn't been done since before she became ill; she spent more time with the children. But the very thought of going to the supermarket made her so uncomfortable she would feign illness so her husband would do the shopping. When her mother invited her to go shopping or out to lunch she declined the invitation, claiming that she had too much work or wasn't feeling well.

A year slipped by before she realized that she was afraid to leave the house. Her domestic situation was nearing a crisis. Her husband was furious with her because he was still doing all the shopping and their social life was nonexistent. The children's teachers had called her numerous times to come to school to discuss problems. Because she never showed up at the meetings, the teachers assumed that she was not interested in her children. Her mother was angry with her much of the time because they had ceased doing things together. The only people she saw on a regular basis were her husband, the children, and her mother, and she couldn't talk about the way she felt with any of them. Her reactions were so bizarre she was sure that she was going insane.

She had read about people with somewhat similar problems,

but they had had chemical imbalances that could be helped with medication. If her problem was a chemical imbalance, it wouldn't make any sense that she could feel perfectly comfortable one minute, then perfectly horrible the next because of a passing thought about leaving the house. Obviously her chemistry couldn't have been changed so radically by just a thought.

NORA'S story is a typical example of the development of a phobia. The details and circumstances vary from person to person, but specific points are consistent.

The phobia-prone person has a generalized sense of vulnerability or inability to cope with life's problems. This often occurs at a time when the person must assume greater responsibility and/or her self-confidence is severely tested, as when a student leaves college and must begin to make major life decisions or when a woman becomes a mother and realizes she is totally responsible for the life of another person.

In Nora's case many things were testing her ability to cope. Because her husband was out of work, she was financially responsible for the family. He was drunk much of the time and unable to offer her physical or emotional support. Worse yet, occasionally in drunken rages he would hit her or the children, and she felt incapable of protecting them or herself from his senseless violence. She blamed herself for the children's problems in school; her confidence as a mother was undermined. When her mother became ill, she was flooded with frightening thoughts: What if her mother were to die? What if their roles were to reverse and she had to take care of her mother? What if her own problems were too stressful for her mother and were making her ill?

When Nora stepped off the bus that cold evening in February she experienced a panic attack. During a panic attack the entire being is under siege. The mind is overwhelmed by thoughts and images of disaster, the body feels like it is flying apart—the heart beats wildly, the legs and hands shake out of control, breathing is difficult, there is a sense of light-headedness or faintness. To make matters even worse, a feedback loop operates that escalates both the disaster images and the physical distress. It operates like this: The mind says, "I'm in danger!" (This may not even be a conscious thought, nor need it be a generally accepted or realistic danger.) When the mind says "danger," the emergency alert system in the body goes into action and shoots adrenaline into the system, which makes the heart beat faster, and so on. The mind responds to these alarming sensations by thinking, "There's something terribly wrong with my body!" With that thought (which is another version of "danger"), the physical sensations intensify. The mind assesses the situation as dire and concludes, "I'm going to die, I need help."

There is a similar feedback loop in effect with feelings of vulnerability and the panic attack. A panic attack confirms our sense of vulnerability. Because the source of the disturbing sensations is a mystery, and the management of sensations so seemingly impossible, the solution the phobia-prone person arrives at is to be extremely careful not to do anything that might induce the sensations. That usually means avoiding all situations and/or places where one has experienced anxiety in the past. This increases the sense of vulnerability. The phobic person lives with the fear that another attack is "out there waiting for me." She has difficulty talking about her fears because she doesn't really understand what is happening herself, and attempts to explain the overwhelming dread and terror to someone who has never had a panic attack are usually met with a blank expression and advice to "get hold of yourself." This creates a great feeling of isolation. The isolation intensifies the sense of vulnerability because the person feels very different from the rest of the world and somehow basically faulty or inferior.

Another point common in the development of a phobia is fear of the sensations themselves. A phobic person believes that the sensations, unless stopped, will lead to a final disaster. "Disaster" usually means some form of loss of control or disintegration of self—it may mean death from a heart attack or stroke or insanity or loss of consciousness or loss of bladder control. At this stage there is a shift in the perception of the danger being "out there" to being an internal danger.

Common conditions in the development of a phobia are:

    A sense of vulnerability or inability to cope
    A feeling of isolation
    One or more panic attacks
    A fear of the sensations themselves

Nora's circumstances created fertile ground for the development of a phobia. The overwork, the abusive husband, the temporary loss of her major support person all fed her sense of vulnerability. Her panic attack left her feeling that even her body was not able to support her or keep her safe and confirmed her inability to cope. The experience of consulting doctors and not finding a reasonable explanation for the disturbing physical sensations created a sense of isolation.

After the second panic attack Nora's perception of danger shifted from an external cause or event to the internal. She began to translate her sensations into feelings of a final disaster (in her case, the final disaster she feared was death or insanity). Therefore she avoided all situations that might bring on the disturbing sensations. Avoidance in itself creates yet another trap for the phobic person. The phobic person's primary thought is, "These sensations are so dangerous I must monitor myself at all times and do nothing that might bring them on." Nora was so frightened of the sensations that she never allowed herself to test her hypothesis of danger. Her only solution was to avoid. Her life became so restricted that the limitations themselves created a whole new set of problems.

When I met Nora she had not been out of her house in more than three years, but she was by no means inactive. After about a year of being housebound Nora started a day-care center in her house in order to relieve the stress on the family finances. The basement of her house was attractively painted, carpeted, and furnished with children's furniture and play equipment. With the aid of two hired assistants she cared for ten to fifteen children every weekday at various times during the day. The assistants did all the shopping, banking, and other errands necessary to maintain Nora's household.

Her husband worked as a long-distance truck driver and was absent much of the time. This was both good and bad; he didn't present a constant abusive presence, but he still offered no physical or emotional support to her or the children.

During our first appointment I informed Nora about agoraphobia and assured her that she wasn't going crazy or harboring a dreaded disease. I explained the anxiety scale, the importance of maintaining a diary, and that a part of our work would involve leaving the house. Nora had been calm and relaxed during most of the interview, but when the discussion turned to plans of going outside she became noticeably distressed.

"Look at me!" she said. "If I get this anxious just talking

about going out, how will I ever be able to handle actually going out?"

"Was there a time in your life when going outside wasn't anxiety-producing?" I asked.

"Oh yes," she said. "Most of my life I loved going places. When I was still in high school I took a train to Florida by myself. On our honeymoon my husband and I went to the Virgin Islands—it was wonderful."

"You're talking about going out now and you're not at all anxious. Why is that?"

"Because then I didn't have this problem. Now I know that when I go out I get anxious."

"So it's the anticipation of getting anxious that makes you anxious," I said.

"Well, maybe, . . . " Nora said slowly,

"I'd like you to write that down in your diary, then when we start to work in vivo we'll pay particular attention to whether it's the actual situation or the anticipation of anxiety that's making you anxious."

Nora and I worked together every Saturday afternoon. Her mother, who had been enlisted as a support person, joined us every other Saturday. Progress was painfully slow. For many weeks the best we could do was to drive the car slowly back and forth in the thirty-foot driveway.

One day (for reasons I don't remember) after backing out of the driveway, instead of straightening out and driving forward, I continued to back down the street until we were more than half a block away from her house. I stopped the car and looked over at Nora staring straight ahead. She looked over at me and with a big smile said, "This is wonderful, isn't it."

"Absolutely wonderful," I agreed.

"Let's go back now," she said.

Back in the driveway, Nora exploded with excitement. "Wait

until.Mother hears this!" she said. "That's the farthest I've been in years, and I was only a little anxious. I think there is hope, I really do!"

"Why was this time so different? How come you were able to do it with so little anxiety today, but in the past you would always be at an 8 or 9 [on the anxiety scale] by the time we got to the end of the driveway?"

"I'm not sure," Nora said, "but I think because you went backwards and I was able to keep the house in sight it didn't seem to be so scary."

During the week Nora repeated the backwards trip several times with her mother. The following Saturday when I arrived at her house her mother was there with a half-dozen photographs she had taken of Nora's house. The photos had been taken from different angles and different distances; a few pictured the two children standing in front of the house.

"I thought that if being able to see the house kept Nora calm, photos might help too, and we'd be able to go forward," her mother said.

I owe most of my best therapeutic techniques to either the people I've worked with or to their support people—and this idea was one of the best. Going nose first this time, we slowly inched our way down the street while Nora, sitting beside me, stared at photos and repeated over and over to herself that the house was still there, and she was feeling OK. This time we made it across the intersection and onto the next block.

"Nora," I said, "we're in the 400 block now. I'm going to make a U-turn here and head back toward your house. Can you look up now?" Her anxiety elevated slightly when she looked around and found herself so far from home, but lowered again once her house came into view. Instead of returning to her driveway, we parked down the street from her house and talked about the experience.

"It's amazing," Nora said, "my thoughts were so clear! In the back of my mind I kept saying to myself, 'I gotta get home. What if something happens? I need help and I gotta get home.' But in another part of my mind I was saying, 'I don't have to rush home! Nothing's going to happen, and in the unlikely event something should happen, I have Mother and Randy [Raeann] here to help me.' It was a real struggle but I think the sensible me won."

Nora had a good, steady foot on the road to recovery. She was able to see that by reality testing the scary thoughts she could control the anxiety. As she continued to make progress, her mother armed her with more photographs of buildings on the street where she would be traveling.

After we had been working together for about six months, Nora suffered a terrible setback. She and her mother had been sitting in the parking lot of a supermarket preparing Nora for a short trip inside when, "out of the blue," her anxiety level hit 10 and she had a full-blown panic attack.

Nora and her mother were both alarmed by the attack and again began to wonder if the problem weren't physical. Again, Nora went to a doctor, who said that it was just nerves. Nora cancelled therapy with me, saying that she was just going to have to resign herself to being a nervous person.

About a month later Nora's mother called me. "I know what's wrong with Nora—so does she, but she won't talk about it. I wish you'd come and see her again."

I had a pretty good idea what was wrong with Nora too, but I believe in the right to have secrets, even when they might be self-defeating. "I can't see Nora against her will," I told her mother, "but I'll give her a call and see how she's doing."

"YOU'VE been speaking to my mother, haven't you?" Nora said accusingly when I called.

"Yes, she's real concerned about you. She's hoping that you'll try therapy again—you'd been doing so well."

"Well I'm not doing well now, I'm right back at square one." She was crying as she talked. "My doctor said that it was too much pressure for me, that it was making me sick."

"Your doctor said that the therapy was making you sick?" I asked incredulously.

"Well, not exactly, but it's made me very nervous again and I don't think it's good for me." With that she hung up.

Less than a week later, Nora's mother was on the phone again. "Nora's really bad. She cries all the time, she doesn't get out of bed—she needs help. She really needs help; her husband won't pay for therapy but I will. Please go and see her."

"I can't see her against her will," I repeated, "but I'll call her again."

"ARE you mad at me?" Nora asked when I called. "I wasn't very nice to you last time we talked."

"No, I'm not mad, Nora, but I'm really wondering what's going on. You said that the therapy was making you nervous, but now that you're not in therapy you seem to be even more nervous."

"It wasn't really the therapy . . . well, yes it was, in a way . . . well, not really, but kind of—indirectly, if you know what I mean. It's complicated, I can't explain it. What did my mother tell you?"

"She said that you were spending a lot of time in bed crying and that she was worried about you."

"What else did she say?"

"She said that she didn't think that your husband would pay for therapy, but that she would and that she wanted me to see you."

"My husband never did pay for therapy. Did she tell you what she thought my problem was?"

"No, she said that she thought she knew, but she didn't tell me."

"Do you know?" Nora asked.

"I think I could make a few guesses," I said.

"I don't know what to do," Nora said.

"Why don't we talk about it."

"Do we have to get into the car?"

"Not if you don't want to."

"OK," she said.

I was pretty sure I knew what Nora was going to tell me; not because I have clairvoyant capabilities, but because I'd heard it before in similar circumstances (a rare example of the advantages of age and experience). On that cool fall afternoon in Nora's living room I found it hard to make eye contact with her because in my soul I felt that I had violated a private space in her. She didn't want me to know her secret, but I knew it, and she knew that I knew it.

She offered me coffee and cookies, and I accepted to make her more comfortable. She fiddled with the cushions on the couch, then turned to me and said, "You must think I'm terrible."

"Why would I think that?" I asked.

"Because I am terrible."

"What makes you so terrible?" I asked. A long silence followed.

Finally, Nora asked, "What would you say if I told you that I often think of killing myself and my kids?"

"I'd ask you why."

"Because I don't see any other way out."

"Out of what?"

"Out of this situation."

"What situation?"

Another long silence. We sipped coffee to maintain some sense of normality. Looking into her coffee cup, Nora slowly began. "You know, sitting in that parking lot with my mother I got the sense that I could be completely normal again—free of this shit. I had the thought that I could get rid of Bill, dump all my responsibilities, and start all over again."

"What's wrong with that?" I asked.

"That's horrible!" she said. "Getting rid of my husband and children! That's horrible!"

"The act of getting rid of them can be horrible, but the thought is sometimes irresistible, and doesn't really cause anyone any harm."

Nora looked at me hard for a long time, then finally said, "That wasn't all I was thinking," she said. "I was really thinking that if I got better I wouldn't have to put up with Bill's shit any longer."

"There's a big difference between not putting up with someone's shit and getting rid of them."

"Well, yes, but my idea was that I would just leave; leave Bill and the kids and go somewhere where no one knew me and start fresh."

"That still might be a possibility. The other possibility is to tell Bill that you won't put up with his abuse. That if he drinks he's going to have to stay at a motel, and ask the kids to help out a little so that you see them as more than just 'responsibilities.'"

"I can't tell them that!" Nora said.

"You mean getting rid of them would be easier than setting limitations."

"Of course," Nora said laughingly, "if I got rid of them I wouldn't have to hear their complaints."

NORA'S terrible secret was that she feared that if she got better she would want to, or be free to, leave her husband and children. I wanted her to realize that although that might be an option, there were also several others, and that she didn't have to cripple herself in order to be what she thought of as a "good person" and stay with an abusive husband.

We resumed therapy and quickly regained lost territory. Within a couple of months Nora was traveling freely within her small community. Then suddenly her husband became quite ill. Doctors couldn't find anything wrong with him, but he couldn't keep food down and he became dizzy and light-headed when he tried to drive.

"I think he's another nut," Nora said when we talked about him.

"Well, I guess we should invite him into our club," I suggested.

"I can't talk to him, and he hates you, so lots of luck!"

RELUCTANTLY, Bill agreed to a joint meeting. He was a big bear of a man; well over six feet tall and powerfully built. He had a full black beard and hair down to his shoulders; he walked like a sumo wrestler. He was the kind of guy you genuinely didn't want to make mad.

"I understand that you don't really like this idea, Bill. Why is that?" I asked.

"I think you're a quack."

"What does that mean?"

"You're not a doctor."

"What have doctors done for you?"

"Nothing, they're quacks too."

"So what do you have to lose with me?"

"Plenty. You're telling my wife to dump me."

"I am?"

"You're not?"

An unfortunate part of my work is that I'm often viewed as an opposition party by the people I need to help me help the client. In this case, I must admit that my sympathies lay more with Nora than with Bill.

"No," I answered honestly, "I'm trying to figure out what's going on here."

"What's going on here is that Nora's trying to get rid of me and that you're helping her."

The words had a familiar ring, but my intention was never to help Nora get rid of Bill. My job was to help Nora overcome her agoraphobia, but if both she and Bill thought that the consequences of Nora's recovery would be the dissolution of the marriage, it wasn't going to work.

The vast majority of victims of agoraphobia are women. Agoraphobia can create overwhelming stress in relationships. The agoraphobic person becomes extremely dependent on her partner, and that dependency generates resentment in both parties. The partner is resentful because he feels used and manipulated. The agoraphobic resents being helpless and dependent on someone who resents her. The relationship wraps itself around these problems and, to the people involved, appears to be held together by them.

There are usually two versions of how this works. Nora's version was: "If he thinks that I can take care of myself he'll leave me," or, "If it weren't for this problem, I'd get out of here and do something fabulous." Bill's version was: "If I thought she wouldn't die without me, I'd get out of here," or "If she were able to, she'd dump me in a minute." Often these beliefs aren't consciously stated; they present themselves as vague feelings of anxiety when either of the parties senses change. So although the apparent intent is to be free of agoraphobia, unseen forces are working against that effort. Unless those forces are brought to light, the work will be subtly sabotaged, and the agoraphobic person will either become discouraged by the lack of progress and drop out of therapy or, as Nora did, find it too stressful to continue.

Magic thinking played a big part in Nora's life. Every time she had a nasty thought about someone, it was quickly followed by the guilt and fear that if something bad happened to them, it would be her fault because of the nasty thought. She also imagined that one day she would wake up, miraculously changed, walk out the door, and leave forever her business, her home, and her family. She had neglected to attend to the fact that before she attained the ability to walk out the door forever, she would experience a lot of changes and gain a lot of understanding, which might make the idea of walking out the door forever the least attractive option.

I encourage people to talk about the effect their recovery will have on their relationship. When I hear, "I'd leave my husband if I could," I try to get the husband in on at least a few of the sessions, because invariably he feels threatened by the changes his partner is making. After working with hundreds of agoraphobics, I know of only four who have left their relationship after recovering. Most found that the relationship was strengthened once they were free of the burden of agoraphobia.

Bill's style of handling difficulties was with force or more exactly, the threat of force. Because of his ferocious appearance he usually didn't meet with a lot of direct opposition. While Nora was housebound, there was no threat to his stability; although he complained about having to do "her work" and never going anywhere with her, he knew that she wasn't in a position to get rid of him. When he saw Nora getting more independent he got scared; he also got headaches, dizzy spells, and stomach distress that didn't seem to have an organic cause. His mysterious illness made him even more scared, because he believed that he held the relationship together by being strong and powerful; if he were to be sick, Nora would certainly leave him. So he blustered and bullied more until Nora wished that she could leave him but was prevented from it by the agoraphobia. Understandably, Bill viewed my role as aiding and abetting Nora's escape. I needed to get Bill involved so he could be a part of the changes that were taking place in Nora's life.

During our joint session I explained to Bill how thoughts can create anxiety, and how the scary thoughts and the physical sensations feed on each other and intensify into a panic attack. I described the physical sensations of a panic attack and asked him if he had ever been in a situation where he thought that his life was in danger and felt similar sensations. He answered with a snort. I had thought that the three of us could go out in the car together so he could see how I work with Nora, but she didn't want to do that; she was afraid that he would get mad and yell at her, making her more nervous.

At the end of the session I asked if they thought another joint session would be helpful. Nora was noncommittal, but Bill hemmed and hawed, then said he wasn't sure he really understood what was going on and asked if he could have a session alone with me. I asked Nora if she had any problem with that.

"Why do you want to do that?" Nora asked him. "Do you want to talk about me?" Nora was clearly surprised and more than a little worried.

Before Bill could answer I said, "You know Bill, I can give you all the information about agoraphobia and anxiety disorders you'll ever want to know, but I can only give you as much specific information about Nora as she gives me permission to talk about. Whatever is said in a session is absolutely private, but that works for both of you. What you might tell me is just as private as what Nora tells me."

"Yeah, I kinda thought that's the way it worked, but I thought . . . like maybe if I knew more I could get Nora to drive with me."

"What do you think, Nora? Would that be OK with you?" I asked.

"Well, yeah, I guess so."

Before I left we arranged for two appointments: one with Bill alone, the other with Nora and her mother. While I was walking to my car Nora sidled up next to me and whispered, "Don't tell him anything I've told you!" I squeezed her arm in silent assurance.

BILL and I sat in the living room while Nora was downstairs with the fifteen kids in her day-care group. He looked pained and uncomfortable. We started out with small talk—he asked if the side roads were icy. "Not too," I said. "But I had to drive slowly."

"Bad time of year for driving," Bill said.

"Yeah," I agreed.

Finally he leaned forward, clasped his hands together, and said, "You know, I'm really worried about Nora. Do you think she can get better?"

"She has gotten better."

"Yeah, yeah, I see that, but can she get *all* better?"

"Sure, if she keeps working on it and other problems don't develop that get in her way."

"Oh." A long silence followed; then finally Bill said, "You

know those things you were talking about last week? I've had them."

"You've had panic attacks?"

"Yeah, awful ones. I thought I was going to die. I couldn't get my breath, my heart was pounding so hard I thought that that sucker was going to crash right through my chest, the top of my head felt like it was going to blast off, I really thought I was going to die."

"Yeah, that sure sounds like a panic attack," I agreed. "What do you think caused it?"

"Nothing caused it, I was just barreling down the road working my way through traffic trying to get to the warehouse before it closed so that I could unload my trailer and head back again without getting stuck with an overnight; when all of a sudden—BAM—there it was."

"What did you do?"

"I pulled over to the side of the road and just sat there for a while, wondering what had hit me. Then I got on my CB, just to hear another voice, and I shot the shit for a while and seemed to feel a little better. I headed out again but missed the warehouse and had to stay overnight."

"When did this happen?" I asked.

"The big one about six months ago. I've had a few smaller ones since then—but now I'm scared. You don't have to tell Nora, do you?"

"No, as I said, this is private. But why don't you want to tell her?"

"Well, she sees me as this big strong guy who can take care of everything—I don't think she'd like it if she knew I had problems. I know you can't tell me, but I think Nora wants to dump me. Sometimes I get the feeling that she hates me. You know, she won't go out with me, even to the store, but she goes out with her mother."

"Uh-huh, well, maybe we ought to discuss that during another joint meeting. But tell me, are your panic attacks what
your mystery illness is all about?"

"Maybe. When nothing showed up on the tests the doctor
said that I should be on tranquilizers, but he wouldn't prescribe
them because he knows I drive trucks and drink a lot—but
Nora probably told you about that."

"What happens when you drink?"

"Ah, sometimes I drink too much and get out of control and
break up a few things and slap Nora and the kids around. I
don't mean to hurt them, you know, I just lose my head."

"I'll bet if you slap someone around they really know they've
been slapped—maybe you should quit drinking."

"Yeah, I should. I don't think it's good for my stomach either."

THAT was the only session I had with Bill privately. I offered to
refer him to another therapist, but he said that he didn't want
to waste time with a bunch of quacks. He came in on a joint
session about once or twice a month, and he asked very good
questions concerning how thoughts create anxiety, and reality
testing. He maintained his bullying manner, and when the
issue of Nora not going out in the car with him came up, Nora
said, "I'm afraid to go out with you. If I turn the corner wrong,
or I take too long at a stop sign, you yell and me and make me
nervous."

"I don't yell at you!" Bill yelled.

"You're yelling now," Nora said.

"I'm not yelling! If you two pussies can't take the way a man
sounds, that's too damn bad!" he yelled and stormed out of the
room.

Nora and I looked at each other and shrugged.

For our next joint session I came prepared with a tape recorder. "What's that for?" Bill asked.

"I'd like all of us to be able to hear what we sound like when we talk to each other," I said.

"Yeah, sure, that's for my benefit, isn't it," Bill said.

"Yeah, pretty much," I agreed.

After a few stiff minutes we all forgot about the tape recorder and started discussing issues normally. Soon a heated issue came up and Bill raised his voice.

"You're yelling again," Nora said. "I never want to talk with you about these things because you can't talk like a normal human being—you've got to yell and shout and stamp your feet. I don't want to be subjected to this."

With that Bill took off again on a high-volume rant.

"Bill, Bill, wait a minute. You can resume this after a while, but right now I'd like to be able to play this back and listen," I said.

While the three of us listened to Bill, his expression changed noticeably. When it was over, I turned off the tape player and asked, "What does that sound like to you, Bill?"

"It sounds like that guy's a real asshole," Bill yelled, and left the room.

I would like to say that that event changed Bill forever, but it didn't. It did, however, make him a little more aware of what he sounded like, and he seemed to make more of an effort to be reasonable. About a month after that session Bill went on a rousing drunk that ended with him in the hospital with twenty stitches in the back of his head and a broken wrist. Although Nora was traveling at that time, she refused to go see him in the hospital (the same hospital where she had had her first panic attack). She also refused to let him come back to the house unless he promised to go to AA.

By this time Nora was free enough of the symptoms of agoraphobia that she could have ended the marriage if she chose, but she realized that she really did love Bill. He was very protective of his family, he was totally reliable (when he wasn't drinking), he could be very, very funny, and she understood and accepted his garrulous style. But she wouldn't tolerate his drinking any longer. I think that to her his abuse had been more acceptable than having to worry about whether he was out getting his head cracked open again.

Nora and Bill are getting along better now than they did before her bout with agoraphobia. She drives around on her own, does the shopping, meets her mother for lunch, and the whole family made a trip to Disney World—the first vacation they had been on in years. Bill quit drinking, and his mystery illness faded into oblivion. A number of years before, Bill's family had let him know that he wasn't welcome, but he and Nora have resumed a relationship with them again. They go out together now and have a normal social life. Nora describes them as "Beauty and the Beast."

The support Nora got from her mother was a major factor in the success of her therapy. Another factor was that Nora could remember a more "normal" time of her life when she enjoyed traveling and was willing to practice and work hard between our sessions. The people who do the homework and practice on their own invariably make better progress.

CHAPTER SIX

Jerry Couldn't Leave a Subway Station Without Picking Up Litter

When I spoke with Jerry on the phone for the first time, he was relentless in questioning my qualifications. Where was I trained? What methods did I use? How long had I been working with obsessive-compulsive disorders? How many OC people had I seen? What was my success rate? When I suggested that he tell me a little about his problem he said, "You wouldn't understand it, nobody does." In spite of his conviction that I wouldn't understand his problem, he made an appointment.

At ten minutes past six the buzzer rang. Jerry was forty minutes late.

"I couldn't get out of your subway station." Jerry said in explanation.

"You mean it was closed off?" I asked.

"No, it was too messy."

"You were anxious about getting dirty or contaminated?"

"No, I had to clean it up."

"Oh," I said as I watched Jerry bend over, pick up a strand

of dog hair from my carpet, inspect it, and put it in his pocket. "Let me guess, Jerry. Your problem is that you have a compulsion to pick up every bit of dirt or litter you see for fear of someone getting hurt and you being held responsible for their injury."

Jerry looked at me, "How did you know that?"

I resisted the impulse to say "Elementary, dear boy"; I told him that many of the people I work with have similar problems and that my subway station frequently gets cleaned up by my clients.

In the few minutes we had left I was able to get an unilluminating history and a sketchy idea of the extent of Jerry's problem. As I always do during the first session, I explained the anxiety scale and asked Jerry to keep a diary recording his episodes of anxiety.

The following week Jerry arrived a half hour late.

"Jerry, you're wasting your money spending half your session with me cleaning up the subway station. What we'll do then, is next week as soon as you get off the train, call me and I'll meet you at the station."

The third week at five-thirty sharp Jerry called me to tell me that he was at the subway station. It took me less than five minutes to get there, but when I arrived I found Jerry with a big canvas bag over his shoulder scurrying around picking up litter.

"Jerry, remember what you told me last week? You really don't want to be doing this. Come on over here and talk to me."

"In a minute; I've just got a little more to do."

I leaned against the wall and watched while Jerry scoured the station for empty soda cans, pieces of paper, cigarette butts, etc. After fifteen minutes I said, "Time's up Jerry. Let's go." Reluctantly he followed me up the stairs. Again we only had about half an hour of the session left. I still didn't have any sense of Jerry except that he was a litter collector. I wanted a chance to talk with him, to look at his anxiety diary, to get an idea of his anxiety levels, and find out how much of his time was spent in the grip of his compulsion.

Directly south across the street from the subway station is a little square with benches. To save time I suggested we sit there and talk rather than return to my office. Jerry surveyed the overflowing litter baskets and broken bottles and asked, "Are you crazy?"

For our next session Jerry agreed to call me before he left his office so I could be on the subway platform waiting for him to arrive.

When I saw him step out of the subway car, I rushed over to his side, grabbed him by the elbow, and quick-walked him through the turnstile and up the steps.

"Now," I said when we got to my office, "I want to know what's going on with you."

"I thought you knew! I have to pick up everything I see because I'm afraid that someone will get hurt and I'll be held responsible."

"I know generally what the problem is, but I want to know the specifics. Do you really pick up everything, and everywhere, or just in subway stations and on my carpet? How do you imagine people will hurt themselves on a dead cigarette butt? Who made you responsible for the safety of New York City's subway riders? Are you responsible only for the stations that you use or for all of them? If someone hurts himself in a subway are there 'responsibility police' who track you down and charge you? What will they charge you with—'dirty subway station homicide?'"

"Whew," Jerry said wiping his forehead, "I've never been asked so many questions."

"These are the things we're going to be working on, but first

I'd like a very specific list of the places where you pick things up, the circumstances (the end of the day, the beginning of the day, if you're alone or accompanied by someone) and the kinds of things that you pick up."

"Briefly: everywhere, all the time, everything."

"No, no, I don't buy that. We just walked out of a subway station and down two well-littered streets, and you didn't pick up a thing."

"That was different, I was with you and I can reassign responsibility—you may be tracked down by the 'responsibility police.' "

"And what will happen to me?"

"You'll be arrested and charged with litter homicide?"

"Come on, get straight," I said.

"I don't know what will happen! I don't understand it at all. You're asking me to be sensible when this problem is totally senseless."

"But sensibility is where safety and normality reside."

Up until this point Jerry had been upbeat and slightly teasing, but his mood quickly changed to despair. "Maybe, maybe not," he said. "But that's beside the point, because I just can't control the need to pick things up."

"Why can't you control it, Jerry? What happens to you that you seem to be forced against your will to do things that you don't want to do?"

"I get this awful feeling—it's like a black cloud that comes over me. It's a horrible feeling of doom—that something terrible is about to happen. It takes me over and I feel like my head is going to explode, and I'll go stark raving mad. The only thing I can think of is to pick things up so that everyone will be safe. While I rush around picking up, the sensation disappears."

"After you've cleaned up the subway station do you feel good?"

"No. The sense of doom is gone but then I feel disgust with myself."

"You're trading the sense of doom for disgust, so you really don't win no matter what you do. How do you imagine that someone will be injured by the litter in the subway station—what's going to happen?"

"I don't know how it will happen, it just will."

Jerry was an investment banker, so he had to have a pretty good grasp of reality in other aspects of his life.

"Jerry, what would you say to me if I asked you to put your life savings in an investment that I felt would be good but couldn't tell you why; in fact, I hadn't even really thought about it?"

"I'd say, 'In your dreams, lady.' "

"Uhmm, yeah. I'd get an overwhelming sense of doom if I were about to plunk thousands of dollars into a new business. How do you decide to make an investment?"

"The company is looked at pretty carefully. We look at the books, the track record of the principals, the strengths and weaknesses in the market, the competition, and so on."

"What happens if in a meeting you ask someone what the competition is like and they say, 'I don't know?' "

Jerry chuckled and shifted in his chair, "Anyone who's come that far knows better than to say 'I don't know.' "

"But hypothetically, what would happen?"

"Well, after he'd been replaced, we would find out about the competition."

"Oh, so you don't fool around, you make sure that you've got clear, hard facts."

"We can't afford to fool around."

"But you're willing to invest your life in a belief that you recognize is senseless, and to accept 'I don't know' for a reason. How come you're willing to fool around with your life like that?"

"Sounds like we're going to be playing 'forty questions.' "

"I don't think we'll be playing at all; I think you'll find it hard work. And I think we can narrow the questions down to about two essential ones: What do you think will happen if you don't pick up litter? What are the facts that support that expectation?"

Jerry brightened up and sat forward, "Really," he asked, "that's all there is to it?"

"Well, yes, that's basically all there is to it."

FOR the next couple of months we started our appointments in the subway station, only instead of rushing Jerry right out we observed the situation. No people were injured by the litter. We watched people come up and down the steps, and we witnessed no accidents. We used a hand counter to try to keep track of the number of people we observed. Every week Jerry entered the facts into his diary: "April 20, 5:30–6:15, over 123 people through station, no injuries."

His assignments had been to observe people in his own subway station for one hour twice a week and to enter the facts into his diary, but Jerry always had dozens of really good reasons why he hadn't done his assignments—didn't have time, took taxis all week, ran into a neighbor in the station, would have been too awkward, and so on. After weeks of no evidence of work on his assignments I said, "Jerry, we've been observing people walk through litter in my subway station for months and nothing terrible has happened, but in all this time you haven't spent a single hour observing in your subway station. What do you think is going on, why aren't you doing your assignments?"

"Oh, no," he said, backing away from me and putting his hands in the air, "here it comes again—I can tell by the tone of the voice; the set of the mouth—the 'Socratic Method.' Notice how she doesn't say, 'You lazy, lying, lout, get out and do your work.' She asks, 'Jerry, what's going on here?' "

"Well, what *is* going on?"

Jerry rubbed his hands together, looked up at the ceiling, and said, "Nothing I can say is acceptable. I know that you don't want to hear, 'I don't know,' or 'I just can't,' but that's all I have to say."

"Have you been asking yourself the two basic questions?"

"I don't even remember what they are."

"They are: What do you think will happen? and What are the facts that support that expectation? Let's write them down so that when you get anxious you'll have a prompt to remind you of what you're supposed to be asking yourself."

"Yeah, well, I'll try," he answered.

We continued to observe people in my subway station, then we moved to the littered square across the street; we never saw an incident of injury from litter. As pedestrians walked past empty cans, bottles, bags, I asked Jerry what he thought would happen.

"Based on multitudinous past experiences, I would have to say, probably nothing."

More weeks went by observing nothing happening, but still Jerry didn't work on his assignments.

ONE beastly hot day after I'd been working with Jerry for about four months, I was running late with my appointments and rushing to get out to meet a client who would be waiting for me on a busy street corner, when the phone rang. It was Jerry.

"I only did it because you said nothing would happen," he said. "I walked right through and didn't pick up anything but, there was a lot of dangerous stuff there. I don't think I can handle this—I don't know what to do. I'm afraid to go back, I think I'll call the police and see if anyone's been killed. This is terrible, you said nothing would happen, it's your responsibility."

"Jerry," I said, with impatience probably evident in my voice, "the mortality rate from subway litter is zero!"

After a short, stunned silence Jerry said, "I don't need to be patronized by you!" and hung up.

I headed for my appointment feeling irritated. Irritated that Jerry hung up on me, irritated with the way he said, "it's your responsibility," irritated because I was hot and rushed and tired and feeling that too many demands were made on me. When I got home that evening I kicked off my shoes and started to go through my mail when it occurred to me, as I thought about my conversation with Jerry, that it was the first time that Jerry had attempted to do an assignment. "I shouldn't have been so impatient with him," I told myself.

At our next appointment Jerry had a lot of difficulty talking about the terrible experience he had had the day before. He didn't want to tell me the level of his anxiety, but finally he admitted that it was a 10 on a scale from 0 to 10—a full-blown panic attack. His method of dealing with anxiety in the past had been to either totally avoid situations that might create anxiety or to immediately give in to the fears and pick up the offending litter. While he worked with me, he successfully placed all responsibility for whatever disaster might occur on to me.

"Did you write in your diary what happened?" I asked.

"No, I was too nervous to just sit and write."

"Did you ask yourself the two basic questions?"

"What questions?"

"Jerry, don't you remember? I had you write them down. The questions are: What do you think will happen? and What are the facts that support that expectation? Let's go over it now. What did you think would happen?"

"This is a waste of time," Jerry said. "We both know that nothing would have happened."

"Now we know that, but *then* what did you think would happen?"

"This is going to sound really crazy, but then I just knew that someone was going to be injured or killed, and I would be held responsible. When I called you, I was actually afraid that the police were about to come and get me. I was afraid to go back to the station because it would be like walking into a trap. But I couldn't stand not knowing if anything happened."

"What did you do?"

"This is so crazy—I feel like I really lost it. After I hung up on you I went back to the station and hung around at the top of the steps for a while. I didn't see any commotion so I went downstairs, looked around, then told the token clerk that I'd heard that there'd been an accident at the station and was worried about my wife, who wasn't home yet. The clerk said that he'd been there for several hours and during that time there'd been no accident. I started to walk away but was still worried and thought that maybe he hadn't understood me, so I went back and asked him again. He repeated that there'd been no accident. I got to the top of the stairs, but it was still gnawing at me. I was sure that there must have been an accident, so I went back and asked him again. This time he looked at me as though I were a nut and yelled that there had been no accident, and to get out and leave him alone. I was so humiliated; I was furious with you, you were the one who got me into this. I didn't think it would be so painful, I don't think I can do that again."

"Let's hope that you won't have to," I said. "But a part of the work is to put yourself into the situation without assigning all the responsibility to me, and to always ask yourself the two basic questions. Do you think your anxiety level would have been different if you had asked yourself what facts you have to support the idea that someone might have gotten hurt or killed?"

"No, I don't think so, because I was beyond reasoning with myself. It was just raw unthinking fear."

How can it be, we might ask ourselves, that someone as intelligent and well-grounded in reality as Jerry can suffer from such an illogical condition? Let's go back to the concept of magic thinking. Jerry, in the privacy of his own mind, decided that he was responsible for the safety of all the people who went through the subway station. Implicit in his belief is that everyone else held him responsible as well; that if anyone was injured in the subway station, the police, or whoever, would somehow know that Jerry had passed through that station at about the same time, and would also know where he had gone, pursue him, and arrest him. When Jerry isn't in an anxiety-producing situation and we ask him who assigned him that responsibility, he recognizes how totally illogical the premise was.

When he is overwhelmed with anxiety, he can't think logically; he responds the same way Henny Penny did. He convinces himself that he knows that something terrible is going to happen because he *feels* that something terrible is going to happen. Because he feels that something terrible is going to happen, something terrible *will* happen. This vicious cycle of fear feeds on itself, escalates, and generates the same distressing physical sensations that accompany real calamities. In the grip of this fear Jerry (and Henny Penny, and all the other magic thinkers we have been considering) loses touch with reality and responds to his inner scene of disaster (getting arrested for injury or death caused by subway litter) and his very disturbing physical sensations. The fastest route to relief is to leave the situation immediately (as with phobia) or to perform a ritual (for Jerry that is picking up all the litter in the subway station).

If Jerry had been keeping a diary, he would have discovered that his anxiety doesn't fall out of the sky: there are always clues that lead up to a panic attack. When the anxiety can be confronted at lower levels, it can be controlled before it escalates into a full-blown panic attack.

The morning preceding Jerry's panic attack he had left his apartment while in a rage with his wife. He had wanted her to pick up his laundry (a difficult chore for him because he worried that the lint in the shop might start a fire). His wife refused, saying that she had too much to do that day, and added that she was tired of running his errands like a servant. In his rage Jerry had violent thoughts about his wife ("I wish she was dead! I feel like killing her!"), and then felt horrified with himself for having thought such abhorrent things. Jerry estimated that when he left his house that morning his anxiety level was already about a 7 or 8.

He took a taxi to work, feeling that he wasn't up to dealing with the subway stations, and when he arrived he found that a major deal he had been working on for a number of months had fallen through. His thoughts were: "I can't do anything right. I'm washed up. I'll be out on my ass. I'm a total failure." His anxiety level was still hovering around 7 or 8.

Over lunch with a couple of colleagues his anxiety level dropped to about 2 after several drinks, but later in the afternoon it rose again to about 7 because he was worrying and obsessing about some of the things he might have said with an alcohol-loosened tongue.

Jerry left work early, taking the subway home. When he walked through the subway station, still feeling the effect of the drinks he had had at lunch, his thoughts were, "Fuck it, I don't care what happens to anyone." He expected to find his wife at home when he arrived. Not finding her, he remembered the violent thoughts he had had earlier and said to himself, "What if something has happened to her? I might have caused it by wishing her dead." When he remembered that he had walked through the subway station not caring what happened, and not picking up "dangerous" litter, his anxiety soared to 10. At that point he had called me.

If I had been able to spend time on the phone with Jerry, I'm sure he could have gotten his anxiety under control, not necessarily by reality testing (which I'd been trying to get him to do), but by reassigning responsibility to me. He probably would have said to himself, "Fine, I've told Randy about it; now if anything happens it's her responsibility."

During our next two sessions Jerry gave me a more complete view of his problems. It wasn't just subway stations that gave him problems. At work he couldn't keep secretaries because he wouldn't allow them to use perfume, hairspray, or white-out at their desk; he considered these products to be highly flammable and was afraid that a spark from the telephone might start a fire. If a chair was out of place he was afraid someone would stumble over it; if an umbrella wasn't properly put away he was afraid that someone would fall; if the carpet mud-guard wasn't perfectly flat he was afraid that someone might stumble. Rarely was he able to keep a secretary for more than a month or two.

His worries at home were mostly controlled by his having secretly assigned responsibility to his wife. Early in their marriage when Jerry worried about poisons and fires, his wife, having become exasperated with him, had said, "Jerry, I love you, but you're a nut—get out of my kitchen!" To him, that statement amounted to tacit agreement to assume all responsibility. He arranged his life so that he never went anywhere new without her. He called her attention to all the hazards he saw ("There's a pencil on the floor; the corner of that carpet is turned up; there's a spray can close to the stove; a broken bottle is on the ground"), thereby shifting the responsibility for possible disaster onto her. She had no idea that Jerry had a serious problem; she just knew that he seemed to be very dependent. She attributed the occasions when he didn't make any sense to his being preoccupied with business.

Jerry had a whole series of litanies that he repeated to himself throughout the day. Some litanies were designed to counteract the power of a violent thought, some were designed to shift responsibility. Each of them had to be said exactly right seven times. If he wasn't sure that he'd said them right, he would have to start over from the beginning; if he lost track of the number of times he had said a litany, he would have to start all over again, because either more or less than seven times meant that he really wanted the terrible thing to happen.

He had magic systems for just about everything he did. When he dressed in the morning he had to put everything on in strict sequence (if he put his pants on before his shirt and tie, that meant something terrible would happen). Before he could put even a single dollar into his wallet he had to check all the bills to be sure that they faced the same way and were arranged in sequence according to denomination—otherwise financial ruin was inevitable. Before he made a telephone call he had to check the surrounding area to be sure that it contained nothing flammable. Even though he assigned responsibility to his wife and me, his time with us was often marred with bad thoughts (he confessed that he often had the thought that I was stupid and didn't know what I was talking about), which would negate the assignment of responsibility.

Jerry's anxiety level was usually around 7 or 8. His life was spent staving off disaster.

After he had given me a fairly complete description of his situation he said, "That's really why I didn't keep a diary. I'm always anxious; if I had to write down every episode, I wouldn't have time to do anything else."

"Why didn't you tell me any of this before?" I asked.

"It was too complicated and crazy sounding. Picking up subway litter is the most recent development in the ongoing nuttiness; it's also the most potentially humiliating. If anyone I knew saw me doing it I'd really be embarrassed, so I felt that that was the most urgent problem."

Jerry was right in deciding to start work on the most recently established problem, but if I had known the whole story I would have had him working on several fronts at the same time so that he would have been learning to identify and control lower levels of anxiety by reality testing and cause-and-effecting. Mostly what he learned during the months we worked together in the subway station was how best to shift responsibility onto me. Even the reality testing wasn't that important because he told himself that the facts didn't apply to him.

When Jerry originally came in to see me he was in a crisis state. Often when people come in to see me they are having a crisis. They want relief immediately and aren't willing to go through the tedious process of diary keeping and reality testing. Usually I can offer some relief just by assuring them that they aren't crazy, and that other people have had similar problems and have conquered them. Jerry found temporary relief by shifting responsibility for all the disaster he imagined might happen onto me. For a while that worked, but he hadn't touched the source of his problem (the magic thinking), so nothing really changed. The fact that Jerry decided to stay in therapy even though he was furious with me and felt that I had failed him was a hopeful sign. This time we started at the beginning.

Jerry and I made a comprehensive list of situations that he found anxiety-producing, and he promised to make four entries a day into his anxiety diary, analyzing each of the entries by using the two basic questions: What do I think will happen? and What facts do I have to support that expectation?

AT this writing I'm still working with Jerry. He's made tremendous progress: he's had the same secretary for over six months; he doesn't point out dangers to his wife; he rarely picks up litter in subway stations; but he still has a long way to go.

Jerry has been very good at keeping his diary, but even though the entries are exhaustingly repetitive and he admits that he has no facts to support the expectation of something terrible happening, he stills suffers high levels of anxiety because of that old obsessive-compulsive voice in his head that says, "But it could happen—this time it might be different."

Although he's reduced the number of situations where he depends on litanies to keep himself and the world safe, he does occasionally get into uncontrollable litany-saying sessions when he feels the need to undo a bad thought. Much of what we're currently working on are the consequences of his bad thoughts. "How is thinking that some guy is an SOB going to cause anything bad to happen to him?" I ask time and time again.

"I don't know, it just will," Jerry answers each time.

"Why is it your responsibility? If he's really such an SOB, don't you think other people are thinking similar things about him?"

I asked Jerry what advice he might give to other magic thinkers: "Resist the urge for quick relief. At the moment, nothing is easier than doing the ritual or saying the litany, but that just gives the problem more power. My problem was like an eight-foot monster and I was just a little kid standing next to it. By fighting it and not giving in to the nutty thoughts and the horrible feelings I feel I'm almost the same size now. Eventually I'll be bigger than the problem and it won't be able to push me around anymore."

CHAPTER SEVEN

JANET, THE BUMP LADY

THE woman who had everything was sitting on my couch, telling me one of the most bizarre stories I'd ever heard. At forty-one, Janet was tall, slim, blond, and incredibly beautiful. Her family was established old money, high society. Her husband was a key executive with a Fortune 500 company, her two kids were in posh private schools—and Janet's life was a mess. In order to leave her Connecticut mansion to come to see me, Janet required at least one bottle of wine. If she were not "sedated," the normally hour-long trip would take four or five hours because she would have to stop and retrace her route, looking along the roadside for bodies of people who might have been hit by cars.

Janet said that she had always been apprehensive about driving and overly concerned about running over small animals that might run onto the road. She lived in a neighborhood where the houses are set on large pieces of property, hidden from the road by trees and accessible by long driveways. The area was semirural, with wooded sections and quiet roads, and often wild animals (squirrels, rabbits, and the like) could be seen crossing the road; occasionally there would be evidence of an animal that didn't make it. When her kids were little and she had to drive them to their activities, she would drive so slowly they would tease her, "Come on Mom, we have to get there today. You want us to get out and push?" She drove so slowly she was a hazard on major highways. Because she held up normal traffic flow, she used the back roads and allowed extra time, and in this way she managed.

But one day about six years prior to coming into my office, Janet was driving her daughter to riding lessons when she felt a bump and thought she had hit something. She stopped the car, got out, and looked around and under the car but didn't see anything. She got back into the car and started to drive away. "Maybe the body was under the wheels where I couldn't see it," she thought. She stopped the car again and walked back to where she had originally stopped—still no body in sight. She got back into the car. "Maybe it's a small body and it's stuck on the wheels or under the car somewhere." She got out of the car again and crawled underneath, looking at all four tires and the underside of the car—still no body. Janet returned to the car and delivered her daughter to her riding lessons, but the thought of having hit something was constantly on her mind.

Several days later she was returning from shopping when she felt a bump while she was driving along a wooded part of the road. She got out of the car and looked underneath; she circled the car, looking at the side of the road; she drove the car five feet forward and got out and looked again; she crawled underneath the car and looked at the tires and the underside of the car, but she found no body. Finally she got back into the car and continued the drive home, but the thought of having hit something nagged at her. When her husband came home that evening, she told him that she thought she had hit something on the road while driving.

"Well, that happens even when you're careful," he said. "Sometimes they run out so fast, and they're so low to the ground, you can't see them."

Her husband's statement, which was meant to be reassuring, tormented Janet. The way she translated it, it meant, "No matter how careful you are, you will still be killing things." She made a note in her diary, "In less than a week I've killed two animals."

Soon, on every trip in the car, Janet thought she hit something. If the kids were with her she made them get out of the car and help her look for the body. The kids, of course, gave her a hard time.

Janet soon expanded her search area to include several feet into the woods, just in case the animal had crawled away after being hit. A twenty-minute trip into town could take two hours. In her diary she noted, "Since last month I've killed twenty-five animals."

Janet obsessed to her husband about hitting animals. "I hit two things today. The first one I hit about 9:20 when I was on my way to the village. It was about thirty feet from the intersection with Shady Road when I felt the bump. I got right out to see if I could catch it but it must have crawled into the woods to hide. I spent half an hour looking for it but couldn't find it. The other one was when I was returning at 4:10. I can't stand it that I keep hitting things. I think of all those poor suffering animals dying in the woods. Can't we do something? Can't we put one of those things on the front of the car like train engines used to have to keep from hitting cows?"

Her husband was also getting reports from the kids about how weird their mom was acting. It took forever to get anyplace because several times along the way she stopped the car and ordered everyone out for a body search. The kids were afraid to invite friends along because Janet's behavior was so crazy it embarrassed them. Her husband, who at this point was very concerned and worried about Janet, suggested that she was under a great deal of pressure and it might be best if she just rested for the time being. He would arrange for help to do the shopping and run the errands.

About a month later her husband called from the local train station. He had taken the car to the repair shop for a minor adjustment, but there was some problem and the car wasn't ready. He was stuck at the train station without transportation. He asked if Janet felt able to pick him up in her car.

She actually felt good getting into the car again and easing it down the driveway. Dusk was approaching. When she turned the lights on she noticed a hiker with a backpack on her side of the road. She moved over to the other side of the road to pass him. When she looked up into the rearview mirror she saw nothing but an empty road. "Oh my God," she said aloud, "I've hit him." She slammed on the brakes, got out of the car, and ran back to the spot where she had passed the hiker. She got down on the road looking for some signs of blood, but it was getting dark and she couldn't see well enough. She ran back to the car for a flashlight. With the flashlight she ran back and forth along both sides of the road and went into the woods looking for him.

After about twenty minutes a car approached from the other direction, and she flagged it down. "Help me," she said, "I accidentally hit a hiker and I'm sure he's dead or dying but I can't find his body." The driver of the other car was a neighbor who knew Janet and her husband but had no idea of the difficulties Janet had been having. At first he helped Janet look for the injured hiker, but after ten minutes without success he asked her how she knew she had hit him. Janet explained how she had seen him, passed him by, then all of a sudden he disappeared.

"But Janet," he said, "he could have walked into the woods to take a shortcut, or he could have disappeared over the crest of the hill. Just because you didn't see him doesn't mean that you hit him. If anything, it's the reverse; because we can't find him it must mean that you didn't hit him."

Janet was inconsolable; she was positive that she had hit the hiker and that he was lying mortally injured somewhere in the woods or beside the road. She felt compelled to find him. She resumed her frantic searching. By then the neighbor realized that Janet wasn't acting rationally, so he suggested that he take her home and they get Philip, her husband, to help them look. "Oh no," Janet said, "I was supposed to pick Philip up at the train station an hour ago."

Philip was beside himself with worry. He had called home to hear that Janet had left long ago. He was about to call the police to see if she had been in an accident when he saw the neighbor and Janet getting out of a car. Janet was disheveled, with wild-looking hair, smudges on her face, and dirty, torn clothes. During the trip back to their house the neighbor explained how he had found Janet, while she sat in the back seat crying.

The family doctor prescribed tranquilizers and total rest. Janet's husband hired a chauffeur so Janet wouldn't have to drive. Months went by. Janet didn't leave the house; she spent a lot of time in bed, reading and relaxing. She was really feeling much better when her daughter asked if she could attend a school play in which she had a leading part. Janet very much wanted to see her daughter's performance and with a chauffeur to drive her, she couldn't imagine a problem.

On the day of her daughter's play Janet settled into the back seat of the car. As the chauffeur picked up speed, something on the side of the road caught Janet's eye.

"Stop," Janet shouted, "there's a body lying beside the road." The chauffeur slammed on the brakes, and Janet dashed out of the car, closely followed by the chauffeur. When they arrived at the spot where Janet had seen the "body," the chauffeur said, "Oh, it's just one of them black garbage bags. For a while you had me real scared." Then to his astonishment Janet proceeded to empty the contents of the garbage bag, turn the bag inside out, looking at both sides, return the contents to the bag, then take the bag back to the car and put it in the trunk.

They continued down the road for another few hundred yards when Janet again shouted for the chauffeur to stop. This time the "body" turned out to be an old tire by the side of the road.

Janet never made it to the school play. When her husband and daughter returned home that evening Janet was still out on the road looking for bodies.

For the next several years Janet was basically housebound. She quit attending social events; she missed the kids' school activities; when she had to go out she medicated herself with a potentially dangerous combination of tranquilizers and alcohol to the point where she was almost comatose.

DURING our first appointment Janet's speech was slurred. She took an inordinately long time to answer the most basic questions. She nodded and her eyes seemed to be closing as we talked. Her husband gave me most of the background information. I explained that the central part of therapy would be exposure. In her case we would be spending a fair amount of time driving around. I explained that I couldn't work with her unless she was sober. Philip assured me that the only time Janet drank was when she had to go somewhere in the car. "But Philip," I said, "we'll be working in the car." He promised that he would deliver her sober for the next appointment.

Our plan was that Philip would go home after work, pick up Janet, and drive back to Manhattan for a late evening appointment with me. We chose late evening because just south of my office in lower Manhattan the traffic is very light at that hour. Philip arrived right on time. I went downstairs to join them in the car, and found Janet stinking drunk.

"Philip," I said, "this isn't going to work."

"It will work," he said. "We'll drive around and I'll tell you what Janet would do, and you can tell me what you would do." A dedicated support person can make a significant contribution to the success of the therapy, so I decided to give it a try. We headed downtown to a construction site that was usually deserted at night. As he drove he pointed out things along the street that Janet would insist he stop for so that she could get out and inspect. The purpose of her inspection was to see if it was a dead body. I suggested that Philip role-play Janet. (Janet was snoring loudly in the back seat.)

"There!" Philip said, "There's a dead body!" He slammed on the brakes. "I have to get out and check it." He was pointing to a fire hydrant.

We continued to drive around while Philip pointed out things that Janet would insist were dead bodies. In addition to having to stop for every conceivable type of litter, Janet would also stop every time she felt a bump. It was clear that she wouldn't get very far on a New York street.

The following week Philip showed up again with Janet drunk in the back seat. We drove around with Philip calling my attention to the most imperceptible bumps and insisting that he had hit something and pointing out every piece of litter on the street claiming that it was a dead body. I had him describe each of the dead bodies to me in detail—their size and shape and physical features. He accurately described every fragment of refuse and rubbish we encountered along the way, and none seemed even vaguely similar to a dead body. How easy it was to reality test with Philip! Toward the end of the session I again

expressed my misgivings about working with Janet. Her combination of alcohol and tranquilizers not only negated any
chance for therapy but was also very dangerous; her doctor
should be informed about it. Philip and I could role-play forever, but unless Janet could be consciously involved it would-
n't do her any good. Philip looked straight ahead into the distance while he listened silently to what I said, but before he drove
away he said with grim determination, "We'll be in touch."

A month later I heard from Janet. "Philip and I would like
to resume therapy," she said. We arranged for an evening appointment, and I wondered what condition I would find Janet
in. When they arrived, to my great delight, I met Janet sober
for the first time. Janet's doctor had been horrified when he had
heard of her alcohol abuse and threatened to have her hospitalized unless she stopped drinking. (It turned out that Janet
was drinking a great deal more than Philip knew, or would
admit to.) Because the drive to Manhattan was so stressful for
her, they drove down the evening before our appointment and
spent the night in a hotel to give Janet a chance to relax before
the therapy session. I was impressed with their determination—that boded well for a successful outcome.

Philip was at the wheel of the car while Janet and I sat in the
back seat. Because she had been so incapacitated with drugs
and alcohol during our first three sessions I had the impres-
sion that Janet was a passive, spiritless, broken woman. I was
wrong. Unfortunately, at that moment most of her spirit expressed itself in anger. She was angry because she had the
problem. She was angry that she had lost six years. She was
angry that she hadn't been able to get effective help. She was
angry because no one understood her suffering. And most of
all she was angry with herself because she knew how irrational
she had become but was helpless to change it. Philip slowly
drove downtown to the construction site where we would be

working. Janet slumped down into the seat and put her hands over her eyes. Every now and then she would shout, "Philip, be careful!" or "Philip, I felt a bump!" He would patiently answer, "I am being careful," or "That was just a pothole."

When we arrived at the construction site I was appalled to see that it was an even worse mess than usual. In addition to the usual detritus of the city, on the streets were huge hunks of wood, barrels, and four-foot wads of rolled-up wire. This would be a real baptism of fire for Janet. Philip stopped the car; she took her hands from her eyes, looked around and said, "Oh God." I agreed. She told me that everything she saw out there looked like dead bodies to her. I asked her to describe the wad of wire to me. She said it looked like a dead body. "Where is the head?" I asked.

"I don't know, but it looks like a dead body; I have to check it."

"We can go out and check it together, but first tell me if it is lying down or sitting or standing," I said.

"I don't know what it's doing, I have to check it."

"Look," I said, "If it's dead, it can wait awhile. First tell me . . ."

The dead body could wait but Janet couldn't. She got out of the car and ran over to the wire and started turning it around and looking through it. Philip and I were right behind her. "Is it a dead body?" I asked when we got up to her.

"You know it's not a dead body," she turned on me furiously.

"But Janet, if I know it's not a dead body, why don't you know that?"

She put her head in her hand and cried softly, "Because I'm crazy, that's why."

I got into the back seat with Janet, had her put her hands over her eyes, and asked Philip to drive back to my office. When he stopped at my door Janet put her hands in her lap.

"You won't work with me any more, will you," she said.

"As long as you continue to show up for appointments sober, I'll continue to work with you. Between now and next week when we meet again, I'd like you and Philip to practice in the car and see how far you can get without checking for bodies. Keep a diary of your practice sessions and describe your thoughts: why the object looked like a dead body, what you did about it, and what the reality was." As I was talking she took notes. When I finished, she looked up, smiled wanly, and said, "Consider it done."

When I went down to meet them for the next session, Janet was sitting in the front seat with Philip. I greeted them and asked Janet if she had her eyes open during the trip from the hotel.

"Yes," she said. "I've had my eyes open a lot lately," and she handed me her diary for the week. Every evening after Philip arrived home from work they had gone out to the car. She had six pages of diary entries. Some evenings they didn't get out of the driveway, but on a couple of evenings they got three or four hundred yards down the road. A very abbreviated version of Janet's diary looked like this:

Task: "In car, trying to drive like a normal person."

DATE/TIME	THOUGHT	ANXIETY LEVEL	RITUAL OR RESPONSE	REALITY
Wed 7:00	dead body	9	checked	a dead bush
Thu 7:00	dead body	8	checked	garbage bag
Fri 7:30	dead body	6	reality tested	an empty six-pack
Sat 2:00	dead body	9	checked	unidentifiable junk
Sun 4:00	dead body	5	reality tested	same dead bush
Mon 7:00	dead body	8	checked	very dead squirrel

"Janet, does anything about these diary entries surprise you?" I asked.

"It all surprises me," she said. "First of all, the fact that I'm getting into the car sober after six years surprises me. On a beautiful spring day with the dogwood in bloom, the fact that all I have on my mind is dead bodies surprises me. I used to love spring. I always went to the garden and cut fresh flowers for the house; now all I do is worry about dead bodies.

"Also, that I could possibly imagine that an empty six-pack was a dead body is insane. While I sat in the car I could see the word 'Miller' on it. I really don't understand it myself, but at the time I genuinely believed it to be a dead body. The same is true about the dead bush. It's an old boxwood on the edge of our property that died last fall. We've been meaning to have the gardener replace it but just haven't gotten around to it. I see it every day from the dining room window, but when I get into the car, all of a sudden it becomes a dead body."

"What about the squirrel?" I asked. "You finally found your dead body. What did you do about it?"

"Yes, the poor little thing. We got it off the road and put it in the woods. It had been dead a long time, so I didn't feel responsible for killing it, but I still felt sorry for it. If it had been a person that would have been a different matter, of course."

"But it wasn't a person. And you didn't find any dead people."

"No, no dead people. Philip suggested that I turn my diary into a scrapbook of dead bodies. I've bought a Polaroid camera. When we're out driving I'll take a picture of everything I think is a dead body, make a note of where it was, and keep it in a scrapbook so that before we leave the house we can review the scrapbook and know what to expect."

I am indebted to Philip for that wonderful, creative suggestion. The Polaroid scrapbook is a technique I've suggested to many of my clients, and it never fails to help the person establish a graphic history of his experiences and see the reality when he gets caught up in obsessive-compulsive thinking.

Instead of returning to the construction site, we found a deserted side street. Philip moved to the back seat; Janet and I were in front with her behind the wheel. She hadn't driven for several years, so she was understandably cautious. She put the car in gear and slowly inched forward. We had gone about thirty feet when she stopped suddenly and said,

"I felt a bump."

"So did I," I said. "What do you think it was?"

"I think I hit someone. I'd better get out and look."

"The street has been deserted since we arrived, how could you have hit someone? There's been no one here to hit."

"They could have been sitting on the curb or they could have fallen down and been lying in the street. I have to check."

Janet ran out of the car and back down the street to where we had started. I joined her. She was looking on the street and crossing back and forth, checking the sidewalks on both sides of the street. "What do you expect to find?" I asked.

She looked at me with anger, "You know what I expect to find! I expect to find the body of the man I hit."

"How do you know it was a man? Did you see a man? How do you know you hit anyone? All you said is that you felt a bump. Could there be another reason for feeling a bump?" No answer. She had gone back and forth from the corner to the car, looking frantically for the body at least a dozen times, and she was obviously getting tired. "Janet, can you think of another reason for feeling a bump? Why don't we look in the street for a pothole that might explain the bump?"

Janet leaned against the car and put her head down, exhausted, and said quietly, "Of course we'll find a pothole to explain the bump; I'm not stupid."

"Then why do you get into the body search?"

"I don't know. The thought comes into my head and it just takes over. I get this awful urgent feeling that I have to get out and search for the body even though a part of me knows that it's crazy—that there is no body. But the thought takes control and impels me to search. I don't feel that I have any will left."

Janet described the obsessive-compulsive condition exactly and succinctly. The victim feels powerless to resist the urge to perform the ritual or to banish the thoughts, even though she knows that the thoughts aren't based on reality.

When we got into the car I asked Philip to walk about twenty feet ahead of us and sit on the curb so that Janet could see that a person on the street would be perfectly visible. We took a blanket out of the trunk, rolled it up, and laid it in the street so that she could see that if someone *was* lying in the street she would see them. Then I asked her to enter into her diary all the results of our reality testing for the night. Her diary entries confirmed that not only could she clearly see a person on the street, but also she could easily tell the difference between a rolled-up blanket and a person.

Janet and Philip continued practicing every evening. Janet accumulated the world's biggest photographic collection of roadside junk and made uneven progress. Some weeks she would be elated and report that she had driven a couple of miles without checking; some weeks she would be in despair and tell me that she couldn't even get out of the driveway, or that she had to get out and check every lump and bump on the road.

"I often feel like I'm two people," Janet explained. "The obsessive, nutty part of me is *this* big (she put her hand over her head as high as she could reach); the real, rational, sensible Janet is *this* big (she held her hand level with her waist). Sometimes the real Janet gets suddenly bigger and can overpower the nutty Janet, but other times the nutty Janet takes over and makes me do things that I know are crazy. But I feel the real Janet getting stronger and stronger. I just wish it were more predictable. If I knew that this week I can drive two miles; next week I'll be able to drive two and a half miles; the week after I'll be able to drive three miles, and so on, I'd feel more secure. But it's up and down without any sense or reason to it."

Janet and Philip were beginning to get disheartened because progress wasn't rapid enough. When I reminded them that Janet had been incapacitated for six years, but now—in less than six months—she no longer drank, she had substantially reduced the number of tranquilizers she was taking, she was again socially active, and she traveled freely as long as Philip was driving, they agreed to reassess their concept of "progress." They had been focusing on what Janet couldn't do rather than looking at how her life had changed for the better—not all progress can be counted in miles.

One cold and rainy evening in late fall while we were working on our deserted streets, we decided to try an area that was unfamiliar to Janet. It proved to be a bad decision. The street was more commercial than our usual streets. It had more cars and pedestrian traffic than we were used to, and more cars parked along the curb. Janet drove slowly alongside the parked cars. It was clear that she was getting apprehensive, so I suggested that she turn at the next corner and return to our old streets. We could try this street when the weather was better. Janet nodded without taking her eyes off the street and continued to the corner. At the corner we could see that the gutters were overflowing and water was over the curbs. Janet hesitated a moment, then eased the car through the water and around the corner. She stopped the car about fifteen feet past the corner and said low and ominously, "There's a body under the water."

"The water is only about five inches deep," I said. "If there was a body there we would be able to see it."

"There's a body under the water, I know it." She was out of the car and on her way to the puddle before I had a chance to help her reality test the possibility. The puddle encompassed the entire near side of the intersection on both sides of the street. Some of it was only an inch or so deep, but near the curbs it was deeper. When I reached Janet she was standing in the deepest part of the puddle poking around in it. "Janet," I shouted over the noise of the traffic and the rain, "if there were a body in the water we'd be able to see it."

"I have to find it, I know there's a body in here somewhere."

"We'd see it, Janet, bodies are deeper than four or five inches."

Janet got down on her hands and knees in the puddle and started pulling up all kinds of unspeakable things from the gutter, but no body. I was afraid that she would be hit by a car coming around the corner, so I ran back to get Philip. When Philip and I returned Janet was on the north side of the street thrashing around in that puddle. She looked up at us, her face twisted with anguish, "I can't do it," she said, "I can't check all these puddles."

Gently Philip took her arm and pulled her out of the puddle, "You don't have to," he said. "There is no body." He took the blanket out of the trunk of the car and wrapped it around her and eased her into the back seat. Soaked to the skin, my hair dripping water into my eyes, and shivering uncontrollably, I went to the greasy spoon nearby and got us some hot coffee. The three of us sat in the car, silently sipping our coffee for a long time. Then, staring intently into her empty coffee container, Janet said, "I'll never do that again. I'll never let it take control of me like that again."

And it never did take control of her like that again. She and

Philip continued to practice every night. But the practice sessions became more normal outings, such as going to the movies with Janet driving both ways. Gradually fewer and fewer photographs of "dead bodies" were added to the scrapbook. One day Janet noticed that two months had gone by without a new addition.

I worked with Janet and Philip for a little over a year. One evening toward the end of our session Janet said, "Remember when I said that the nutty Janet was this big and the real Janet was only this big? Well now I feel that the real Janet is just as big as the nutty Janet, and I think that pretty soon the nutty Janet will only be a scared little girl."

When she started driving alone again, Janet and Philip stopped coming to see me, but Philip continued to work with her. He was a perfect support person. He was patient and understanding, he helped reality test but remained steadfast against being drawn into Janet's rituals. He was also extraordinarily creative in finding ways to assist Janet toward her goal. When she decided that it was time to use highways but found that maintaining the required speed on the highway was difficult for her, Philip installed a special horn in his car and offered to follow her on the highway. Every time her speed fell below fifty miles an hour, he honked.

I wonder what the other drivers thought when they saw a big Mercedes sedan followed by a racy Jaguar honking to the tune of "I'm a Yankee Doodle Dandy."

(For more information on my work with Janet see pages 253–55 in chapter 15, "How to Get Better."

CHAPTER EIGHT

NORM: HIS BRIDGE PHOBIA LED HIM INTO ALCOHOLISM, MESSED UP HIS MARRIAGE, AND ALIENATED HIS KIDS

NORM was thirty-four years old when he had his first panic attack. He was returning home with his wife and three small kids after visiting his dying father. Norm, his brother, and two sisters gathered every Sunday at their parents' home for dinner. Although they all knew that their father's health was rapidly deteriorating and he had a very short time to live, they pretended that everything was just fine and Dad would be back to normal in no time. The Sunday dinners and the charade had gotten increasingly stressful over the weeks. Sniffles could be heard at the table, and some weeks Norm would barely make it to the car before breaking into tears.

On this particular Sunday, as they were getting into the car Norm's three children began fighting. Norm became so upset with the racket he left his wife in the car to quiet the kids while he went up the street to get a drink.

When Norm returned they left Philadelphia in heavy traffic and headed for the bridge across the Delaware River toward their home thirty minutes away in New Jersey. As he got on the bridge he suddenly became aware of his rapidly beating heart and uncontrollable shakiness. His mouth was dry, and he felt a queasiness in his stomach and a frightening feeling that he wasn't really there in the car, he was somewhere else observing with detachment a strange look-alike Norm driving over a bridge. As he was inching along in stop-and-go traffic he thought, "I'm going to go crazy, lose control, and drive over the edge of the bridge." As soon as he got off the bridge he abruptly pulled over to the side of the road, fell forward on the steering wheel, and continued to shake and gasp for air. His wife was terrified, and thinking that he was having a heart attack, got out of the car and tried to get help from passersby. But drivers zipped past, paying no attention to her. After ten or fifteen minutes Norm's heartbeat slowed and the shakes left him. His wife drove the rest of the way home.

Several days after Norm's first panic attack his father died. During the period of mourning his wife drove the family back and forth from their home across the bridge to Philadelphia. About a month went by before Norm had the occasion to drive alone over the bridge. Rushing to a business appointment, he was on the approach to the bridge when his heart started to beat wildly, and he became so shaky he was afraid he would lose control of the car. He gripped the steering wheel with all his strength and, with beads of sweat rising on his face, he crept along. He noticed that as he got past the apex of the bridge the sensations abated a bit. Once off the bridge his mind went to the problems he anticipated at the business appointment. His day in Philadelphia ended late, and it was evening before he started home. As he headed for the bridge he thought, "What if IT happens again?" With that, his heart started to beat rapidly, and he felt shaky, weak, dizzy, and had difficulty breathing. Confused and upset, Norm pulled into a gas station and called his wife to come and get him.

THE job he had at the onset of his phobia required that he travel to Philadelphia and Washington, D.C., regularly. He lived in southern New Jersey, and traveling to those cities required going over sizable bridges. At first Norm had his wife drive him to his appointments, but gradually, even with his wife driving, he began to panic as they drove over a bridge. He had gone to several doctors, fearing there was something physically wrong with him, but they pronounced him in good health. He began to take tranquilizers on the days he had to go over bridges, but they didn't alter that overwhelming sense of dread that came over him.

Norm discovered that the addition of a couple of ounces of vodka in his morning orange juice effectively chased away that sense of dread; but the combination of his morning cocktail and tranquilizers had a disastrous effect on his job. At meetings he would mumble, ramble on senselessly, or just stare intently at some distant point in space. After several months of dubious performance, he stumbled into a meeting one morning a half hour late, knocked over a carafe of coffee, and promptly fell asleep, only to be rudely awakened by his boss advising him in loud and uncertain terms that he was no longer employed.

His first reaction to having been fired was one of welcome relief—he would never have to drive over a bridge again. Norm's relief was short-lived when his wife forcefully reminded him that he had a family to support. He assuaged his guilt and shame with more vodka. As money got tighter and tighter, he calmed his worries with just a tiny bit more vodka. Fortunately, when sober Norm had a fine business head. After a year of floundering he and his wife started a successful business in their home.

NORM came to see me when he was in his late forties. Their business had become very successful. He had managed to avoid

driving over bridges for fourteen years without noticeably re-
stricting his life, he claimed. He and his wife went frequently
to New York via tunnel, and they had flown to Europe a couple of times, but a planned trip to California had been aborted
because he thought about the bridges around San Francisco
and became too anxious to go. He probably would have continued avoiding bridges except that his oldest child would be
graduating from the University of Pennsylvania in spring and
the next oldest was in school in Baltimore, so he either had to
forget about seeing his kids graduate or start driving over
bridges again.

Oddly, Norm never connected the stress of his father's illness and death with the difficulty on the bridge those many
years ago. To him it was as though the two situations occupied
separate compartments with no bearing on each other. The
original panic attack on the bridge was of a totally mysterious
origin to him. It was my guess that he had displaced all of his
feelings of fear and rage and helplessness over losing his father
onto the bridge. Had he been able to recognize that the physical sensations he experienced were manifestations of thoughts
of the anticipated loss of his father, he probably would not have
become phobic.

Our first session was spent developing an understanding of
the problem. When considered in the context of Norm's life
the feelings of fear and helplessness were appropriate—but it
was vital for Norm to know that it wasn't the bridge that caused
those feelings. It had been so long since Norm had attempted
to drive over any bridge that it was impossible to establish a
hierarchy of difficulty, so his assignment for the week was to
drive around the area with his wife to see how he felt driving
on overpasses and low bridges.

Norm arrived at our next appointment with some very surprising information. "I thought," Norm said, "that bridges were
just this isolated little problem and all I'd have to do was drive

over a few bridges and that would be it, but last week when I was trying to establish a hierarchy for us to work with I discovered that everything I do is calculated to avoid bridges. For ten years I've taken the same route to my in-laws' because I know there are no bridges along the way. There's a shorter route that I could take, but it involves two bridges. I say that I don't take it because it's not as scenic, but I've been lying, even to myself—I don't take it because of the bridges. When I go to New York my wife always comes along. I've told myself I'm doing her a big favor to take her into the city to shop, but that's not true. I take her along because before we get to the high overpasses approaching the tunnel we switch places and she drives. Another thing I've been doing and didn't even realize— I'm ashamed to admit it—I won't let my wife go anywhere without me. In the back of my mind I think, 'What if I have to go somewhere and there's a bridge on the way?' so I locked her with me in this trap. I had no idea how much it has affected our lives."

WHEN we think about Norm's background, his situation isn't all that surprising. His whole family denied the fact of his father's illness until the man died. Norm denied his feelings about his father by in effect saying to himself, "I can deal with Dad's dying, but I can't deal with bridges." That he presented himself to me as a totally together kind of a guy with this tiny little problem was consistent with the way he managed difficulties—by denying that they exist (at this point he still hadn't divulged to me the extent of his drinking). It also became apparent that avoidance had become such an automatic response he wasn't even aware of it much of the time.

Norm had kept a detailed diary for the week:

DATE	ANXIETY LEVEL	ACTIVITY	THOUGHT
6/12	2	starting out on new road with wife—turned back	What if there's a bridge?
6/13	1	making appointment with new salesman	Where will I meet him?
6/13	2	fight with wife	What if she leaves me?
6/14	2	driving to in-laws	I'm going to have to take the other route.
6/14	3	talking to Tom (son)	What if I can't make it to his graduation?
6/15	3	meeting new salesman	What if he wants me to introduce him to Philadelphia clients?
6/15	3	fight with wife	She hates me.
6/16	4	working in office	I'm really crazy.
6/17	4	working in office	I won't be able to do what my therapist asked.
6/18	5	driving to therapist	She's going to be mad at me.

Norm's diary revealed several interesting issues. The first thing I noticed was that eight out of ten of the recorded thoughts were in the future tense, so the thoughts that created the anxiety had nothing to do with what he was doing. For instance, in the last entry (driving to therapist—she's going to be mad at me), it wasn't the driving that he was having difficulty with, it was the thought of my being mad at him.

"Norm," I said, "I'm wondering about your numbers. Here at the beginning of the week your level is a 2 thinking about going over a bridge and later it's a 5 when you're coming to see me. Would it be easier for you to go over a bridge than to face an angry therapist? Also, with a 10 being your first panic attack, which was really a horrible experience, a 2 is just a drop in the anxiety bucket; how come you turned back when your level reached 2?"

Norm looked at his diary as though he never seen it before, squirmed a little, and said, "I'm not sure. It was really hard coming here this afternoon. I had all the old feelings, the rapid heartbeat, difficulty breathing, I was real uncomfortable."

"What about the 2 when you were driving with your wife?" I asked. "Why did you turn back at such a low level?"

"I guess because it was so easy. I knew my wife wouldn't bitch at me if I turned back, but I could just hear you say, 'Why are you wasting my time? What the hell are you doing here if you're not going to work at this?' "

"I see," I said. "You're saying that you know you can goof off with your wife but you don't think that you can goof off with me."

"Maybe," said Norm, smiling sheepishly. "But then maybe I was just angry with myself and I put my words in your mouth."

"Are you angry with yourself?"

"Sure," he said. "I'm furious. As I looked at my problem and saw how pervasive it's been, and how I've used my wife and lied to myself all these years, I got really disgusted with myself."

"What do you want to do about it?" I asked.

He dropped his head and exhaled deeply. "I don't know," he said. "That's what makes me so crazy. I know that I can't go over a bridge—if I do I'm afraid I'll go insane or die of a stroke or a heart attack or something."

"What will make you die or go crazy?"

"Those feelings, they're so terrible."

"But Norm," I said. "I know they're terrible, but they haven't made you die or go crazy before, so why will they now?"

"I'm older now," he said. "Maybe my heart can't take it."

"What did your doctor say?"

"He said that I'm strong as a horse."

"Let's get in my car and I'll show you a couple of low overpasses and you can decide if you want to drive over them," I said.

Norm and I drove to an overpass about fourteen feet high over a four-lane highway. We parked the car on the side of the road and walked back and forth across the overpass without difficulty; then I asked Norm if he could drive across it. He got into the car and drove across the overpass, turned around and came back again.

"That was great Norm, what was your anxiety level?"

"I really didn't have any anxiety," he said. "It was easier than I thought it would be— no big deal."

"But it has been a big deal for fourteen years," I said. "How come it all of a sudden changed?"

"I just looked at it for what it is—it's a two-lane road that goes over a highway. It will only take me fifteen seconds to drive across it and I can stand anything for fifteen seconds."

"So just by telling yourself, 'I can stand it,' you sidestepped all anxiety?"

"It seems that way."

To reinforce Norm's successful technique I said, "So by giving specific dimensions—'It's a two-lane road that will take me fifteen seconds to drive'—you made it manageable. That's good to know. Let's try another overpass."

The next overpass we came to was over the same four-lane highway but was arched rather than flat. Again, we parked the car and walked across it first. Then Norm got in the car alone and drove across—and sat there. He didn't turn around to come back. I waited for a while, then walked over to the car. Norm was just sitting there, staring at the steering wheel.

"What happened?" I asked.

"I blew it."

"What did you blow?"

"I blew my cool," he said. "The front wheels barely got onto the overpass when my level hit an 8. I was totally out of control."

"What do you mean you were out of control? You didn't stop, or back up, or drive off the edge—how were you out of control?"

"All the old garbage again," he said. "My heart was pounding and I felt shaky. I don't think I'll ever get out of this."

"What's your anxiety level now?"

"Oh, it's only about a 3 now, but it really spiked up to an 8 when I started out."

"What happened to 'I can stand anything for fifteen seconds'?"

Norm shrugged. "I guess I forgot that," he said.

"Do you really think that you blew it and that you were totally out of control?" I asked.

"Yes, in a way," he said. "Instead of recognizing that it was only a little overpass and telling myself that I could stand it, I went back to the same old garbage."

"Did you think that you'd get rid of fourteen years of garbage on one overpass?"

"That doesn't sound realistic, does it?" he conceded.

I wanted to find out what Norm was telling himself while he drove over the overpass that made his anxiety level jump to an 8, so I got into the car on the passenger side; Norm turned the car around and headed back to the overpass.

"I can tell you right now that one of the scariest thoughts was that I'll never get rid of this problem," he said. "But you're right, I can't really expect to get rid of it on one overpass. Ummm, now it's the arch that's bothering me; I can't see what's on the other side. My level just jumped to about an 8 again."

"What do you think might be on the other side?"

Norm turned to me and with a laugh said, "My level just dropped to a 2 because I can see that that was a nonsense thought—I know what's on the other side, I just came from there."

"How can you tell the difference between a nonsense thought and a non-nonsense thought?" I asked.

"Well, it's pretty clear that if I tell myself there could be something scary on the other side of the overpass after I've just come from that side and know what's there—well, that has to be nonsense because it doesn't agree with what I already know."

"Oh, so you're saying that a nonsense thought is one that contradicts your own reality."

Norm would never have believed me if I had told him that those terrible feelings are caused by his own thinking, but during that session he had a chance to observe his anxiety level jump from a 2 to an 8 because of a "nonsense" thought.

Fourteen years of terror at the thought of driving over bridges had sensitized Norm to the situation. His catastrophic inner scene was of losing control (through illness or insanity) and driving over the side of the bridge or overpass.

Norm had experienced his inner scene of disaster, and that caused his heart to beat rapidly. He told me that the scariest thought he had was that he'd never get over the problem; the rapid heartbeat seemed to confirm that thought. Norm had told me earlier how disgusted he was with himself because of his panic, so the thought of never being able to get rid of it must have caused him considerable anguish. By the time I had gotten to the other side of the overpass, Norm had added yet another scary thought, "I was totally out of control." (What he really meant here was not that his actions were out of control, but that overwhelmed by his inner scene, his thoughts were out of control.) This too seemed to be confirmation that he would never get over the problem.

Already primed for anxiety because of one bad crossing, we went over the overpass again. Scary thoughts will reproduce like rabbits unless they are reality tested, but they must be elicited before they can be tested. When we were together and he verbalized his scary thoughts, the outcome was quite different. Norm's thought, "There's something scary on the other side," was so clearly indefensible that he was able to dismiss it as a nonsense thought immediately.

Norm's personal belief system was also a factor in predicting ultimate failure to recover from the phobia. He assumed that he would or should get over fourteen years of phobic reaction in one trip over an overpass. He believed that a high level of anxiety was the same as being totally out of control. It actually gave him a great deal of comfort when he recognized that even during his worst panic attack he wasn't "out of control." At no time did he endanger himself or his family; he drove over the bridge and pulled off the road fully in control of the car.

Our next session included Norm's wife, Marge. I hadn't met her before but Norm had described her as being loving, supportive, and understanding. They came into the office and took seats at opposite ends of the room. Norm's assignment for the week had been to drive over the same two overpasses with his wife and to continue his diary, adding another column on the right entitled "Rational Response."

"Well, how did the assignment go?" I asked.

Norm shifted in his chair and looked out the window. Marge answered, "Not so good."

"Oh, why not?" I asked.

"He wouldn't do it."

I looked at Norm.

"I tried, but I just couldn't get myself to drive over the over-passes."

"That's the way it always is with him," Marge said. "If there's a way of getting out of something, he will. He'll always take the easy way out without thinking of anyone else."

Norm sat up straight and in a bellicose voice said, "Are you telling me that for the past twenty years I've been taking the easy way out and not thinking of anyone else? Take a look at what you've got, lady. I work myself ragged so that you and the kids can have a nice house, and cars, and all the clothes you want. You have more than anyone I know, and you aren't exactly overworked."

Not intimidated by Norm's manner, Marge said, "I'm sick of your problem. It's 'My nerves this, my nerves that.' All you talk about are your nerves. The only places we ever go are to my parents and your doctor. Now you have a chance to do something about your problem and you're ducking out on that, too."

Marge did not sound like the "loving, supportive, and understanding" wife Norm had described to me. Two diary entries of the week before came to mind: "My wife hates me." "What if she leaves me?" Norm was probably denying that his marriage was in trouble.

"Marge, tell me what happened. Did you drive to the over-passes with Norm?"

"I don't want to talk about it," she said with a shrug. "This is a waste of time and money."

"Norm, do you want to tell me what happened?"

"Well, I got to the first overpass and my level was about a 3, and I remembered how bad it was last week when we did it and just couldn't bring myself to drive over it again."

"How bad was it last week?" I asked.

"It was terrible, I hit an 8, I was totally out of control."

"You hit an 8 on the second overpass, and then only for an instant. On the first overpass you had no anxiety at all. And I thought we had determined that even though your level was high you were in complete control the whole time."

"Oh yes, I had forgotten that."

"Humpff," from Marge.

"Well I did forget it. So many things happened last week that I forgot that I drove over the first overpass."

WHEN we put ourselves in Norm's place, his "forgetting" is perfectly understandable. He told me at the first session that he was afraid that if he went over a bridge, he would die or go crazy. When his level went up to an 8 it was as though his worst premonition would come true, and he felt out of control. It is to be expected that he would remember the most devastating part of the session. It was hard for Marge to understand Norm's "forgetting." She interpreted his behavior as avoiding responsibility and manipulating her into taking care of him. If she was to function as Norm's support person, we would have to help her to see the situation from his point of view.

"Marge, is there anything that really scares you?" I asked.

"I can't stand snakes, but aside from that nothing scares me."

"That's how Norm feels about bridges," I said. "The thought of driving over one terrifies him. He gets the shakes and the shivers and his heart beats wildly. Is that the way you feel when you think about encountering a snake?"

"Yes, but a snake is different. It's real. It's alive, it could bite or do something."

"A bridge is real too. Norm thinks he could have a heart attack, go crazy, or die. And he believes it as much as you believe in the dangerousness of the snake."

"But that's crazy."

"Who's to say what's crazy? Besides, getting mad at him for being crazy hasn't solved anything—and it sounds like you've been mad at him for a long time."

"I've been mad at him since he screwed up our trip to California. That was over five years ago. Since then he hasn't even tried to go anywhere."

"It will be hard for you to be his support person if you're going to be mad at him all the time. Do you think you'll be able to turn off your anger while you work with him?"

"I'll try. Do you think he can get over this? I don't even care if he can never drive over the Golden Gate or Verrazzano Bridges, as long as we can go somewhere without him getting crazy."

"Norm, last week we discovered that one of your coping techniques was to estimate the amount of time it would take to get across the overpass and tell yourself that you could stand the anxiety for that period. Try using that again during this week. Let's repeat the assignment with you and Marge driving over the same overpasses we did last week. Does that sound manageable?

"While you're working on bridges together it's going to be very important that the two of you clearly and specifically communicate your feelings to each other. How about both of you using the 0 to 10 scale on all feelings? So Norm, when you're anxious you identify the level from 0 to 10; and Marge, when you're unhappy or upset you use the scale too so that Norm will really know how you feel."

CLEARLY, Norm had a lot of problems, but the only one he admitted to or expressed a willingness to work on was his phobia of bridges. Marge, on the other hand, feeling used and manipulated, was pressing for Norm to pay attention to the fact that she was extremely unhappy in their relationship. I felt certain that if the sessions focused too much attention on the marital difficulties, Norm would drop out of therapy, but if we ignored those difficulties, we would lose Marge's cooperation. So I tried to balance their conflicting interests.

In an attempt to get Norm to be aware of his own self-defeating expectations, I asked him to establish some short-term goals for the next month.

"Well, I have to get to Philadelphia."

"Is it reasonable to think you can do that in a month?" I asked.

"Maybe not," he said. "Maybe what I should do is to figure out how long it takes to get over the bridge and then work up my endurance time on the overpasses. And I can compute the time it will take by how rapidly I'm building up my endurance to the anxiety."

"That sounds like a good idea. So you're saying the short-term goal is to build up your endurance over the month, and then continue to build it up until you're ready for the bridges over the river. That means that we should be doing longer over-passes with lower anxiety over the months."

AT the next session, I could see that Norm was becoming over-whelmed with the demands being made on him. First the pressure of having to get to Philadelphia, then Marge expressing her unhappiness with the relationship, must have been very threatening. I could see that he wasn't at all happy with the way things were going. Marge had indicated that the work on the assignment had been quite successful, so I changed the subject in order to reinforce Norm's strengths.

"Marge told me a little about the success you had with last week's assignment; can you tell me more?" I asked.

"It went much better this week. We drove around and found a couple of overpasses and a little bridge over a creek. First Marge drove over them while I timed her with a stopwatch. The longest one took twenty-five seconds. Then I drove over each one alone in the car, telling myself that I could stand it for fif-teen or twenty-five seconds, and it worked! The highest my anxiety went was about a 6 and that was on the little bridge.

The thought was, 'Pretty soon I'll have to do the bridge over the river.' But I was able to identify that as a nonsense thought because I wasn't on a big bridge then, and that little bridge wasn't really scary.

"I've been keeping my diary with the additional column with 'rational response' and I'm amazed to see how much I anticipate trouble. Marge is right when she says that when I get somewhere I always want to turn right around and go home again because I'm always thinking, 'What if this happens, what if that happens.' I'm never in the present. But I've never actually looked at what I tell myself and assessed it. This week when I did, I realize they're all nonsense thoughts."

NORM'S DIARY:

Date	Anxiety Level	Activity	Thought	Rational Response
6/17	4	going to overpass	I can't do it.	Maybe I can, maybe I can't, but it's not dangerous.
6/17	5	looking at overpass	It's too high.	It doesn't make any difference how high it is, I won't drive off it.
6/18	4	going to in-laws'	I've got too much work to do.	It will get done, it always does.
6/19	4	looking at bridge	There's water underneath.	So what, I'll stay on bridge.
6/19	6	on bridge	I have to go to Philadelphia.	Yes, but this bridge is manageable.

I was really surprised to see Norm's diary. I would have guessed that either he wouldn't have identified the thoughts because he was so into denial or that he wouldn't be able to respond to them rationally. "Norm," I said, "you've done a really great job at identifying the thoughts and responding to them rationally. Did your anxiety level come down with the rational response?"

"Yes, pretty much once I saw how ridiculous it was. After all, why should I worry about water under the bridge; I don't plan to swim it, I'm going to drive over it. I don't know where those thoughts come from, but they seemed scary until I started to question them."

THE three of us continued to work together. They came to see me Saturday mornings, and during the week they spent a couple of hours three times a week driving over bridges and overpasses. As Norm became more confident with his driving, Marge started spending more time away from the house alone. Within a few months they were discussing the possibility of Marge taking a part-time job. We spent several Saturdays driving along the Delaware River looking for "easy" bridges. When we found one, first Marge would drive over alone while Norm and I timed her, then we would drive over together with Norm in the back seat recording his thoughts with a tape recorder; next, he would drive over with Marge and me in the car, and finally he would drive over alone, all the while recording his thoughts and rational responses. Occasionally several trips with Marge or me driving were required before Norm could take the wheel.

One morning while Norm was driving and Marge and I were in the back seat, she turned to me and said, "I'm so pleased with the way things are going. I can't even remember the last time Norm got drunk."

"Oh," I said, feeling like a dope because I had completely forgotten that part of Norm's problem. He had always arrived sober for his appointments with me, and except for our first session when we briefly discussed his drinking, it hadn't come up again. Although we had never worked directly with Norm's drinking problem, as soon as he started to feel some sense of control in his life the need to anesthetize himself with alcohol diminished. Frequently this is the case with people who use alcohol to manage their anxiety, but too often it becomes a problem in itself that needs specialized help.

AFTER about six months Norm was able to drive over all the local bridges and overpasses, the high overpasses approaching the tunnel into New York, and most of the bridges from New Jersey into Pennsylvania north of Philadelphia. He still couldn't manage the three major bridges into Philadelphia or the bridge into Delaware. Interestingly, Marge didn't care. She was delighted with the progress he had made and her new-found freedom. Her anger toward Norm lessened as soon as she became a part of his recovery. As she developed a better understanding of his fears, she was able to appreciate how hard he was working at overcoming his problem. Norm still wanted to work on the three bridges into Philadelphia. So we kept working.

Norm mastered the Philadelphia bridges in time to drive to his son's graduation. He and Marge regularly drive to Baltimore to visit their daughter.

THE partners of phobic and obsessive-compulsive people are often angry. Their lives are limited by their partners' limitations, and they frequently feel used and manipulated. It is hard for a partner of a phobic person to understand the terror the phobic person feels. Partners often say something like, "Don't be silly, it's only a cat," or "Get hold of yourself." When they do understand and can put their anger aside, they make the best support people. Without Marge's help Norm's recovery would have been much more difficult.

CHAPTER NINE

STEVIE, THE BOY WHO WOULDN'T EAT

"I HOPE that this therapy won't take too long," Stevie's mother said. "His illness has already cost us plenty. By the way, why are you charging us for two hours?"

I was sitting in a very beautifully and expensively decorated living room in Stevie's Fifth Avenue apartment.

"If Stevie came to see me in my office I would only charge for one hour. But it takes me three-quarters of an hour to get here; an hour with Stevie; another three-quarters of an hour to return to my office."

"I don't see why I should pay you for sitting on the subway," she interrupted.

I chose to ignore her comment, " . . . how long the therapy might take, that's hard to say. It depends on Stevie's willingness to work, his motivations, what other problems we might have to deal with . . . "

Again she interrupted, "There are no other problems. Stevie has everything. He's bright, he goes to the best schools, he has everything a boy could want."

I looked up to see a thin, pale boy with dark, unruly hair standing in the doorway. I smiled at him; he returned the smile with a lopsided smirk. Stevie was seventeen, but he looked much younger. Stevie had been referred to me by a doctor who was seeing him for intense psychotherapy. The doctor knew that I did in vivo and exposure work with phobias and obsessive-compulsive behaviors and thought that it might be helpful for us to work together with Stevie. It was hard for me to reconcile the obvious affluence of Stevie's surroundings with Stevie's mother's parsimonious attitude toward his therapy.

I suggested that Stevie and I go somewhere where we could talk. He led me into the library. When we got inside, he leaned against the door and whispered, "She's a real ballbuster, isn't she."

"Well," I said, "I don't know if I'd say that. But I'll bet she's real hard to talk to most of the time."

"Yeah, she's a pisser."

"What about your dad?"

"I don't have a dad. We live with my stepfather. He's a jerk, but a rich jerk. He pays to keep us quiet. 'Here's fifty: now be quiet.' "

"You must get a lot of fifties that way."

"Sometimes, but I pay for it in other ways," he said.

Stevie seemed so casual and breezy it was hard to believe that he was the same boy Dr. G. had described. He had dropped out of school (one of the best, of course) before the end of term because he was so beset with fears of food contamination. Much to the alarm of the school authorities, he had stopped eating. They tried to entice him with special foods without success. In error they treated him for anorexia nervosa, which he didn't have (his fear was not of gaining weight but of poisoning by food). When Stevie became aware of the inappropriateness of the therapy he decided that all adults were jerks and that no one would be able to understand or help him. In spite of his mother's pleading and demanding and his stepfather's bribes, Stevie still wouldn't eat. When they took him to see Dr. G., he was down to about ninety-five pounds. After Dr. G. saw him a few times, he decided to bring me in on the case.

"So what is this stuff I hear about you not wanting to eat?" I asked.

"Yeah. Crazy huh?"

"I don't know," I said. "Why don't you tell me about it?"

"Well, there's all this shit in the environment. Nuclear waste is the good stuff. That won't kill me for another thirty years and in the meantime I can glow in the dark. But the rest of the garbage—the antibiotics they feed the cattle, the insecticides they spray on the vegetables, and the PCBs they use to package the food—that stuff is dangerous."

"What's your solution?" I asked. "Right now you look like the famous ninety-eight pound weakling, and unless you've got something brilliant up your sleeve I can only expect that you're going to get a lot skinnier. It looks to me like the immediate choice is to be poisoned by nuclear waste in thirty years or starve to death in six months."

"Hmm, not too bright, huh?"

"Not in my book. There must be some kind of a compromise."

Stevie was a very troubled but funny, funny kid. His spirit and sense of humor made many of our exposure sessions feel like high-school pranks.

On one occasion when we were working on the escalators leading to the commuter trains in the World Trade Center (he was also afraid of contamination by crowds), he found himself on an escalator behind someone who was smoking a cigar. Because Stevie was fearful of contamination by smoke, he pulled his T-shirt up over his head and rode to the top of the escalator with his bare back and belly exposed. At the top of the es-

calator we were greeted by a security guard who pulled us
aside, "Hey, what are you guys doin'?"

I gave him my card and, in my best professional manner,
said that I was an in vivo therapist and we were practicing on
the escalators so that this lad would be able to use the commuter trains to visit his grandmother.

"Well you can't do that vivo stuff here," he said. "If he wants
to see his grandma that's OK, but no vivo stuff."

After we got around the corner I lit into Stevie. "What on
earth are you doing? You looked like a weirdo. You can't pull
your clothes off in public and not get into trouble."

"Hey, that was great!" Stevie said. "How did you come up
with that grandmother rap?"

"Forget about the grandmother rap," I said, "what about the
weirdo rap?"

His face fell. "Are you mad at me?"

"Stevie, I'm not mad at you, but if you walk around looking
like a weirdo you're going to get in trouble. And if you walk
around looking like a weirdo with me we're both going to get
in trouble. I'm too old to get in that kind of trouble."

"You're not too old," Stevie said, "you're wonderful."

Stevie totally missed the point, but he missed the point so
endearingly, what could I say?

Let me hasten to add, however, that not all of our work was
so entertaining. Most of it was hard, tedious, and repetitive.
Our first order of business was to get food into Stevie. He was
convinced that all food was contaminated. Stevie had eaten
nothing for weeks. He had lost weight rapidly. If he couldn't
get his act together soon he would be hospitalized against his
will and fed through a tube.

"Stevie," I said, "I don't care what you eat, but if you want
to stay out of the hospital you have to eat something. How
about french fries?"

"You want to kill me with cholesterol?"

"No, I want to keep you from killing yourself by starvation. If you don't eat you're going to be sent to the hospital and all kinds of artificial crap is going to be put into a vein in your neck, like it or not."

"You're just like everyone else," he said. "You don't understand."

"I can't understand if you don't explain it to me. Give me the details. What thoughts do you have when you start to eat? What does it feel like in your body?"

Every time Stevie thought about eating, another thought about contamination or poison popped into his head. He became so distressed at the thought of poison that he was unable to eat. We reality tested poison: If food is so poisonous, how do people live to ninety? How come we don't see dead bodies in restaurants? Why are there any people around at all, because they all eat food?

Since everybody ate food, and not everybody was dead or dying, we discussed the fact that something must be wrong with his theory. We spent many hours in supermarkets walking up and down the aisles, looking at the food, reading the ingredients on the labels (a discouraging pastime), trying to find some item of food that Stevie would be willing to eat. Finally, he decided to try some cottage cheese. (Because it was white, if it were contaminated he could see it; it was low in cholesterol; and it wasn't too processed.) We looked at all the expiration dates on the containers of cottage cheese; we checked to make sure that the seals hadn't been tampered with; and after an exhausting inspection chose a container that looked clean, intact, and had a distant expiration date. Back in his kitchen he opened the container. "It looks yukky," he said.

"It looks a whole lot better than a feeding tube," I said.

"Yeah, but I have this awful feeling that if I eat it I'll barf."

Stevie was probably mistaking nausea for anxiety sensations. I encouraged him to have just one taste. He refused.

"Why won't you taste it?" I asked.

"Because once I get it inside me I'm stuck with it and I'll get sick, or be poisoned, and then it will be too late."

"Why will you be poisoned if millions of other people aren't? And let me remind you that your solution of not eating is not exactly keeping you safe and healthy."

"You made your point, but I still feel like I'm going to barf."

Slowly Stevie took the spoon. "I can't do it. You taste it first," he said.

A nice piece of Brie or Camembert is very much to my liking, but I hate cottage cheese. I dipped the spoon into the container anyway.

"How is it?" Stevie asked.

"Not great, but not poisonous. Now you try."

Stevie took a spoonful and put it in his mouth and swallowed fast. Then he quickly took several more spoonfuls.

THAT was the beginning of Stevie's eating crusade. After cottage cheese, he thought that bananas might be safe because they come prewrapped by nature. We found a health food store in his neighborhood where he could buy organically grown vegetables and cereals. Each time he was about to try something new he paced the aisles, picked up an item, studied it, put it down, and picked it up again. "What do you think about while you stalk the food?" I asked.

"Oh, mostly I think about all the garbage that's in it and how long I have before it kills me. Just the thought of it makes me feel sick. My throat closes up so I can't even swallow. I hate this—I wish I didn't have to eat. It's like poking myself in the eye with a stick."

Many containers of food were purchased and then thrown away because he couldn't bring himself to try them. I was always willing to be the first taster. Often I would taste something and Stevie would wait until the next appointment to see if I had died before he would try it. We hung around fast-food places to see if the people who ate there got sick or died. (During our observations McDonald's and Burger King had a zero mortality rate.) We watched a homeless person pick a cigarette butt off the street and smoke it—he seemed to suffer no ill effects.

In three weeks Stevie gained seven pounds, but every ounce of it was a struggle. When he tried something new he would often put a microscopic amount in his mouth and then quickly spit it out. Again he would try with another microscopic bit. I suggested that he just hold the food in his mouth and taste it for a while before he spit it out—sometimes he did. His thought was always, "I'm going to be poisoned," but since I had tasted it first I wanted him to explain why he would be poisoned and I wouldn't. On one occasion he impulsively bought an ice cream bar from a vendor in the park. He ate it quickly, and on finishing had a panic attack. He began hyperventilating, complained of not being able to breathe, was dizzy and weak. He felt that he was about to faint. I told him that the sensations he was having came from anxiety, not poisoning, and if he would do slow, deep breathing most of them would go away. He was too agitated to hear me, and insisted on going to a hospital to have his stomach pumped. He was convinced that he was dying. We were in Central Park at Fifth Avenue and 80th Street; the closest hospital was at Lexington Avenue and 77th Street, and I suggested we jog there. By the time we got to 78th and Park Avenue we were both out of breath, so we stopped to rest.

"How are you doing?" I asked.

"I think maybe I'm not dying after all," Stevie said sheepishly.

"I don't think so either. I think you had a panic attack, and I think the next time you get those sensations if you do the breathing exercise Dr. G. taught you, it won't be nearly as scary."

When we assessed Stevie's past experiences of suspected poisoning and compared them with the most recent episode, he agreed that they'd all been panic attacks too, and were not symptoms of being poisoned. He was both relieved and upset to learn that he had not been poisoned: relieved because he didn't have to feel that sensitive or vulnerable to contamination, upset because if those terrifying sensations could come from nowhere, he couldn't control them, and he would never feel safe. It was hard for Stevie to totally believe that the sensations came from his own thoughts and that they could be controlled by staying in reality and doing the breathing exercise to counteract the hyperventilation.

BECAUSE Stevie's condition was considered critical he was seeing Dr. G. three times a week and me twice a week. I concentrated on getting Stevie to eat while Dr. G. worked with him on his many other problems. He never discussed his home problems with me, but I learned from Dr. G. that Stevie had a twin brother who was being hospitalized for OCD. His brother was a "washer," and his many cleaning rituals had driven the family to such distraction that the stepfather in effect had said, "Either he goes or I go." An older sister was living with relatives in California because of difficulties with the stepfather. His natural father had died when Stevie was about ten; his mother remarried less than a year after his death. Stevie had a lot of bad feelings about that.

His trouble with eating didn't start until after he went away to prep school. A family friend had thought that it would be a good idea to send the twins to different schools to make them more independent. Stevie was sent to a school in New England, while his brother stayed at home and attended a local school. At first it seemed that Stevie had suddenly become health conscious. He quit eating junk food and became a vegetarian. But as time wore on, more and more foods gave him what he believed were "poisoning" symptoms, until finally he didn't feel safe eating anything. His brother, in the meantime, started washing. He took several two-hour showers each day and would change his clothes four times a day because they were contaminated. He yelled at his stepfather for doing "dirty" things (putting his briefcase on the table, etc.). Just before Stevie came home from school, his brother was sent to the hospital.

My work with Stevie took place right around the time of the Tylenol poisonings. Stevie was convinced that there were a lot of "nut jobs out there" who were liable to poison him. He was afraid to eat in restaurants because a disgruntled or crazy employee might poison the food. He was afraid to walk through crowds or on busy streets because a crazy person might throw poison or acid on him. And he thought that inhaling any amount of smoke would give him lung cancer. The easiest to reality test was the immediate killing effect of cigarette smoke. We spent several sessions sitting in the bus terminal watching from a distance as people smoked one cigarette after another without showing ill effects. A couple of the people were regular inhabitants of the bus station, and we saw them week after week, smoking incredible amounts without suffering.

We stood on 42nd Street and Eighth Avenue (a hangout of many crazy people) to see how many people threw acid or poison on passersby. None did.

When we started working in restaurants, I made it a rule that Stevie could not spit food out. If he felt that he absolutely had to get it out of his mouth he could discreetly put his napkin to his lips and quietly ease it into his napkin. Restaurants were very hard for Stevie because they offered the possibility of crazy people contaminating his food in the kitchen and another type of crazy person throwing poison or acid in his hair or over his shoulder into his food while he ate. To ease his fear about someone throwing poison or acid on him we always arranged for him to sit with his back to a wall where he was able to watch people. He promised to tell me if anyone threw poison or acid on me. We started out by ordering tea and toast. On our first restaurant encounter he inspected the two pieces of toast on his plate and declared them contaminated by unidentifiable grains. I exchanged our plates and put some jam on one of the pieces of toast and began to eat.

"Stop!" he shouted, "I can't be responsible if anything happens to you." The people around us put down their silverware and discreetly watched us while I calmly continued to eat the toast.

"I'm serious," he said. "Don't eat that, it's poison."

The waitress came over to our table. "Is something wrong?" she asked.

I looked at Stevie for a moment to see if he was going to say anything, then I smiled at the waitress and said, "I don't think so." She looked nervously at Stevie, then did a half shrug and walked away. Stevie crossed his arms and slumped down in the chair. I continued to eat the toast.

"You made a fool of me," Stevie said sullenly. "I tried to save you and you made a fool of me."

"Stevie," I said quietly and gently, "I really appreciate your concern for me, but you were imposing your irrational fears on me, not real-world fears. Look, I ate both pieces of toast and nothing has happened to me." In spite of my surviving the two pieces of toast, Stevie proclaimed that restaurant to be hopelessly contaminated and refused to return. We did find another restaurant where he could sit with his back to the wall and watch for possible acid or poison throwers. Again we ordered tea and toast. Again he picked each piece up and inspected it carefully. I could guess what he was thinking. "I'm still alive, aren't I?" I said.

"I'm not so sure." he said grimly. He bit off a tiny piece of toast, chewed for a while, then put his napkin to his mouth. He waited awhile and bit off another tiny piece, chewed, and again put his napkin to his mouth. He repeated this about five times. I asked him why he wasn't swallowing. "I can't," he said, "my throat is too tight." I suggested that he wait awhile, have a sip of tea, then try again. Before we left the restaurant Stevie had chewed up and spit out one and a half pieces of toast, but the remaining half piece of toast was actually swallowed. We declared our second restaurant encounter a success. As we walked back toward his apartment, he put his arms in the air and said, "Today Leo's Coffee House; tomorrow Lutece."

In three months Stevie was eating—not well, but eating. He had gained twelve pounds. His weight was no longer considered a critical issue. We were going to public places, walking down busy streets, and eating in restaurants (although we never did make it to Lutece). During this period his mother didn't bother to conceal her active dislike of me. Although she insisted that I come to the apartment to pick up Stevie, she continued to resent having to pay me "for sitting on the subway." She didn't like the fact that I wasn't a famous doctor like Dr. G. (Stevie said that she thought I was a quack, and he would tease me and call me Dr. Duck, or tell me not to flap my feathers.) Most of all I think she hated the fact that Stevie and I got along well together. On one occasion when we were planning an exposure task she passed the library door just as we both started laughing about something. She entered the library in a barely controlled rage and said she couldn't see anything amusing about the situation and asked us to meet in the downstairs lobby in the future.

Shortly after the library incident Stevie's stepfather called to say that Stevie and his mother had gone to London, and he wouldn't be needing my services any longer. I heard from Dr. G. that after a month in London, Stevie returned to his school in New England that fall weighing about 115 pounds and eating a reasonably well-balanced vegetarian diet.

Over the years I've received postcards from him. He finished school, went to college, and got a girlfriend. Stevie is now in his twenties; the last card I received said,

> "Dear Dr. Duck,
> Egads, I'm fat! Do you know any good diet quacks?
> Best regards, Stevie."

Because both Stevie and his twin brother suffered from OCD, it's a safe guess that he had inherited a propensity for it. Add to that the many life stresses he experienced (the loss of his father, his mother's remarriage, and the separation from his brother), and Stevie was on fertile ground for a good case of OCD. Why his problem manifested itself as a fear of food contamination and his brother's as a fear of dirt, I don't know. In spite of his inherited propensity for OCD, I doubt that he will ever have a problem with it again. Stevie's mind was quick and rational and he easily understood the concepts of magic thinking and reality testing.

CHAPTER TEN

GRACIE, THE WOMAN WHO SPENT EIGHT HOURS A DAY BATHING

GRACIE was fifty-three when she sought help. She had been obsessive-compulsive as long as she could remember. Even as a small child she worried about dirt and contamination; she was afraid of animals, birds, and bugs because of the diseases they might carry. In school she had no friends. She carried her hands up against her chest, clutched into fists so that she wouldn't accidentally touch something. Her classmates called her weird. If the teacher asked her to write on the blackboard she panicked at the thought of touching chalk.

Using the school bathroom was a nightmare. She couldn't touch the bathroom door because she was afraid of the germs. She would stand at the door until someone else came to open it. The other girls gathered around and made fun of her until eventually someone would come out and she'd slip in before the door closed. She opened and closed the door to the stall with her foot, and used the toilet balancing on one foot while she held the door closed with the other. On leaving the stall she took a wad of toilet paper with her to turn the faucet handle at the sink. After she washed her hands, she'd leave the water running and return to a stall to get more toilet paper to turn the water off (she couldn't use the original wad of toilet paper because that had been contaminated by her dirty hands). If other girls were in the bathroom at the same time, they teased and tormented her. Knowing that she was balanced on one foot, they would push the door to try to knock her off balance, or they would try to prevent her from going back to a stall to get clean paper. Occasionally they would come directly out of a stall and touch her, which caused her to break into tears of panic and trigger a washing ritual that would take so long she would be late for class.

Gracie was very bright; in spite of her difficulties she received excellent grades. She won a scholarship to a prestigious women's college, which required her to live in a dorm. Her contamination fears became more widespread and the rituals more involved and time-consuming. The dorm had a large communal bathroom. Before Gracie could use any of the bathing facilities she had to spend several hours scrubbing the walls, the sinks, and the bathtubs. She would wait until the other dorm residents were in bed before she started her scrubbing and bathing rituals. Some nights she wouldn't get to bed until four or five in the morning.

She was afraid of shoes because they touched the dirty pavement. No one could come into her room wearing shoes. In the first two months of college three roommates filed protests and refused to room with her.

Her reports and papers were always overdue because if there was a smudge or an inkblot (these were precomputer days) on any part of the work, the entire report had to be redone. Everything she handed in was rewritten eight or ten times. She dropped a course because one day while sitting in class she saw (or thought she saw) a mouse in the classroom. All the books she had with her at the time were also contaminated. Gracie threw them out.

The hours Gracie spent in the bathroom washing increased. Sometimes while drying off she couldn't remember if she'd washed her feet, so she would go back and shower again. Then she wouldn't be able to remember if she'd washed her hands, etc. . . . A completed shower required about three hours. Eventually Gracie's fears and the endless work required to satisfy the compulsion became so overwhelming that in despair she dropped out of college and returned home.

At twenty Gracie returned home to live with her parents and two teenage brothers and was clearly getting worse. Soon she believed that every part of the house was contaminated except for her bedroom and the bathroom.

Gracie was furious with her family; she felt they were intentionally contaminating her. She wanted them to take off their clothes before they entered the house and perform other rituals, but her family flatly refused.

Gracie spent six and eight hours a day in the bathroom. In total exasperation, her father removed the latch from the bathroom door, attached a twenty-minute timer to it, and gave the boys permission to go into the bathroom and get Gracie after the timer went off. Gracie's solution was to wait until the family went to sleep and spend her nights washing and her days sleeping.

Thirty-two years slipped by this way. In time Gracie's brothers grew up and left home, her father died, and her mother became very ill. Gracie never left her room except to go the bathroom, where she continued to spend most of her nights washing. Her mother left meal trays on a table next to her bedroom door. Gracie read books, which she ordered through the mail, and watched TV.

When Gracie's mother became ill, Gracie was afraid she'd be contaminated by her illness. One of the brothers put an intercom between Gracie's and her mother's room, and they spoke with each other all through the day. It wasn't until a nurse employed to take care of her mother asked Gracie why she didn't try to get help for her obsessive-compulsive problem that Gracie realized that she wasn't crazy and could get help.

I WAS spending two days a week working in a small rural community in New Jersey when Gracie's mother called me. Gracie and her mother lived about twenty minutes away in another small town. It took several months to set up an appointment with Gracie. First her mother called and wanted me to come to the house without Gracie's consent or knowledge, but I was not willing to do that. I insisted that Gracie call me so I could explain the concept and procedures of therapy. Finally Gracie called; she seemed interested in therapy but extremely hesitant. Establishing a time for an appointment was difficult because Gracie was still sleeping all day and washing all night. She would get up about six in the evening and have breakfast and watch the news on TV; then she would start her washing rituals. The only time she thought she might be able to fit therapy into her schedule was between the hours of three A.M. and five A.M. Tuesday or Thursday.

One may wonder how a woman who sleeps all day and washes all night could have such a fixed schedule. With Gracie, I later learned, days and times had magic qualities. Monday was dirtier than Tuesday; Thursday was the cleanest day of the week. The cleanest hours were between three and five A.M.

Gracie was an avid reader, but she wouldn't touch magazines or newspapers because they were dirty. She ordered many books from publishers and book clubs and opened the mail wearing plastic gloves, which she'd then throw away. She would read only at certain hours and on specific days. Self-help books could be read any day except Monday (if she read them on Monday the information would be negated).

Mysteries and romances were severely restricted to Saturday between the hours of seven and eleven; otherwise the murders and sex in the plot would make her dirty.

I didn't know about any of Gracie's magic during the months she would call and ask me to see her at four in the morning or to make a special trip from New York to see her on a Thursday. Her manner was whiny and demanding ("Well why can't you see me at four A.M.? People who need help need it when they need it, not when you're willing to see them."). She seemed to be so removed from normal social awareness that I wasn't particularly eager to see her. But increasing pressure from her mother and brothers and my being the only person in the small community with experience working with OCD willing to make house calls destined us to work together.

Gracie refused to see me on Friday because that day I would be coming from New York and would be dirty from the city. Saturday evening was out because I would be dirty from seeing other "crazy people." That left Saturday at 8 A.M., when I would be coming to her fresh from a shower and uncontaminated by the world and other people.

Gracie's house was a substantial, well-maintained house in an upper-middle-class neighborhood. Set well back from the street, it was landscaped with old oak trees, flowers lining the walkway to the door, and big, glossy holly bushes surrounding the house. Her mother, who met me at the door, was a gracious older woman. She walked with difficulty and was clearly very ill. She apologetically informed me that Gracie wasn't feeling very well and that perhaps she could give me the information I needed for the initial interview.

On the second Saturday I was to see Gracie, again her mother met me at the door and said that Gracie wasn't feeling well, but she would be glad to discuss Gracie's condition with me. I obtained more details about Gracie, her problem, and how it had affected the family. The third Saturday, when Gracie still wasn't feeling well, I gently but firmly said that I didn't want to hear any more about Gracie, I wanted to speak with her. We went up the stairs and stopped at a closed door across the hall from a bathroom. Her mother knocked: no answer. Her mother knocked again; still no answer. "Gracie dear," she said, "Ms. Dumont is here and needs to talk with you." No answer. I knocked hard.

"Gracie," I said, "I can't help you if you don't talk with me. I'm not going to come back again."

A muffled response.

"What? I can't hear you."

Another muffled response. Her mother translated. "She says she's afraid."

"What are you afraid of, Gracie?" I asked.

"I'm afraid that you are dirty and you'll make me dirty."

"Would you feel safe talking with me through the closed door?" I asked.

When I was young and idealistic I had a vision of myself doing therapy in a tasteful modern office, wearing a crisp white jacket over my just-short-of-ultimate-chic street clothes, discussing deep psychological issues with brilliant talents. But there I was on a drippy Saturday morning in a shabby raincoat and running shoes, squatting in front of a closed door in the hallway discussing my relative dirtiness with a woman who hadn't been a part of the real world for thirty years.

"Gracie, will you talk with me through the closed door?" I asked again.

"I'll try."

Our third, fourth, and fifth sessions were conducted through a closed door. At first I tried to stay within the structure of cognitive/behavior therapy (set short- and long-term goals; establish a hierarchy of fearful situations; plan manageable exposure sessions, and assign homework), but it became impossible. Gracie was difficult to talk with. When I asked her a question she would repeat nonsense phrases over and over again. If I asked her what the phrase meant she would say, "That's for me to know and you to find out." When I asked her what she was afraid of she said, "Dirt, dummy, dirt, dirt, dirt." When I asked her why she was afraid of dirt she said, "Because it's dirty, dummy, dirt is dirty." When I asked her what would happen if she were to get dirty she said, "Dirt, dirty, die, dirt, dirty, die." "Do you mean that you're afraid that if you get dirty you will die?" I asked. No answer. "How will dirt make you die?" No answer.

About halfway through the fifth session, after staring at the door and hearing nothing but long silences and nonsense phrases, I began to have serious misgivings about being able to help Gracie.

"Gracie," I asked, "do you want me to continue to come?"

No answer.

"Gracie, when I don't hear anything from you I don't know what to do. I get the feeling that you don't want me here."

No answer.

"You know what I'll do, I'll leave now and not plan on coming back again until you call me." I felt unsettled about the situation. I told myself that Gracie was a lot more disturbed than I had originally thought.

Later that night Gracie called. "Ms. Dumont, this is Gracie. I'll expect to see you next Saturday morning at eight o'clock."

"That's fine," I said, "I'll see you next week." On the phone Gracie sounded normal (irritating but normal); on the other side of the bedroom door she sounded irrational.

For session six I was still squatting in the hall talking to a closed door.

"Gracie, I don't understand why you can talk to me on the phone but you can't talk to me when I'm here."

"Dirt, dummy, dirt, dirt, dirt."

"Are you afraid to have me standing so close to the door because you think I'm dirty?"

No answer.

I made a daring leap of logic. "Gracie, you know what I think? I think that when I stand here you're so afraid of my dirt that you can't talk because you're saying litanies to keep yourself safe. Is that right?" I heard soft crying on the other side of the door. "Is that right, Gracie?"

"Yes, that's right."

Gracie was consumed with fear. Normally washing would help to relieve the fear, but I was standing between her and the bathroom. She calmed herself by repeating her litanies over and over again.

I thought Gracie might be an excellent candidate for medication. Often when people are so anxious they can't think or concentrate on the cognitive/behavioral work of therapy, medication will calm the fears enough for our work to be more effective. But Gracie was not only fearful of medication, she wouldn't let a doctor examine her. On several occasions her mother's doctor had offered to look in on her or prescribe a minor tranquilizer, but Gracie would have none of it. Another option for Gracie would have been the OCD inpatient program at Temple University, where she could get intensive therapy, but she was too fearful to subject herself to such extreme treatment. I described the options of medication and an inpatient program and told both Gracie and her mother that I didn't think continuing our sessions in their current form would be helpful. Gracie was silent on the other side of the door. Her mother looked away from me sadly, and again I left Gracie's house feeling unsettled. And again I heard from her later that night. She had been thinking about what I'd said. Medication or an inpatient program were totally unacceptable to her. She had called her brother Charlie and enlisted his aid in putting in another intercom that I could use. (I couldn't use her mother's intercom because her mother's illness would contaminate me and then she could never let me in her room.)

Four months after my initial contact with her mother I still hadn't laid eyes on Gracie or had a normal conversation with her. My end of the intercom was installed at the foot of the stairs within view of her door. I picked up the receiver and buzzed her room. "Hi Gracie, I'm here," I said.

"I know," she answered, "I saw you coming up the walk. Your car is dirty."

She was back to the rational but irritating person I recognized on the phone. "Does my dirty car make me dirty?"

"I think so," she said.

"What will happen to me because I'm dirty from my car?" I asked.

"You'll get sick," she answered.

"When?" I asked.

"What?" she asked.

"I said, 'When will I get sick?' Will it be today, or next week, or next year? When?"

"I don't know," she answered.

"I'd like you to enter into your diary that today I arrived in a dirty car, and then keep track of me to see if I get sick. OK?" Finally, I was able to make the first effort to get Gracie to identify her thoughts, to think in terms of cause and effect, and to reality test.

On the intercom Gracie very rarely responded with nonsense phrases. When I heard long silences I guessed that she was saying a litany, and I would ask her what scary thought she had gotten that she had to exorcise. Usually it was a "bad" thought about me (that I was stupid or ugly) and her belief was that having a bad thought about me would negate our work. Gracie was doing "either-or thinking" (if I don't know everything about everything, I'm stupid; if I'm not as attractive as the people on TV, I'm ugly). She believed that if she had any negative thought about me it would negate the therapy. She sort of kept a diary. Many of her anxiety-producing thoughts were so scary she was afraid to write them down. She numbered her scary thoughts (but wouldn't tell me what the numbers referred to). Her diary read:

DATE/TIME	THOUGHT	ANXIETY LEVEL	RITUAL OR RESPONSE	REALITY
Tues. 8:30	#3 & 6	8	washed hands for 30 minutes	must get rid of the dirt
11:30	#14	6	said litany seven times	must get rid of the dirt
3:15	#8	7	said litany seven times	must get rid of the dirt
5:30	#2	9	washed hands for 45 minutes	must get rid of the dirt

Clearly, Gracie and I would have a disagreement about "reality," but I decided to leave the lower numbers (the most scary) alone for the time being and see if I could chip away at the less scary items.

"I can see how washing your hands gets rid of dirt," I said, "but how does saying a litany get rid of dirt?"

"It's symbolic dirt!" she answered, impatient with my stupidity.

"Oh," I said, "will symbolic dirt cause a symbolic illness?"

"Of course it does, what do you think an obsessive-compulsive disorder is?"

No doubt about it, Grace was very well read. Gracie often used intellectualization as a way to avoid the work of identifying the frightening thoughts, analyzing cause and effect, and reality testing, and she was able to intellectualize circles around me.

MONTHS went by, and I still hadn't seen Gracie. All our sessions were conducted over the intercom. I thought she must be doing the work because she spent a fair amount of time reading her diary entries to me. But the content of her thoughts was no clearer, because of her secretive numbering system. I often had the feeling that I didn't know what I was doing with her, as though I were trying to fine-tune a delicate piece of machinery in total darkness. I watched for the slightest bit of improvement but saw none. In the beginning I'd asked Gracie to keep track of the amount of time she was spending on washing and saying litanies in the hope that we would see the time gradually diminish. It didn't. I was about to discuss the apparent lack of change with Gracie when I arrived one morning to find her brother Charlie waiting for me. "We want you to know how pleased we are with Gracie's progress." he said to me.

"We?" I asked, "Who's we?"

"Gracie, our mother, and me," he said. "We were beginning to think that it was hopeless, but now we see that Gracie can get better, and it's so encouraging that I'd like to work with you to help her." I couldn't have been more surprised if he had told me that I'd finally convinced him that the sky is green and he wanted to go forth and spread the word.

"Charlie," I said, carefully weighing my words, "I'm really

glad to hear you say that. Where, in your opinion, has Gracie made the most progress?"

"Oh, she's so much more open," he said. "This is the first time in twenty years I've been able to have a conversation with her. She's real again, she's not always off on some nut case that I can't understand. We talk."

I liked Charlie. His offer to work with me was the best thing that had happened in that household. My time in the community was limited, and it was clear that Gracie would need longer-term care than I was in a position to provide. Charlie offered a good solution.

"Have you spoken with Gracie about this possibility?" I asked.

"Yes I have," he said, "and she's all for it." So was I! In almost every case I prefer that the family be involved with the treatment of the obsessive-compulsive person. They are with the sufferer day in and day out, twenty-four hours a day. I spoke with Gracie on the intercom, and it was clear that she did indeed want Charlie involved.

FIVE months after my initial contact with Gracie's mother, Charlie joined me as a cotherapist. He was able to enter her room (he had installed the intercoms), whereas I was not; he spoke with her every day; I spoke with her an hour a week. I was glad to have Charlie's help. I gave him information on cognitive/behavioral treatment of obsessive-compulsive disorders. He came back with very good questions. When I suggested a specific approach with Gracie, he responded with suggestions based on his knowledge of her. Charlie was able to gain access to Gracie's room and do exposure assignments with her—I could not. With Charlie's help Gracie started to make rapid progress.

SIX months after my initial contact I saw Gracie for the first time. She stood in the open door of her bedroom talking to me while I was at the foot of the stairs. I had tried to imagine what Gracie looked like during those months that she was incognito.

Overweight, I thought, due to inactivity; long, unkempt gray hair; shapeless housedress and slippers. I was wrong! Gracie was slim, with short, strawberry blond hair that framed a pretty, well-proportioned face. She looked very "au courant" dressed in a T-shirt, slacks, and running shoes, and much younger than her age.

Soon Gracie, Charlie, and I were meeting in the living room. After I touched the sidewalk outside Gracie would touch my hands and see that nothing bad happened to her. Next I touched my dirty car and touched Gracie. Again, nothing bad happened to her.

Please understand—this was not easy.

Each time we did something new Gracie experienced great distress. She was sure that she would die or go crazy if she couldn't immediately wash or perform rituals. Charlie and I reminded her that she had had the same feeling on numerous occasions, but she never died or went crazy. When Gracie suddenly went silent we knew that she was saying litanies or removing herself from us. "Gracie, what's the thought? Let's 'cause and effect' the thought. How can thinking about something dirty make you sick? If we think about a million dollars will that make us rich?"

My first experience of Gracie's bedroom was something of a shock. I had thought that someone so obsessed with dirt would have to have a sanitized room to live in. Except for her desk and bed, the room was in chaos. I suspect I could have written my name in the dust on the windowsill, things were lying around on the floor—it was not what I expected. She saw me looking at the windowsill. "I know, it's dirty," she said. "It's too dirty for me to touch it, so I can't clean it."

"Why don't you have the cleaning woman come in to clean up?" I asked. Gracie worried that the cleaning woman wouldn't do it right. She might put a dirty cleaning cloth on a clean surface and contaminate everything. When an area of her room became "dirty" Gracie designated it as a "no-man's-land." Over the years the dirt encroached on her until the only "safe" area of the room was the immediate space around the door, her bed, and desk.

Gracie and I had progressed to working together in the bathroom to reduce her washing time. First I demonstrated how I washed my hands while Gracie counted to see how many seconds it took. Then Gracie tried it while I counted. "OK," I said, "Ready. Set, turn on the water and pick up the soap, one, two, three, put the soap down and rinse your hands, four, five, . . . "

With me counting and keeping pace Gracie was able to wash her hands in thirty seconds (her old record speed was twenty minutes). This was obviously a winning technique. We made a tape recording with me counting and keeping pace. Charlie installed a tape recorder in the bathroom, and every time Gracie went in to wash her hands she turned on the tape recorder. We also worked on reducing the number of times she washed her hands. Gracie worked out a wonderfully creative reward system for herself. Every day, just for having the courage to get out of bed, she awarded herself ten dollars. Each time she washed her hands, she deducted twenty-five cents. If she washed her hands forty-four times during the day, she carried a dollar debit over to the next day. If she washed her hands only twenty times during the day she had a five-dollar balance to add to the next day's ten, for a total of fifteen for the day. The idea was to amass enough money to buy a "success present."

We used the same technique to reduce Gracie's showering time from two or three hours to fifty minutes.

A year went by and I still didn't know what most of Gracie's thoughts were (she continued to use her numbering system), but we had started walking down the street. Gracie's most compelling goal was to walk to the small bookstore in town (about a four-block walk). For a woman whose entire activity for thirty years had been walking across to the hall to the bathroom, this was an arduous task.

Gracie still walked with her fists clutched and held against her chest in order not to touch anything dirty, so she looked a little odd on the street. Charlie, who was known in the community, felt self-conscious walking with us, so very often he stayed home while Gracie and I worked our way toward the bookstore. Our usual procedure was to walk about fifty feet before Gracie would say that she thought something dirty touched her and she wanted to go home and wash. We would reality test the thought—what could be so dirty? Why weren't other people running home to wash? In the past she had had similar fears and nothing bad happened, why was this time different? Why was it that I could be subjected to this "dirt" all the time and nothing bad happened to me? We must have presented a peculiar sight to anyone watching.

Finally, more than a year after we had started work together, Gracie opened the door to the small, neat, privately owned bookstore. The owner was waiting on a customer at the service desk. Gracie and I stood just inside the door. With her fists clutched against her chest and her eyes closed, to my utter surprise Gracie yelled, "I want . . . " whatever book it was she wanted. In shock the two women looked at us still standing in the doorway. They exchanged hushed words and studiously avoided looking at us again. Gracie let out a loud sob, turned, and ran the entire four blocks home.

Back at the house she attacked me. "That was terrible," she said. "I was never so embarrassed and humiliated in my life!

How could you let a thing like that happen? I can't trust you at all. I'll never be able to go out again."

I had totally overlooked the fact that Gracie hadn't had a normal social exchange outside of her family in thirty years. "Gracie," I said, "let's not lose sight of what you just accomplished. For the first time in thirty years you walked down the main street of town and entered a store. That's terrific! Unfortunately, your social skills stink, but we can work on them just like we worked on getting you out of the house."

It was very easy for Gracie to lose sight of her progress, because her comparisons were based on "normal" activities of "normal" people. In fact, during that first year Gracie had made phenomenal progress. She had cut her obsessive washing down from six to eight hours a day to about three hours. She had righted her upside-down schedule and was active during the day and sleeping at night. She was sitting down in the dining room and eating meals with her mother, and visiting with family members (she had never seen her niece and nephews until just a few months prior to our bookstore episode). Gracie's progress really was terrific; even feeling self-conscious was a sign of progress. But now her distress was so intense she wasn't able to hear any suggestion of progress.

"You think I look weird," she shrieked at Charlie, "don't you! That's why you won't go out with us." Charlie reddened, squirmed in his chair, and studied his hands. "Well, the hell with you! The hell with all of you!" Gracie yelled, and stormed up the stairs and slammed the door. Charlie and I exchanged guilty looks. We both knew that Gracie looked weird. With her fists held tightly against her chest, she walked stiff-kneed and leaned backward, her eyes squeezed closed most of the time.

Two weeks later when I got out of my car to begin the session with Gracie I saw Charlie at the door with a video recorder taping my walk to the house. He and Gracie had been working on Gracie's "style" by video taping her walk and comparing it to other people's. Gracie had been walking weirdly for forty years; she had to learn how to walk like a "regular" person.

When people ask me what the rate of cure is, I never know what to tell them. Will Gracie ever be completely "cured?" Probably not. But when I left after working with her for two and a half years, she was walking normally and going to the bookstore to buy books by herself. She had contacted an OCD group and was offering hope and help on the telephone to other sufferers. She was making arrangements to return to school and get her degree. She had a satisfying relationship with both her brothers (although Charlie remained very special to her) and their wives and children. She was able to be with, touch, and help her increasingly frail mother. When I left the community we set up a schedule; either she or Charlie would call me in New York once a month to tell me about progress or problems and get advice. After six months I didn't hear from them anymore. I like to think that when I have made myself obsolete I have been successful.

PEOPLE have asked me why Gracie's family didn't get help for her sooner. Her mother told me that when Gracie started having problems in the 1950s they took her to doctors and psychiatrists, but nothing helped. After one psychiatrist recommended institutionalization, they stopped looking for help and decided to maintain her at home in whatever way they could. Behavioral therapy wasn't used for OCD until the 1970s, and effective medication has been available only for the past six or eight years. (For more information on my work with Gracie see page 252–53 in chapter 15 "How to Get Better.")

CHAPTER ELEVEN

DAVID FEARED HE COULDN'T HOLD ON TO HIS JOB BECAUSE HE SO DREADED GIVING SALES PRESENTATIONS

THE PHOBIA of public speaking and its close cousins, social phobia and performance anxiety, are among the most common of phobias. The common denominators are the fear of negative evaluation by others and a driving perfectionism that leads to unrealistic expectations about performance or behavior. The magic thinker believes that if he is perfect he will be successful and loved by all, and if he is not successful he is worse than nothing. The magic thinker with performance anxiety believes that he knows how others are evaluating him. The assumption is: "I know that everyone thought I was a jerk, because I felt like a jerk." Performance anxiety sufferers project their own feelings about themselves onto other people; because they hate themselves for being imperfect, they assume that others do too.

These phobias present a problem for the therapist because it's not usually possible to accompany the violinist into the orchestra pit or the actor onto the stage. I have, however, attended "toastmaster" meetings with people phobic of public speaking and gone to single bars with socially phobic people (for strictly therapeutic reasons). Much of the work is done by assessing tape-recorded performances and examining belief systems.

DAVID was twenty-eight years old and making a very comfortable living as a division sales manager for a major pharmaceutical company. He had an MBA from a prestigious eastern university. The next obvious step in his career would be to general sales manager and ultimately to marketing director. However, David had come for help because he was afraid he wasn't going to be able to hold onto his present job, let alone plan on climbing the executive ladder.

Once a month all the division sales managers in his company gave a presentation to upper management; twice a year sales managers were required to give a presentation to the board of directors. When David came for help he had given four presentations, each one a little worse than the last. He had decided that he would quit his job before he would do another. I needed to know what David was feeling and thinking while he gave the presentations.

"It's terrible!" he said. "I really feel like I'm going to die. Even before I have to start to speak—you know, when I'm waiting for my turn—I start feeling like I'm going to suffocate. My heart is banging, my head is throbbing; I can't breathe. It's like there is no air in the room. By the time I get up to speak the room is spinning and I don't even think I can get to my feet. My mouth is so dry it feels like my tongue is going to get stuck to the roof and I won't be able to talk.

"I have to stand there forever trying to get myself together enough to be able to focus on the paper and get the words out. When the words finally do come, my voice is squeaky and shaky and I have a weird sense of not really being there. I feel totally out of control and I'm afraid that I'm going to pee my pants and start screaming and babbling.

"Articles on public speaking always tell you to pick friendly faces out of the audience and make eye contact, but I can't do that. I'm not in that room, I'm not that person standing there squeaking and shaking. Everything seems unreal—I'm unreal, the people are unreal, it's just a weird, horrible feeling.

"When I get into that head there isn't anything I can do. I've tried relaxation and it doesn't work. I've tried to think of something pleasant and my mind doesn't work. Nothing works; I feel like I'm going to go crazy or die." Just telling me about the difficulty left David distraught and exhausted.

"When you get into your speech does it seem to get a little easier?" I asked.

"No," he said. "I just barely make it through. By the time I'm finished I'm sweating like a pig and totally out of control—I know I've made a fool of myself."

David was telling himself at least two things that really couldn't be accurate. He couldn't have been "totally out of control," and it's doubtful that he made a fool of himself.

"What do you mean when you say that you were totally out of control?" I asked.

He gave me an exasperated look and said, "I couldn't function—I was wiped out."

"Oh. Well, what happened after you gave your last presentation?"

"Fortunately, mine was the last one on the agenda. So when I finished we broke and all went for lunch. I had to have a couple of stiff ones before I really calmed down."

"Where did you go for lunch?"

"There's a place about three blocks from the office that's not too noisy or crowded—we go there for lunch quite a lot."

"How'd you get there?"

"We walked, it's not that far."

"Oh, I thought you said you couldn't function."

David flashed a look of irritation at me. "What I really meant was that I just couldn't think any more."

"Did you order your own lunch?"

"Of course I did," he said, his irritation growing. "What I really mean is that I was totally wiped out, exhausted."

"Did you finish your presentation?"

"Yeah, I don't know how though."

"So if I understand you correctly, when you gave your last presentation you felt really, really terrible. You had a sense of unreality, you were frightened, shaky, and couldn't talk normally, but somehow you did it without fainting or wetting your pants or going crazy. And then afterward you went out and had lunch."

It was clear that David didn't like my interpretation of the episode. Grudgingly he said, "Well, yeah, but when you say it that way you don't get any of the intensity of it. I *really* thought that I was going to die."

"Have you ever had that feeling before?"

"Yeah, every time I've given a presentation."

"Have you ever died before?"

"Oh come on," he said, "you just don't know how bad it feels."

"Honest, David, I do know that it feels really bad, but when you've had that feeling—how many times, four times?—and each time you say 'Oh my God, I'm going to die,' but don't die, we have to look at why that misinterpretation persists. Do you know where that feeling comes from?" I asked.

"Yeah, from adrenaline—my doctor explained it to me when I thought I was having heart attacks."

This came as a surprise to me. David had said nothing about his "heart attacks" in his initial interview. I wondered about

three issues: David's "heart attacks," how well he understood
the mechanics of his panic, and how he came to the conclusion that he made a fool of himself during his presentation.

"When did you think you were having heart attacks?"

"That was several years ago. I had this jerky job that I got
right after I got out of graduate school, and in the morning I'd
get on the subway to go to work and start getting these heart
palpitations and felt like I couldn't breathe and had terrible
chest pains. It would happen at least twice a week until finally
one day I thought I was going to die of a heart attack right there
on the Lexington Avenue subway. So I got off the subway at
the next stop, grabbed a taxi, and went straight into the emergency room at Bellevue.

"That was a horrible experience! I thought I was dying and
they're telling me to wait. When the doctor finally saw me he
said it was just nerves and gave me a tranquilizer. I didn't have
a lot of confidence in that guy, so I went to see my own doctor and he ran a bunch of tests and confirmed that it was just
nerves and gave me more tranquilizers."

"What was making you so nervous?" I asked.

"I had to get out of that job. I liked the people and the work
was interesting, but I had to get something better and nothing
was working out."

"If you liked the people and found the job interesting, why
was it so jerky?"

"It wasn't going anywhere. I could see myself ten years down
the road in the same place, doing the same thing with piddling
yearly increases but nothing really big."

"So you felt that you had to leave a job that you liked for
something bigger, but nothing bigger was happening."

"Yeah, I was feeling like every day was just one more day
down the drain. I really had to do something."

"Did the tranquilizers help?"

"No . . . Well, maybe. I took them for a while and the attacks didn't seem to be as bad, you know? I'd still have them, usually on the subway in the morning and sometimes at home alone I'd have them, but they didn't seem to be so bad. Maybe the tranquilizers helped, or maybe it was knowing that they weren't heart attacks that made the difference."

"How long did you take the tranquilizers?"

"Just for a few weeks, maybe a month. I didn't think they were really doing any good and I heard that they could be addicting, and I didn't want to get into anything like that. Also, I read that I wasn't supposed to drink while I was taking them and I'd really rather have a couple of drinks than take a pill."

"What happened with the attacks?"

"I don't know, they just stopped happening. I think about them every now and then when I'm on a subway. But I don't have them anymore, thank God."

"Were those attacks similar to the way you feel when you give a presentation?"

"Oh no, I really feel like I'm going to die when I have to give a presentation."

"But you thought you were going to die then too. You went to a hospital emergency room."

"Yeah, that's true . . . but these really feel different."

"You said that your doctor told you that the attacks are caused by adrenaline. Do you know how that works?"

"Not really, just that the adrenaline makes my heart beat faster and all that."

"Yeah, that's right. That's a part of the 'fight/flight' response. The same thing would happen if a mugger stuck a gun in your face. There would be an instant spurt of adrenaline into your system and your legs would shake, your mouth would be dry, your heart would beat like crazy, your voice would be squeaky. And another thing that most people do when they're frightened, they either hyperventilate (take short, quick breaths) or they hold their breath. But in either case changes in the body chemistry will cause them to feel dizzy or faint. So the thought or awareness of being in danger causes all of these frightening sensations."

"Yeah, but I don't have a mugger's gun in my face when I give a presentation."

"What do you think causes it then?"

"I don't know—that's why I'm here."

"Oh . . . Earlier you said you knew that you had made a fool of yourself when you gave the presentation. How did you know that?"

"Well come on, what do you think I looked like? There I was standing there in front of all my colleagues, hardly able to talk, shaking and squeaking, almost peeing my pants from fright . . . "

"Did any one know that you almost peed your pants?"

"No, but they sure knew that I was nervous."

"Do you suppose any of the other guys are nervous when they give a presentation?"

"Oh sure, to some degree at least."

"Do you think they make fools of themselves?"

"Well, no, but that's different."

"How is that different?"

"It just is."

"Who decided that?"

"I guess I did."

"So you decided that when they're nervous it's OK, but when you're nervous you make a fool of yourself?"

"Yeah, I guess so."

"What reasoning did you use to come to that conclusion?"

"I don't really know."

"It sounds as though you have a different set of standards

for yourself. You're saying nervousness is OK for them, but it's not OK for you. Why is that?"

"I'd be happy with just nervousness—but I'm half crazy."

"What do you mean 'half crazy'? What did you do that was crazy?"

"Well, I could hardly talk."

"But that's nervousness, not craziness. Do you think it might be possible that the other guys feel as though they can hardly talk when they're nervous?"

"Yeah, I've heard them say that, but I didn't think it was the same."

"What do you think makes it different for them?"

"I don't think that they feel as bad as I do."

"What does the degree of feeling bad have to do with making a fool of yourself?"

"I'm not sure. Maybe I think that they can see how bad I feel, or maybe it's because I feel so much worse I can't function as well, so my delivery suffers."

"Has anyone one said, 'Hey David, you really did a terrible job on the presentation'?"

"No, no one would say that."

"If I remember correctly, your boss said that you had done a pretty good job."

"He said that it was well planned and the content was good. But he said that I was obviously nervous too."

"Did he say that you'd made a fool of yourself?"

"No."

"I can't imagine that it would look good for him if every month you got up and made a fool of yourself."

"No, it sure wouldn't."

"So it's likely that if you were making a fool of yourself he would have taken you aside and said something to you."

"Yeah, probably."

"So he's making a distinction between being nervous—which, although it's not optimal, isn't terrible—or making a fool of yourself."

"I guess so."

"David, look at what you're telling yourself. You said that you couldn't function, that you were totally out of control, that you were crazy, and that you made a fool of yourself. It sounds like you're telling yourself a lot of stuff that's not very accurate."

"It's beginning to look that way."

Finally, I got David to see how he was beating himself up. It would have been much faster and easier to have just told him that he was an impossible perfectionist and that he was telling himself a lot of unreal garbage, to stop it immediately, but that never works. I have to circle around and look for threads of evidence that I can pull out and hold up for inspection. Only after seeing the contradictions in the evidence themselves do magic thinkers reassess their convictions.

I asked David to keep a really good record of his anxiety and the kind of things that he was telling himself. I also explained the anxiety scale. I asked him to rate his anxiety level of his last presentation.

"I think that's the worst I ever felt, it was a 10."

"What about when you were coming here this morning? Were you anxious then?"

"No . . . yes, I guess I was. Maybe about a 4."

"What were you thinking about?"

"Just about having to tell someone all this stuff. I thought I'd sound like a jerk. I thought that maybe you'd want me to go for tests because something else was wrong with me, you know, like a tumor or something."

It was so hard to get David to believe that any of his problems might actually be caused by his own thinking. I suggested that he keep a diary so he could see how closely related his panic was to what was going on in his mind.

Here is David's initial diary entry:

TIME/ DAY	ANXIETY LEVEL	ACTIVITY	THOUGHTS
2:00 Tues	4	going to therapist's office	She'll think I'm a jerk or that something's wrong with me.

"This sounds like it's is going to take a lot of time. What's the point of it?"

"Well, remember earlier when I said that all those sensations you feel are pretty much the same as you'd feel if you had a mugger's gun in your face . . . "

"Yeah, and I pointed out that I didn't have a mugger's gun in my face."

"Right. But there must be something going on that makes you respond as though you are in real danger."

"In danger of what?"

"On your way here your anxiety went up to a 4 because you thought that you might sound like a jerk or that you might have a tumor. A big concern about the presentation is looking like a fool."

"But that's not 'dangerous.' "

"It's not? What would you do if you were to pee in your pants and start babbling and faint in front of your colleagues?"

"Oh God, I'd die."

"What would cause you to die?"

"The embarrassment and humiliation—I'd die."

"So now you're telling me that it is dangerous to look like a jerk because the embarrassment and humiliation would kill you."

David shifted in his chair and studied his hands for a while. Finally he said, "Well, it wouldn't really kill me, but I don't know how I could deal with it."

David was committing all of the phobic's typical errors in logical reasoning. He was catastrophizing by telling himself that he would die or go crazy. He was overgeneralizing when he told himself that because he felt horrible in the past he would always feel horrible. Telling himself "I'm a jerk because I think I look like a jerk," was emotional reasoning. He was telling himself "If I'm not perfect, I'm rotten," which is either/or thinking. And he consistently ignored the positive by not accepting the reality that he didn't die or go crazy. In fact, each time he had given a presentation, his boss had told him that he'd done a good job.

EVENTUALLY I learned that David's father was the kind of guy who would ask what happened to the other three points if David came home from school with a 97 on a test. He was having a tug-of-war with himself when his first "heart attack" episode occurred. On the one hand, he really liked his job; the work was interesting and he enjoyed the people. On the other hand he was telling himself that he had to do better. The better job required him to assume more responsibility and involved more stress. The standards David set for himself were like his father's expectations. David believed that it was OK for other guys to be nervous, but it wasn't OK for him. It wasn't good enough that his boss told him he did a good job. He had to do the best job. He feared other people's evaluation of him because his own was so harsh and demanding. We were going to have to question David's need to be 100 percent perfect before we would see significant progress with his public-speaking phobia.

"DAVID, what will happen if you don't give the best presentation?"

"I'll lose my job. They don't keep jerks around."

"But the meaning of 'best' indicates that there can only be one. Does that mean that they fire everyone except the one 'best' person?"

"Uhhh . . . no, they can't do that because they have to have more than one sales manager."

"Are any of the guys bigger jerks than you are?"

"Oh yeah, I don't know how some of them keep their jobs."

"So what is this stuff about having to be the best or you'll lose your job?"

"Well, maybe I don't have to be the best to keep my job, but I really want to be the best."

"Sure you do and that's fine, but you're making it a whole lot harder for yourself when you say, 'Unless I'm the best I'll lose my job.' What do you get if you are the best?"

"What do you mean?"

"What do you get—do you get a big button that says, 'I am the best' or do you get more money, or what?"

"Well, I guess I'd be more likely to get the promotion."

"You mean the guy who does the best presentation gets the promotion?"

"No, not actually. You need the sales numbers before you get the promotion."

"So it sounds like there are a lot of ways to be 'best,' and 'best' in one area doesn't necessarily mean the 'one and only best.' How many sales managers are there in the company?"

"Fourteen."

"It sounds as though you could actually be eighth or ninth best at giving the presentation and your job would still be safe. And the rest of the guys wouldn't necessarily think that you're a jerk."

"Yeah, I suppose so."

BECAUSE David's main problem concerned giving business presentations, it was impossible to work in vivo with him. David came up with the ingenious idea of using his boss as an unwitting support person. Because he felt it was indicative of personal weakness if he revealed his phobia, he told his boss he was taking elocution lessons in order to improve his presentations. He asked him to tape his delivery and invited him to comment on it. His boss expressed pleasure at being involved in David's efforts toward self-improvement.

An essential element of reducing public-speaking anxiety is being completely familiar with the material to be presented and being totally prepared. David rehearsed his presentation in my office. When he felt confident with his delivery, we taped it so we could compare it to the recording his boss would be making. That way we could know exactly how the anxiety affected his speaking.

We arranged to have our appointment on the evening of the day he was to give his presentation. That afternoon David called to say that he wanted to cancel our session. He said that he had made a complete fool of himself and he didn't think he would ever get over his phobia. I encouraged him to come in for the session and listen to the tape before he drew that conclusion.

When David arrived he was carrying the tape recording and the notes that his boss had made of the presentation in a sealed manila envelope. He was more upset than I had ever seen him.

"I'm done," he said. "I'm finished, I made a complete ass of myself. This was the worst one yet. My mind went totally blank and I forgot where I was in the presentation. I babbled like an idiot. I shook so badly I couldn't even hold the paper. I just don't think I can deal with this, I don't know what I can do."

Because the envelope was sealed David assumed that it contained dire news and was afraid to open it. I opened the envelope for him. "David, it sounds like you and your boss are talking about two different presentations," I said.

We listened to the tape together. David's boss's comments were accurate. He said that David's material was very well organized and clearly presented. But his delivery needed work. Overall, however, improvement was evident, and this boss felt that he had done good work.

DAVID and I worked together for another two months. We spent time considering his need to be the best and his fears of negative evaluation by others. When the time came to do another presentation, he again asked his boss to tape it and comment. This time, although he was still anxious, he didn't carry with him the disaster imagery of having made a fool of himself. His boss's evaluation was that David's presentation was very good, and David's self-evaluation was more in line with reality. After he had successfully given the semiannual presentation to the board of directors, David terminated therapy.

I still hear from him from time to time. He did get the promotion to general sales manager and has established a "toastmaster's" group within his company to help other people who have public speaking difficulties.

PEOPLE with public speaking and social phobias fear negative evaluation by others. Very often they will have self-defeating assumptions, rules, or beliefs, such as:

—"If I'm not perfect people will reject me."
—"I have to be the best, otherwise I'm a failure."
—"If people think I'm weak, they'll take advantage of me."
—"It's necessary that everybody like me."

David's thinking was a variation on a common theme of public-speaking phobics: "If I'm not the best, they'll think I'm a jerk, and I'll die of the humiliation."

David was convinced that he was making a complete fool of himself, even though his boss remained positive. Our most important work was to convince David that he could be less than 100 percent perfect and still be pretty good.

CHAPTER TWELVE

MR. MORE, THE MAN WHO COULDN'T THROW ANYTHING AWAY

WHEN I was about fourteen I was drafted into helping my mother and aunt clean out the house of an elderly distant relative who had recently died. I'm not sure exactly how she was related; my memory of her is hazy, but I know with absolute certainty that I had never been in her house prior to the cleaning expedition.

The house was a little bungalow in sad disrepair on the outside. Inside it was stacked to the ceiling with boxes. Leading from the front door was a path about four feet wide with boxes of more or less equal size stacked on each side. The path led to the dining room, where there were more boxes. Piled on the dining-room table and chairs were more boxes. From the dining room the path split off and led to her bedroom and sewing room (both stacked with boxes). The kitchen was the only room with a semblance of normality. In spite of the boxes, the neatness and order of everything was dazzling. The boxes were stacked and aligned with precision, and every box was labeled and sublabeled with a brief description of its contents.

In the bedroom: SHOES—BLACK
Low heels
(out of style)

SHOES—SUMMER
White & beige
(kind of worn)

In the dining room: DOILIES
White & Cream
Large

NAPKINS
White Damask
(for company only)

In the living room: READER'S DIGEST
From 1942 to 1946

The house was a warehouse of her entire life. In awe I wandered along the paths trying to imagine what her thoughts could have been when she surveyed her accumulations. But I realized that such an understanding was way beyond my grasp when I found in the pantry a box, somewhat larger than a shoe box, that was labeled PIECES OF STRING TOO SHORT TO SAVE.

MR. MORE was forty-two years old, single, and lived alone. He was a little overweight and had a slightly rumpled, dishevelled appearance. He worked as an accountant for a large firm, and his constant obsessing on inconsequential matters was affecting his career. He estimated that he spent at least a third of his working day obsessing. He was able to keep up with the work by staying many hours overtime, but the tax season was approaching and his workload would double.

Mr. More obsessed about everything: "Did I remember to turn off the gas or lock the door? Should I have worn gray socks instead of black socks? The black socks look too drab, almost morbid. Will people think I'm morbid because of the black socks? If they think I'm morbid they'll think there's something wrong with me. Maybe I can sneak out for lunch and buy a pair of gray socks and change them, but if I change them, where can I put the black socks? I can't just throw them away. I can't put them in my desk drawer; they might smell bad. What can I do with my black socks if I buy new socks? And what if someone notices that I've changed socks in the middle of the day . . . "

After a phone conversation with his boss he would think, "I shouldn't have ended the conversation by saying 'Have a nice day'; that's too frivolous. He'll think I'm a real twit for saying anything so silly. Or maybe he'll think I'm being a smart aleck. Maybe I should call him and tell him I didn't mean it—but no, I can't call him up and tell I don't want him to have a nice day. Maybe I can call him and have another conversation and end it more intelligently. But what can I call him about? I can't just call him for no reason except to end a conversation . . . "

On our third appointment Mr. More arrived very distressed. "Now I have a real problem," he said. "That other stuff was just nonsense. I can't get into my apartment, and I have to get in because I've got important papers there.

"Why can't you get into your apartment?" I asked.

For a moment he hesitated and then with exasperation said, "Because a stack fell in front of the door." I started to ask, "What stack . . . ?" when a picture of my relative's house with all the boxes emerged from my long-buried memory. "Oh," I said, "I think I understand."

The previous morning on his way to work he had slammed the door shut (he always slammed it to be sure the lock would catch), and he heard a loud crash. When he tried to reopen the door it wouldn't budge. He pushed and pounded without luck. He obsessed about the problem all day at work and then called his brother and arranged to meet him at his apartment door, where well into the night the two of them tried to get into the apartment with no luck. During our conversation he remembered that there was a fire escape outside his kitchen window. (It's not unusual that an otherwise obvious solution can be completely overlooked when a person is distraught.) While he was in my office he called his upstairs neighbor to arrange for Mr. More to crawl out the neighbor's window, down the fire escape, and into his own window. Before he left we agreed that his apartment was in serious trouble and that our next appointment should be held there.

My departed relative's apartment was neat and orderly—Mr. More's was total chaos. The house of my memory had wide, clear paths. In Mr. More's apartment there was no way to walk without stepping on stuff. Everywhere—all over the floor, the couch, the tables—were clothes, dirty dishes, plastic containers, empty bags, newspapers, magazines, books, and other objects of various sizes and purposes.

Mr. More had a problem throwing things away. He remembered that even when he was very little he couldn't bring himself to throw away outgrown clothes. He saved the shells he found at the seashore and the stones he picked up at summer camp; he saved his comic books and all his school papers. His older brother drew a chalk line down the middle of the room they shared, and if any of Mr. More's collection oozed over the line his brother would throw it out. In college he had a reputation for being a slob, but except for a few arguments with his roommate the problem never became a major issue.

The disorder got out of hand when he moved into his own apartment. Because he had a limited budget for furnishings, he picked up things he found on the street—a chest of drawers with one drawer missing, a wobbly chair, a table with a scratched top. The intention was always to fix and refinish the furniture and replace the pieces when he could afford to. Over the years he bought a waterbed and an expensive couch, but the curbside collection continued to grow. He picked up appliances that didn't work, mirrors that were broken, damaged furniture, stacks of magazines, worn clothes, and all sorts of objects of uncertain identity.

Periodically he would set aside a day for "housecleaning," when he typically would pick up item after item, inspect it briefly, and decide that it was still good, or that he would fix it next week, and put it down again, leaving the apartment looking much the same as before the "housecleaning." The collection grew and grew. Newspapers were saved because Mr. More worried that he might have missed an important article and felt that he should reread the paper. Worn clothes were saved because he liked them and he might wear them for painting or cleaning. Plastic containers were saved for storage. He saved grocery bags because they were still good and he could use them again. On numerous occasions his mother had attempted to help him. With his permission she took piles and piles of his things and deposited them on the curb for garbage collection, but each time after she left Mr. More started worrying about the possibility of something really important having been thrown out, until the anxiety was so great he was compelled to bring the things back in. His mother finally refused not only to help but even to visit his apartment. His collection continued to grow.

Mr. More's social life was nonexistent. During his twenties and thirties he occasionally dated, but around the third date he would begin to obsess about his date's reaction to his apartment. He would make such a point of not taking her to his apartment that she would become suspicious and break off the relationship. During his late thirties he maintained an affair with a woman for several years and avoided taking her to his apartment by telling her that he was married. After a couple of years of dating he told her that he was leaving his wife and moved into her small one-bedroom apartment. Soon he began collecting things he found on the street again. Eventually his woman-friend started to complain about the clutter. The clutter increased and the arguments escalated until finally the woman told him that she couldn't live with him any longer.

Mr. More lived in fear that the superintendent of his apartment building would evict him. Once, using a passkey, the super went into the apartment to check for a water leak. He warned Mr. More to clean the apartment or face eviction. Since then every time he ran into the superintendent, Mr. More would give him five or ten dollars and say, "Everything is fine, the place is all cleaned up." But the fear of someone coming into his apartment was always present. Except for the superintendent, I was the first person inside Mr. More's apartment since his mother had left in disgust over ten years before.

The place smelled bad. There was nowhere to sit, hardly any space to stand, and everything was covered with the sooty, gritty dust characteristic of New York. I was beginning to reassess my commitment to in vivo therapy. "One step at a time," I told myself. "First we have to understand what the fear is and then take one small, manageable step toward it."

The first step was to understand the dimensions of the problem. Mr. More and I stood in the middle of the mayhem, trying to establish a hierarchy for the collection. Large items, such as furniture, and articles that had personal meaning were the hardest to throw away. Objects that were interesting (a carved chair leg) or conceivably useful (plastic containers, broken appliances) were next on the list. At the very bottom of the list (therefore the most dispensable) were wrinkled paper bags. We started by wading through the mess. After about twenty minutes we had collected a stack of bags about a foot high.

Our next step was to throw the bags out or to analyze why they couldn't be thrown out. Mr. More didn't seem to be having any trouble during the search and collect period, but as the time to throw the bags out approached I could see that he was becoming agitated. I asked him how he felt.

"Not good," he said, "not good at all. I may have left something important in one of them. There may be an important paper or money in the bags. I really can't throw them out until I've had a chance to check them." I asked him how he felt physically. "Tense, my chest feels like it has a tight band around it, and there's a lump in my throat and a bigger one in my stomach. I have to check the bags, I have a feeling that I left something important in one of them."

"Shall we check them together?" I asked.

"No, you might not do it right. I have to do it myself."

I stood and watched while he picked up each bag, opened it, put his hand in, looked inside, shook it, and put it down again. In some of the bags he found receipts for merchandise or groceries, many of which were seven and eight years old. Each of the receipts he read, smoothed out, and carefully put aside. After he finished the stack he started over.

"You've checked all of these, let's throw them out now," I said.

Mr. More forcefully said, "No! I can't throw them out until I'm sure I've checked them all. There might be something important in one of them."

Two of the most distressing aspects of OCD are the questioning of one's own reality and the need for absolute certainty. Other people are able to trust in their sense of reality ("I definitely remember locking the door"), or they can tolerate uncertainty ("I don't really remember locking the door, but I'm pretty sure I did"). But the OCD sufferer is compelled to repeat an action over and over again. The goal in therapy is to develop trust in one's reality and to learn to accept and live with uncertainty. At this point, however, these were still distant goals for Mr. More, so he had to repeat his checking.

When he had finished, we walked together to the garbage chute and threw the bags down. Back in his apartment I asked him how he felt.

"Great!" he said with a big smile, "I really think I can do it."

"Sure," I said, "we'll work together and eventually we'll be able to get this place cleaned up."

Mr. More's face darkened. "I meant that I thought I could throw out the wrinkled bags, not everything."

Trying hard to keep the dismay from showing on my face, I said, "Right, that's a good place to start." His assignment for the week was to continue to find and throw out bags; to keep a record of his thoughts; and to clear a space for us to sit down during the next appointment.

My assignment for myself was to reassess my own attitudes. Mr. More's place was filthy. It caused me distress just to stand in it. I didn't want to breathe the air; I certainly didn't want to touch anything. I didn't even have the courage to look into the bathroom or kitchen. I really didn't want to have to go there again, but I doubted that sitting in my office and talking about how he should throw things out would be terribly effective. An important part of therapy is the acceptance and positive regard that the therapist communicates to the client. Would I be able to separate my revulsion for Mr. More's lifestyle from Mr. More if every time I saw him I was offended by his squalid apartment? I decided to endure another session in the apartment, gently letting Mr. More know how I felt about it, and then go from there.

For the next session I prepared myself by wearing old clothes and carrying moist paper towels in a plastic bag so I could clean myself off afterward.

"I'M kind of surprised you came back," Mr. More said. "Most people wouldn't have."

Mr. More had spent the entire week clearing a six-foot circle and clearing the junk off chairs. He hadn't done the other parts of the assignment. It seems contradictory that people spend considerable time and money for professional advice and then disregard it, but there can be a myriad of complicated reasons for people not doing their homework assignments. Sometimes it is old leftover resentment from having been a school kid. Or real-life problems impinge, such as illness or an extra-heavy work schedule. Maybe the person lacks commitment and feels that it is a waste of time. Most often it is because the goal was too ambitious.

ALTHOUGH he didn't throw out any additional wrinkled paper bags, he did put aside all those he found while cleaning so we could work on throwing them out together. We had another foot-high stack of bags and old receipts to deal with. I suggested that he tear the bags completely open and spread them out flat. While he was doing that I pulled out more bags and stacked them. When he finished with the first stack, we went to the garbage chute and threw down the bags and receipts.

On returning to the apartment, I noticed that Mr. More was getting agitated. "What are you feeling?" I asked.

"I'm feeling very tense," he said. "I'm feeling that tightness

in my chest and the lumps in my stomach and throat. How do
I know that you know what you're doing? How do I know that
you aren't making me go too fast and will cause me to crack?"
He clutched his chest and said, "Those receipts are gone now,
I can't get them back."

"Why do you need to get them back?" I asked.

"They might be important," he said. "I might need them."

"Why will you need grocery receipts or receipts that are over
two years old?"

"I don't know, but I have to get them back. Maybe if I get
the super he'll open the door to the garbage chute in the basement."

"If you get them back will that terrible feeling go away?" I
asked.

"Yes. I think you're making me go too fast, I can't stand it.
I should never have let you talk me into throwing those receipts
away."

Mr. More's terrible feeling is an intrinsic part of an obsessive-compulsive disorder. The OC victim gets a frightening
thought (in Mr. More's case, it was "What if I need those receipts?"); the thought creates the distressing physical sensations
of anxiety, and the victim relieves the anxiety by performing a
ritual. Sometimes the ritual is saying a litany; often it's washing. For Mr. More it was keeping absolutely everything so he
would always have whatever it was he might need. The most
difficult part of getting over an obsessive-compulsive disorder
is resisting the compelling urge to perform the ritual. Mr. More
was misinterpreting the terrible feeling as an indication that
something even more terrible would happen—he would
"crack." The overriding impulse is to avert that most terrible
thing and get relief. But the OC trap is that every time the person employs the ritual to be free of the terrible feelings, he re-
inforces the OC stranglehold. The dilemma is: allow the terri-

ble feelings and uncertainty and eventually work free of OCD, or perform the ritual and appease the feelings but intensify the OC behavior.

MR. MORE was very angry with me. He felt that I had pushed him too hard and too fast and subjected him to unreasonable danger. I had to encourage him to allow the terrible feelings and help him to see that the feelings would go away without having to perform the ritual. Many OCD treatment programs expose the person to his most fearful situation or contaminant and then prevent him from washing or performing another ritual. So he may have to handle feces and not be allowed to wash his hands, or he may not be allowed to bathe for a week. This procedure really works for the people who are willing to enter the program and stay with it, but many people are averse to subjecting themselves to such a punishing treatment. The anger and stress Mr. More was experiencing could cause him to drop out of therapy. It was very important that I reinforce his ability to think rationally during periods of stress and to allow the feelings.

"Tell me about the receipts," I said. "What were they? What could have been so important that it can make you so miserable?"

"I don't remember what they were, I'm not sure that I saw them all. I shouldn't have thrown them out."

"We went over them together, remember?" I said. "We had two categories of receipts. One was grocery receipts; do you remember the other category?"

"I think it was receipts more than two years old," he answered.

"Right! So out of those two categories, what could be so important?"

"I can't be sure that I saw them all," he said. "I can't be certain that I read them right."

"Would you have been likely to have mistaken a check or a fifty-dollar bill for a grocery receipt?" I asked.

After thinking about it carefully, he replied, "I don't think so."

"So what could have been so important?"

"I don't know," he said, "but I still have this terrible feeling."

"What if we try to get the super to open the garbage chute in the basement so that you can retrieve the receipts? Will the feeling go away?"

"Yeah," he said, "but I can't do that. The super already thinks I'm a nut job, and besides, I'll feel like a miserable failure."

"So what you're saying is that you'll get short-term relief but long-term misery. The decision is yours: what will you opt for?"

Mr. More's distress was severe. He was pacing and gasping for air. "I hate this," he said, "why does it have to be so hard? On one hand, I know it's irrational but on the other, I feel like I can't control it. I feel that I have to get rid of these feelings. But getting rid of the feelings will only cause another set of bad feelings. I really feel like I'm going to crack; I can't stand the stress."

"I know that the feelings are awful, but I haven't known anyone to crack from them; they will go away, and it does get easier," I said. "Let's make a list of things that might really cause problems if you were to accidentally throw them out."

Mr. More's list of things not to throw out contained: credit cards, driver's license, checks, cash, contracts, and official documents.

"How realistic is it that you might have mistaken any of these items for an old receipt or a grocery receipt?" I asked.

"Realistically? Well, it's not too likely, but it could happen," he said.

"What would happen if you were to lose your driver's license or credit cards or cash?" I asked.

"It would be a pain in the neck," he said, "but most of the stuff is replaceable except for the cash, and it's unlikely that it could have been so much money that I'd go broke because of it."

"So what you're saying is that even if you did mistakenly throw out something important the consequences won't really be so dire."

Mr. More breathed a sigh of relief. "I guess not," he said.

By the time I had to leave, Mr. More's bad feelings had abated. His assignment for the week was to continue to throw out the wrinkled bags and to identify and reality test his thoughts as we had just done.

When I arrived for our next appointment I noticed that the cleared circle around our chairs had shrunk to about four feet in diameter. The collection was beginning to close in on us again. However, Mr. More had done all of his homework. Wrinkled paper bags were stacked and ready to be inspected, and he had kept a record of his obsessive thoughts. Asking an obsessive person to keep a diary can be risky: Because obsessive people have a need to do everything completely and perfectly, they may end up spending most of their time working on the diary until it becomes another obsession. But Mr. More's diary was concise, and it identified a number of anxiety-producing thoughts, which came as a bit of a surprise to me. I would have guessed that the majority of his anxiety-producing thoughts would be work related, such as: "Did I do that right? Should I recheck the figures? I should do it over again. What if I made a mistake?" However, they were all thoughts about social situations. "Did I end the conversation too abruptly? They must think I'm a jerk. I shouldn't have worn this jacket." I had been so diverted by the mess in his apartment that I had forgotten that his original complaint was whether or not he should have worn black socks or said "Have a nice day." Again I was reminded that Mr. More had had virtually no social life in ten years. To say that his social skills were lacking is to barely touch the surface of his problem. He didn't have the first idea of how to interact with people on a purely social level. He didn't know how to initiate a conversation or how to end it, or how to deal with any part in the middle. In his work he was very confident; he rarely had concerns about having made a mistake, so he almost never had obsessive thoughts about it. But office parties were totally out of the question. Business lunches were agony; even meeting someone in the hallway was difficult. He would obsess endlessly about what had been said or done.

Mr. More originally came into therapy because of his obsessive thoughts about social situations. He genuinely wanted friends and a relationship with a woman, but he knew that the condition of his apartment and his uncontrollable collecting would be a turnoff for most people. He earnestly wanted to work on both problems. It was his suggestion to spend the first twenty minutes of a session examining his social problems and the remaining forty minutes on the collection.

We started with modest social assignments, such as initiating a conversation while waiting for the elevator. We wrote out scripts: "Hey, what do you think about those Mets?" "Do you think the good weather will stay around for the weekend?"

His personal appearance was a major subject of his obsessions, so he planned to buy a book on dressing for success. I delicately pointed out that even "success clothes" have to be cleaned and pressed in order to be effective. His clothes were strewn all over his apartment, and he usually looked like he'd slept in them. That led nicely to an assignment to pull out all the clothes he could find and take them to the laundry or cleaner's, make space in a closet to store them properly, and to return to the work of cleaning up the apartment.

The work progressed. When Mr. More felt comfortable with elevator conversations he graduated to water-cooler conversations. After we disposed of most of the bags (both wrinkled and "good") and some of the receipts, we started on plastic containers. He kept ten; pretty ones went to the thrift shop, the others to a recycling center. When his clothes came back from the cleaner's and he cleared out a closet for them, we lost our chairs and clean circle for a couple of weeks, but the annoyance of having nowhere to sit and talk motivated him to establish a neat area again.

Just getting to the magazines in Mr. More's apartment took weeks. Each time we started on a new project, he suffered with the old terrible feelings and desperately wanted to retrieve whatever it was we had just thrown out. His assignments were to prepare things to throw out, but he wouldn't throw anything out unless I was with him. He still needed me to help reality test and to allow the feelings. Often he would get angry with me and accuse me of putting too much pressure on him and making him go too fast, even though I always let him decide on the assignments and gave him the option of retrieving the stuff if he wanted to.

At a snail's pace things were being removed from the apartment. Mr. More had begun to wear mostly clean, pressed clothes. Not only did he initiate conversations, he even invited people to lunch on a couple of occasions. Mr. More was clearly getting better.

AT the very start of therapy I always ask the person to establish short- and long-term goals, but OC people often have a hard time with planning because they are so overwhelmed with day-to-day difficulties. Mr. More had originally been unable to set any realistic goals. I felt the time had come for us to sit down together and reassess what we wanted to accomplish and what we needed to do in order to accomplish it. Mr. More had been enjoying small social success recently. His immediate short-term goal was to start dating again. The long-term goal was to get married and have a family. He found that his obsessing at work had diminished considerably. Although he didn't expect to ever be completely free of obsessing, he felt that he could reduce it even more. The techniques of identifying and categorizing the cognitive distortions, as detailed on page 256, and reality testing had worked well for him, but sometimes he found that saying the same thing over and over again had a comforting quality. We agreed that if it was a positive statement ("I like this jacket. It's clean, pressed, and it fits well. I'm glad I wore it"), he could repeat twice. Negative statements ("I shouldn't have worn this jacket. It looks jerky and sloppy") must be converted to positive statements or worked through on a Thought/Consequence chart.

AFTER a year of work successfully getting rid of old receipts, newspapers, magazines, etc., we still weren't able to conquer broken toasters. Mr. More and I were reading different scripts. My script said that each time he accomplished a task things would get easier and easier, until finally the task would present no problem at all and he would simply do it. His script said that one thing had nothing to do with anything else, and that each task was as difficult as the first. The lack of visible improvement was disheartening for both of us, but it was important to focus on his accomplishments during the year. The original complaint of spending excessive time obsessing at work was no longer an issue; a secondary problem of lack of social contacts was vastly improved. I had to wonder why it was harder to throw out broken toasters than to risk rejection or humiliation in social interaction. After struggling with the problem in my mind and finding no reasonable solution, I asked Mr. More if he had any insight into it. "It's not that one is any harder than the other," he said. "They both seem impossible at the time, but it's a whole lot more satisfying to be successful socially. Once I throw out the toasters I still have a pile of junk to deal with and it doesn't seem like I've accomplished much for all that suffering." I should have been able to figure that out. People won't subject themselves to anguish unless the payoff is substantial. After considerable discussion, we decided to concentrate for the time being on further developing Mr. More's social skills. Much to my relief, the appointments would take place in my office.

Mr. More's progress in social matters was already more impressive than I realized. We had been so mired down in trying to deal with the apartment mess that he had neglected to note his accomplishments at work. He had been promoted to a position that would require input at meetings and presentations; he had established two good male friendships; he regularly went out to lunch with other people; he had gone to an office party and enjoyed it; and he was wooing a coworker. The final item was, no doubt, why he had wanted to switch the focus of our work. Mr. More's concept of romantic technique had been inspired by movies and television. Although he was acutely aware of the fact that he could never pass for Tom Cruise, he did have some very basic misconceptions about the "mating game." The most troubling of his misconceptions was that if he asked a woman for a date, he would then be committed to go to bed with her; marry her; have a child with her; buy a house; and start commuting to work. So he was extremely reluctant to ask a woman for a date unless he was absolutely sure that she was the perfect woman and he was prepared to spend the rest of his life with her.

The object of Mr. More's attention was a woman in her twenties, recently divorced, and newly employed at his firm. His fear was that he would invite her out and find himself committed to the "whole marriage thing" (as he described it), only to be shocked to discover that she was not the perfect woman for him. We broke the problem down to manageable steps. The first step was to invite the woman out to lunch. That proved to be abruptly devastating—the woman made it clear that she already had a boyfriend. A rude fact of life that Mr. More had not taken into consideration was that people may come into his orbit with an agenda that does not include him. For several months our work dealt with his depression and obsessive thoughts of being worthless and hopeless. Then we decided to go back to his apartment and work on the problems of throwing stuff out.

Returning to his apartment a year and a half later was "déjà vu all over again." Maybe my tolerance had lowered, but it seemed to me even worse than it had originally appeared. There was no cleared area where we could sit; paper bags, newspapers, and magazines had reappeared; and it was filthy. A strange thing happened—I lost my temper. "This place is disgusting," I yelled at him. "Why are you wasting your money with me? You're not doing anything. I'm not going to sit in this mess while you jerk around with paper bags for another year."

I have a friend who said that she wished she could live her life on tape. Then every time she made a mistake she could erase that section and retape it. Two seconds after I yelled at Mr. More, I truly wished I could retape it. He was shocked; I was shocked. For a while neither one of us knew what to do. Finally I suggested that we go to the corner coffee shop and talk about it. He said that he had thought I was the one per-

son who could understand his problem and accept him; he felt
abandoned and betrayed by me. I apologized for my outburst
and told him how awful I felt about it and tried to make clear
that I accepted his problem and himself as a person while at
the same time I found his living style totally unacceptable. It
was unfair of me; I was changing the rules. Originally I had
been willing to work in his apartment, but then all of a sudden I wasn't. That session was spent in the coffee shop with
him telling me how angry and disappointed he was and that
he couldn't continue our therapy.

A year went by, during which I often thought of Mr. More and
wondered how he was doing, before I received a phone call
from him. He was seriously dating a woman and wanted to
know if I would be willing to work with him in his apartment
again. The conditions he set were that I would have to promise
not to yell at him, and he would promise to maintain a clean
bathroom and clear area for us to sit. I was glad to hear from
him again. I felt I had handled the situation badly and left it
uncomfortably unfinished. I accepted his conditions and
agreed to work with him again.

Mr. More's current long-term goal was to invite his woman
friend to his apartment for dinner. We started, as before, reality testing the importance of wrinkled paper bags, "good" paper
bags, old newspapers, magazines. This time the progress was
significantly faster. Within two months we were preparing to
throw out broken appliances, and a slight improvement in the
condition of the apartment was visible. Gradually and carefully
he started to throw things out between appointments, and I
would arrive to find the piles of rubble reduced and the clear
area increased. The kitchen got cleaned; old, dirty dishes were
thrown out and replaced by new ones. The floor became visi-

ble, scratched tables and broken chairs were thrown out, and new ones took their place. Finally we were able to sit on his couch while we worked on the thoughts, identifying them and reality testing.

This may sound like a miraculous recovery. But in fact Mr. More and I worked together for two years on his problem. During the year that I had not seen him he continued to do the basic work of cause and effecting and reality testing, but he was doing it in the social sphere, which was his original complaint. During those years he learned that the terrible feelings do go away and that the worst never really happens. But most of all, he learned that he could succeed. Once he'd had the experience of success in his social sphere, he had the confidence to seriously attack the collecting problem.

Three and a half years after I had braved my way into the muck and mire, Mr. More invited his fiancée to his apartment for dinner.

(For more information on our work together, see pages 255–62.)

CHAPTER THIRTEEN

SAM, THE SNAKE MAN

SAM DATED the onset of his problem from 9:12 A.M., September 16, 1981. The day started out like every other. His alarm went off at 5:30 A.M. Then he began a long ritual of checking for snakes. He got out of bed and immediately stripped the bed of the blankets and sheets, shook them out, folded them neatly, and put them in a tightly covered cedar chest along with the pillows. He took his large flashlight and looked in the closet, starting from the ceiling on the left, carefully checking all the corners and crevices, working his way carefully past the shelf and the clothes down to the floor, where he kept his shoes. He did the same meticulous checking in the bedroom, living room, and kitchen. An hour and a half had passed before he started on the bathroom, where he checked each corner of the room, behind the toilet, and under the sink. He poured drain opener down the bathtub drain, let it fizz for a while, ran water down the drain for exactly seven minutes, stopped up the drain, and ran water in the tub for his bath. By then it was about 7:30.

He bathed quickly, drying off with a towel he had taken from a metal container, and returned to his bedroom to dress. He picked up his undershorts and shook them vigorously, checked the front and the back, the inside and the outside, then put them on. He repeated this action with each article of clothing.

At 8:30 he left his apartment for the walk to work. During the walk he kept his eyes focused on the sidewalk, stopping only at the same deli he stopped at every morning for a container of black coffee and a plain bagel with cream cheese.

When he arrived at his office building he waited outside the elevator. He entered, pushed the button for the seventeenth floor, and concentrated on the light panel above the elevator door until it indicated that he had arrived. Once in his office, he began a similar ritual of checking.

SAM had two terrible years between September 16, 1981 and the time he called me. He was hospitalized at his own insistence, saying that he had had a nervous breakdown and that the hospital was the only safe place (safe from snakes, that is). Somewhere along the line he was diagnosed as psychotic and medicated to the point of not being able to get out of bed. (He still had terrible fears of snakes but wasn't as wild and verbal about expressing them.) Later he was put in an implosion therapy program where for several hours each day he was required to sit in a small, unfurnished room with images of snakes projected onto the ceiling and walls.

Immediately Sam told me that if I were the kind of therapist who would force him to come in contact with snakes, he would not be interested in seeing me. Also, because he was fearful of snakes curled up under the seats in buses or taxis, or in the dark corners in subway stations, he insisted he could not come to see me; I would have to work with him in his apart-

ment. He lived on the Upper West Side of Manhattan before it
became as fashionable as it is now. Just down the street from
his building was a small square on 73rd and Broadway called
Needle Park. I was not enthusiastic about working in the area,
but I made an appointment to see him, expecting the problem
to be relatively uncomplicated.

Sam's apartment was a walk-up on the third floor of a small
old building. A few minutes after I rang the bell the door
opened about two inches, restrained by a chain on the inside.
His eye peered out at me.

"Hi, Sam. I'm Raeann Dumont; we have an appointment."

He eyed me slowly from my head to my feet, then back up
to my head again.

"Take your coat off and shake it out," Sam said. I put my
bag on the floor and took my coat off and gave it two good
shakes.

"Now fold it up inside out, leave it on the floor across the
hall, and come in."

I looked around the hall at the peeling paint and the broken banister and said, "It's twenty degrees outside and I don't
feel like going home this afternoon without a coat. If you want
an appointment with me you'll have to accept my coat as well."

"What's in your bag? Why is it so big?"

"Because I like big bags. Sam, I'm not crazy about snakes either. I don't have a snake in my bag."

"I thought the theory was that I have to encounter the fear
in order to get over it."

"We'll work up to it gradually. I promise Sam, no snakes."

Sam was a very tall, very thin man in his late thirties. He
smiled grimly and gestured for me to come in. His apartment
was brightly lit by many long fluorescent bulbs and spotlights
shining into all the corners. Everything was white: the ceiling,
the walls, the floors. The furniture was all unupholstered white

wood. I could tell right away that Sam's phobia was more complicated than I had anticipated.

Although Sam dated the beginning of his problem to two
years prior to contacting me, our interview indicated that Sam
had had problems most of his life. As a little boy he compulsively counted his toys and lined them up on the floor in a very
specific way. If his mother inadvertently rearranged them while
cleaning, he would become very upset. At meals, even in the
school cafeteria, he insisted on having a separate plate and
fork for everything. If his mother was serving peas, potatoes,
and meat, she would have to serve it on three small plates along
with three forks.

Sam obsessed about his schoolwork, spending many hours
every day redoing it and making sure it was perfect. After tests
he would obsess about the way he had answered the questions
until he got the test back with the grade. Sam was a straight-A
student all the way through high school, but shortly after graduation he had what he called a "nervous breakdown"; he went
to bed and stayed there for three months.

His parents expected their brilliant son to go to college.
When he buried himself in his bed they tried coaxing, bribing,
and bullying, but nothing would move him. They grew des-
perate. He had always been an obedient, cooperative child; they
could explain this aberrant behavior only as a "brain virus," so
they packed him up and sent him to a hospital, where every
imaginable test was performed. All the results were negative.
He was sent home with the recommendation that he see a psychiatrist. Sam missed the start of the school year, so the pressure to go to college was off. He went to a psychiatrist of his
parent's chosing three times a week and puttered around the
house.

That spring Sam's father arranged for him to take a job in
the mailroom of a large advertising company. Sam's duties

were to sort the mail, deliver it to the proper offices, and run errands. Much to his parents' dismay, Sam loved the job. Sorting the mail was easy; delivering it to the offices was fun because he got to meet all the people; and running the errands broke up the day and added diversions. By getting him the job his father had hoped to demonstrate that without a college education Sam would be stuck in menial, dead-end work. But after about six months of the mailroom job Sam was promoted to an assistant art director. By the time he was twenty-three years old, he had an important management position in a very large advertising agency.

His perfectionism and obsessive attention to details made him an excellent worker, but he was not always well liked by his coworkers. His social life was not nearly as successful as his career. He was tall, attractive, meticulously dressed, and had no problems getting a first date. But if his date was five minutes late, he would stop seeing her. If she had lint (or God forbid, dandruff) on her clothes, if her shoes were run-down or dusty, if her hair was messy, or if her purse was cluttered, he would quit seeing her. If, by some miracle, the woman did not suffer from any of these faults, he would drive her away with his constant need for reassurance.

I experienced his crazy-making demands for reassurance after we had been working together for a few weeks. In the middle of a session he said, "I got a haircut this morning. You haven't said anything about it."

"Oh," I said, glancing up briefly, "I hadn't noticed—looks good."

"If you think it looks good, how come you didn't say anything about it?"

"I didn't really notice."

"If you didn't notice, it can't look all that good."

"Your hair always looks good." This was true. Sam was always well-groomed with clean, trimmed fingernails, every hair in place, and clothes neat, clean, pressed, and coordinated.

"Don't you think the left side is shorter than the right?" he asked.

"It looks the same to me."

"You're not really looking at it! Look at it and see if the left side isn't shorter."

"Sam, I looked and the left side isn't shorter."

"You're probably not looking from the right angle. Stand over there and look."

"I'm not going to stand over there. It looks the same to me, and what difference would it make if it were shorter?"

"It is shorter, isn't it. That's why you asked what difference it would make. I knew it was shorter."

"Sam, what difference would it make?" He looked at me with a stunned expression, as though he couldn't believe I would ask such a stupid question.

"Well, it would be wrong."

"But what difference would it make?"

"I'd look like a fool with one half of my hair shorter than the other half."

"What would happen?" I asked. "Would you lose your job?"

"No, but it would be wrong. It is shorter, isn't it? That's why you're going through this."

"Sam, I really don't see that there is any difference in the length of your hair from one side of your head to the other. I'm going through this to see if maybe you aren't making a big deal out of nothing. Look in the mirror and tell me if you think you look like a fool."

He walked over the a mirror on the living room wall, stared at himself for a while, then said, "I knew it! It is shorter."

"Do you look like a fool?"

"That's beside the point. It's shorter. I shouldn't have let the barber get away with that. I'll go back tomorrow and have him even it off."

On that occasion the therapy session ended before we had a chance to fully explore "what would happen." But there were plenty of other opportunities. Demands for reassurance were made during every session. "Do you think this shirt looks OK with this jacket? Is the collar too wide/narrow? Is the color too dull/bright? Are the sleeves too long/short? Is the fabric too heavy/thin?" I was quickly disabused of any notion that Sam had a high regard for my fashion acumen when I heard him go through the same routine with a cashier while he was cashing a check at the bank. In fact he did it with just about anyone who would stand still long enough.

Another problem that limited Sam's success in the social arena was that he wouldn't go anywhere he couldn't walk to, because he worried about snakes in buses, taxis, and subways. He was afraid to go anywhere unfamiliar because he couldn't be sure that the place was snakeproof.

Although Sam's history clearly indicated problems with OCD at a very early age, snakes didn't become a problem until his late twenties. On an early spring evening he was hanging out with some friends in a bar after work. One of the guys was talking about the company softball game that had taken place on the previous weekend. The man described how he was standing in the outfield while the pitcher and the umpire were arguing over a foul ball. It was a cool day. He stood in the sun with his arms wrapped around himself to keep warm when he felt something funny on his right leg. He looked down and saw a snake curled up around his leg from his ankle to the knee. He stamped his foot and swatted at it with his glove, but the snake clung fast. Then he ran over to one of his teammates to ask for help, but the teammate ran away laughing. He continued to stamp and kick and yell for help. The rest of the guys came running over, teasing him about what a snaky guy he was, and so on, but none of them helped get rid of the snake. While Sam's friend was telling the story he was chagrined that he had panicked because it was a harmless garden snake, but he was also irritated that his teammates hadn't responded a little more sympathetically.

Sam, who had gone to summer camp as a kid, had certainly seen snakes, but he had never thought of the possibility that a snake might get on him. As his friend told the story, Sam found himself getting sick to his stomach. He was afraid to look at his leg and felt impelled to leave. That night he dreamed of snakes wrapping themselves around him.

The next morning when he got up he checked his apartment for snakes. The thought of snakes wrapping themselves around him continued to occur throughout the day. Every time, he violently shook his leg and stamped his foot; he couldn't control the reaction. He left work early that day and went home. He felt so exhausted he just wanted to go to sleep but was afraid that he'd dream of snakes again. To reassure himself that he wouldn't have snakes crawl all over him as he slept, he checked his apartment again. He started in the kitchen, got halfway through and couldn't remember if he had checked under the sink, so he started over. Again when he had almost finished, he felt a nagging doubt that he hadn't checked behind the stove. Sam spent the entire night checking his kitchen for snakes over and over and over again. The next morning Sam called his mother and said that he had had a nervous breakdown and wanted her to take him to a hospital. His mother called his old psychiatrist, who prescribed tranquilizers, rest, and resuming psychotherapy.

For the next six years Sam managed by avoiding, checking, and taking heavy doses of tranquilizers. Until, as he told me, September 16, 1981, when he opened his desk drawer and found a snake in it.

"Sam," I asked, "have you given any thought as to how the snake got into your desk drawer?"

"Sure I have," he said. "That's a part of what makes me so crazy. It was put there by someone who worked with me. That means I can't be safe anywhere; people will torment me with snakes."

"How did they get the snake into the building? Someone walking into a building on Madison Avenue with a snake around their neck would be noticeable. Desk drawers aren't the natural habitat for snakes. Once they got it into your drawer, how did they get the snake to stay?"

"Well . . ."

"What?"

"Real."

"Real what?"

"The snake."

"Sam, do you mean that the snake in your desk drawer wasn't a real snake?"

"Uh, yeah, that's about it."

"What was it? Was it like a rubber snake?"

"No, uh, it was more like a picture of a snake."

"Why did you lead me to believe that it was a real snake?"

"I didn't think you'd take me seriously if you knew it was a picture of a snake. You'd think I was just a nut."

The picture in Sam's desk drawer was a very realistic image of a snake prepared to strike, taken from a nature magazine. Sam responded with the same amount of passion to the picture of the snake as he would have to a real live snake. He had been able to manage his fear of snakes (with many limitations and much time-consuming checking) while it remained a fear of real snakes, but when it became a fear of pictures, images, and thoughts of snakes Sam's life became immensely complicated. Magazines and by extension newsstands became dangerous. Store windows became dangerous; not just pet shops and fish stores, but also jewelry store windows because of bracelets, pins, and necklaces in the form of snakes, and toy stores, which often have rubber or plastic snakes in their windows. The possibility of seeing a snake in some form or fashion was overwhelming. Sam felt so bombarded by snakes that every expedition outside his carefully inspected and controlled apartment was formidable.

Most days Sam felt unable to leave his apartment due to his fears. He took a leave of absence from his job, but his work was so highly valued that his boss arranged for him to work at home two or three days a week. He never returned to the office where he had found the picture of the snake in his desk drawer. On the rare occasions he went to the office building, his boss let him use a small room that had been painted white and furnished only with a drawing table and a chair; there were no cabinets, drawers, or low furniture in which snakes could hide.

Sam made good money while he was working, but he hadn't worked full-time for more than two years. When I started working with him he was under financial pressure because the money he had saved while he was working was beginning to run out, and his boss was pressuring him to either return to work full-time or to quit. On the one hand, Sam felt he had to get rid of his fear of snakes immediately, and on the other, he felt powerless to deal with the fears and wanted to be hospitalized. I was constantly trying to mediate between the two aspects of Sam.

MOST of the people I've worked with are smarter than I am. I don't know if that is more a feature of me or of OCD. Sam was better read, more widely informed, more creative, and he thought faster on his feet—all of which made him extremely difficult to work with. I would say things like, "There really aren't a lot of snakes slithering around loose in New York."

And he would say, "Oh yeah, well I read that in 1958 two cobras escaped from a cage in a guy's car and weren't found for six days." (To an OC victim any possibility becomes an overwhelming probability.)

I might say, "Even though you may find snakes nasty and unaesthetic, the vast majority are totally harmless."

He would come back with, "I read about a woman who was bitten by a 'totally harmless' garden snake in Central Park and later died of an infection."

I could have gone on to say that more people die from being hit by lightning in Central Park than from snakebites; in the entire country, more people die of beestings than snakebites. All of this was, of course, beside the point. The real point was that Sam believed that being in close proximity to a snake (real or otherwise) would make him go crazy.

Here is Sam's hierarchy of fearful objects or situations:

1. Having a snake on me
2. Touching a snake
3. Seeing a snake
4. Being somewhere I might see a snake
5. Thinking of snakes

Sam and I discussed the very real possibility that we might never get to items number 1 and 2. In truth, I was just as happy knowing that I would not have to rent a snake, put it into a little snake carrier and transport it on the subway to Sam's apartment, then, with my own hands, take it out of the carrier and demonstrate how innocuous snakes are.

Sam was noticeably relieved when I agreed that there are millions of people who live full, successful, happy lives without the need to wrap snakes around themselves. But the last three items were really messing up his life. When he did a Hierarchy Chart (see page 297), it became clear that he was fearful of encountering snakes (or pictures of snakes) in the most unlikely places. To make things even more difficult, Sam believed that thinking about snakes would make them magically appear; and of course, practically everything (including the color green) made him think of snakes.

Our exposure and reality testing started by seeing if snakes would actually appear if we thought or talked about them. Sam didn't want to say or hear the word "snake." He referred to them as "the S thing." Every time Sam thought of "the S thing" he silently repeated seven times:

Fire and flame,
singe and simmer,
scorch and burn,
blaze and inflame,
cremate and incinerate.

This litany was designed to drive snakes from his mind. The litany also explained the frequent silences during our conversations.

Sam finally agreed to look at a picture of a snake bracelet. He reduced saying his litany from seven to five times. However, he armed me with a baseball bat with which to club to death the snakes that might appear.

"Sam," I said, "I'll be glad to club the snakes for you, but give me an idea of which direction they are likely to come from. Will they be coming under the door, or from the window, or out of the crack in the wall . . . from where?"

He didn't answer me. His eyes were closed and he was very still.

"Are you saying your litany?"

He nodded.

Ten or fifteen minutes went by. "Are you still saying your litany," I asked.

He nodded again.

"How many times are you going to say it?"

He shook his head slightly, eyes still closed. I waited.

Then Sam looked at me and very softly said, "I can't deal with this. I'm going to go crazy."

"What does it feel like when you think you are going to go crazy?"

"My thoughts feel like they are out of control. As though they are going to go somewhere horrendous and I'll never have another sane thought again."

"Are you having sane thoughts now?"

"I'm not sure."

"How could we test the sanity of your thoughts?"

"When you asked me where the snakes would be coming from—that wasn't sane."

"You mean I wasn't sane?"

"No, I mean that the idea that the snakes would appear isn't sane."

"Oh, you mean that in reality you don't think that snakes will appear."

Sam looked at me with mock anger. "All right," he said. "I know what you've done! You've gotten me to talk about snakes and concede that they probably won't appear."

"That sounds real sane to me, Sam."

Sam and I worked together for three years. We started by looking at a picture of a snake bracelet, and very gradually we worked our way up to pictures of real snakes. We made forays into unfamiliar neighborhoods and looked in pet-shop windows (never seeing a snake, mostly kittens and puppies and birds). We walked through Central Park; we even sat on the grass. All the while we were cause-and-effecting ("What is the medium by which a snake will appear when we think about it?") and reality testing ("How many snakes did we encounter on our last walk down Broadway?").

On many occasions during those three years Sam angrily announced that he was quitting therapy because it didn't work. Always, when we analyzed his diary (he was a scrupulous diary keeper) we found that the incident that set off the checking, the scrubbing, and the litanies had nothing to do with snakes. Very early in our work together when he was still looking at the picture of the snake bracelet (and doing exceedingly well at limiting his litanies), Sam's boss called him to say that if he wasn't able to come back to work full-time by a specific date, he would have to fire him. (See Sam's Exposure Diary on page 250.)

Sam did resume his old job. For the first two weeks I met him at the elevator and together we went into his office and opened his desk drawer. I was identified by his coworkers as "Sam's snake woman." During this period I was on the company payroll because Sam unabashedly announced to the organization, "You guys made me crazy. You guys can pay for making me uncrazy." They did.

AFTER I hadn't heard from Sam for several years, he called me to make an appointment with him and his girlfriend, Annette. They had been seriously dating for several months and had talked about getting married, but all of a sudden he was calling her cold and bitchy and she was calling him demanding and impossible. The problem turned out to be his old crazy-making demands for reassurance. She said she couldn't take his asking her the same thing time and time again. After a few sessions Annette learned to say to Sam, "I see that your cuffs are exactly above the floor in back, and break slightly over your shoe in front. I think the length is just fine. Now that's all." And Sam learned to resist the urge to ask again in greater detail. Sam and Annette got married and have, at this writing, a little boy.

SAM is very successful. I read about him from time to time. He is probably the most brilliant, creative person I've worked with. Even when he was obsessed with snakes, he was witty and clever. He was quick to catch on to concepts and develop them in a way that made them his own. And he was a hard worker. After he had experienced some progress and became convinced that therapy could work for him, he attacked the program and worked at it furiously.

We never did work directly with snakes. Our "graduation trip" was to the Bronx Zoo, where we looked at the critters from behind a half-inch of glass and agreed that they weren't really slimy and certainly wouldn't make us go crazy, but we were glad they were behind glass. (For more information on my work with Sam see pages 246–51 in chapter 15 "How to Get Better.")

CHAPTER FOURTEEN

JOHANNA, FRANK, LARA, AL: SHORT-TERM SUCCESS STORIES

THE preceding case examples described people who had multiple and complex problems; the work with them was frequently difficult and long-term. When I started doing in vivo work in 1975 the majority of the people I worked with had lived for many years with their crippling problems and had no idea what was wrong with them or that they could be helped. They usually did their best to hide their problems from friends and family for fear they would be thought of as mentally ill. If they had sought treatment, they were often told that "it's just nerves" and received tranquilizers or spent many years in analytic therapy discussing the origin of the problem without experiencing any relief from the anxiety.

Over the past seven or eight years my practice has changed because of the aggressive educational campaigns conducted by the Anxiety Disorders Association of America and the OC Foundation. They have let people know that phobias and obsessive-compulsive disorders are common problems and that there is effective help for them. Now I rarely encounter people like Gracie (Chapter 10), who've lived most of their lives with phobias or OCD, existing in a distorted, isolated world of fear; the people in this chapter are more typical of the clients I see today.

JOHANNA: PANICS ON SUBWAYS

Johanna was twenty-three years old when she came to see me. She had graduated from an Ivy League college in the spring and was lucky (and talented) enough to get a job at a literary magazine immediately after graduation. Her mother and older sister were lawyers, and her father was a medical research scientist. The four of them lived in a large brownstone in a very nice area of Brooklyn. When the girls were fourteen and eighteen their parents turned the top floor of the house into a private apartment for them. As a teenager Johanna had all the privacy and independence of her own apartment while still maintaining the security of a loving, concerned family. Johanna's sister had always taken a motherly (and bossy) role with her. When they moved into their apartment together, it was her sister who told her what to eat, what clothes to wear, and when to get home at night. Johanna alternately worshipped and resented her sister.

Although Johanna described her parents as "busy doing their own thing," she considered them loving and supportive. She thought of herself as the "black sheep" in the family because she wasn't as smart, pretty, or socially gracious as her mother or sister.

Her problem started about six months prior to coming to see me. Johanna was sitting on the subway on her way to work one morning, when suddenly, out of the blue, she felt dizzy, light-headed, and unable to breathe. She thought she was going to faint or die, and when the subway came to the next stop she dashed out the door. Still gasping for air, she ran up the steps and hailed a taxi. Since that occasion, every time she got on the subway the same thing would happen.

It was much too expensive for Johanna to take taxis to work every day; she tried taking a bus but it took forever. She continued using subways by going one or two stops, dashing off just before she was about to faint or die, standing gasping in the station until she was able to catch her breath, then getting on the next subway and going another couple of stops. She repeated this sequence until she finally got to work.

During our first session I took a brief history of Johanna. I explained where her frightening sensations came from, the anxiety scale, and how to keep a diary. When Johanna returned for her next appointment, she reported that her anxiety hadn't come out of the blue as she had originally thought. She experienced anxiety when she had disaster thoughts: "If the subway gets stuck I'll suffocate and die. There's something wrong with my brain; I think I'm having a stroke." Johanna spent a couple of sessions in my office learning breathing and relaxation exercises and how to reality test the scary thoughts that would pop into her head.

The last few sessions we spent riding in subways together. At first we sat together while I helped her apply the cognitive and behavioral techniques she'd learned in my office; then we sat at opposite ends of the car; finally, we rode in separate cars.

In six sessions Johanna had learned where her anxiety came from and how to control it by reality testing the frightening thoughts. She understood that what she had experienced on the subway was a panic attack and that, although it felt terrible, at no time was she in danger of dying or going crazy.

Johanna and I may meet again. She tends to be slightly socially phobic. If she has difficulties on her job, or romantic problems, she will call me for help. If she does, I would guess that as with our last project, therapy will be relatively uncomplicated and short-term.

FRANK: PHOBIC OF CROSSING STREETS

During our first appointment in my office Frank gave me a very brief background of his family, in which he assured me that there were no "crazies or nut jobs," then he leaned back. "You'll never believe my problem," he said. "I can hardly believe it myself. I'm thirty-six years old and I'm afraid to cross streets by myself." At that time I was working with two other people who were phobic of crossing streets, so I had no difficulty believing his problem.

Frank had been married for eight years, had two small children, and worked as a salesman for a large textile firm. He had had difficulties crossing streets alone as long as he could remember, but it was only when he started calling on potential buyers in New York City that it became a real problem. Initially he solved it by taking taxis everywhere and having them drop him off right in front of the building where he had an appointment. Just a week previous to Frank's call to me, he had been on his way to an appointment when the taxi driver encountered a street that was closed due to construction. Not being able to get Frank any closer to his destination, he dropped him off a half block away—but what Frank didn't realize was that he was on the wrong side of Sixth Avenue (a very wide, busy street).

"I had a really important appointment that day," he said. "I got out of the taxi not worrying about a thing until I saw that I was on the wrong side of Sixth Avenue. There was no way I could cross that street. I stood on the corner and tried to figure out how I could get across, but it felt like I was looking through the wrong end of a telescope—that street went on forever. I'd get old and die before I reached the other side. I never made it to that appointment. I got a taxi, went right home and stayed in bed for three days—I told my boss I had the flu."

Frank came to the next appointment with a Hierarchy Chart of difficult streets, his Anxiety Diary, and a Thought/Consequence Chart. (See the Self-Help Worksheets in Appendix 2.) From his Hierarchy Chart it appeared that the best place to start our in vivo work would be with narrow one-way streets, so we went to the corner of a side street outside my office.

"This isn't going to work," Frank said after we had been standing on the corner for a while.

"Why not?" I asked.

"Not enough people. I can't hitch a ride."

"Can't 'hitch a ride'?"

Frank explained that when he crossed a street he would look for an "understanding person" waiting to cross. He would sidle up to that person and walk across the street as close to him or her as possible.

"I guess that means you're stuck with me," I said.

"Yeah," he said dismally.

From Frank's Thought/Consequence Chart I knew that his fear was that he wouldn't be able to make it to the other side of the street—in the middle he would collapse or become paralyzed. The first thing we had to do was reality test his theory. "Why will a physically strong, healthy person collapse or become paralyzed?" I asked.

"I'll get so panicky I won't be able to control myself."

"What will make you so panicky?"

"The thought of collapsing or becoming paralyzed in the middle of the street."

Frank was doing circular and emotional reasoning. The thought of collapsing or becoming paralyzed would make him panicky, which would make him collapse or become paralyzed.

"Have you ever collapsed or became paralyzed from panic?"

"No, not actually. I've felt as though I was about to, or that I might, but I never really did."

Frank and I started our in vivo work on a narrow street by first crossing together, walking about three feet apart; then with me following about four paces behind him; finally, he crossed alone with me waiting for him on the far side. I saw Frank twice a week, and between our appointments he spent several hours working with his wife crossing streets. Frank's Exposure Diary indicated that his anxiety was highest just before he stepped off the curb and dropped to about a two or three by the time he reached the middle of the street. From that, Frank learned that he could experience high levels of anxiety and not collapse or become paralyzed.

Within five weeks of our initial appointment we were working on Sixth Avenue (Frank called it "Killer Avenue"). Again, we started out crossing together but walking about three feet apart. During our earlier sessions we had discovered many techniques that made crossing much easier. The most important was for Frank to not look at the far side of the street. When he did he experienced the visual distortion that he had described to me previously, of looking through the wrong end of a telescope. Instead, he looked either at the ground or at the oncoming traffic. Another helpful technique was to establish the number of paces required to cross the street, then as he was crossing, silently count them off. For instance, if a street could be crossed in twelve paces, Frank would start at twelve and count backward, knowing that by the time he reached six or five his anxiety level would decrease.

Our twentieth appointment was Frank's "graduation." We met on the corner of Sixth Avenue where he had had his first panic attack. First we crossed together; then we crossed with me following him. Before the hour was over Frank had crossed Sixth Avenue alone eight times and reported minimal anxiety.

OFTEN during the first appointment people will ask me how long it will take for them to get rid of the problem. There is no simple answer to that question, but I tell them that the longer they've had the problem, and the more ingrained the pattern of avoidance and the harder it will be to overcome it. But, if they really work hard at it, do the homework, and practice between sessions, recovery can happen a lot faster. Frank is excellent proof of that.

LARA: SOCIAL PHOBIC

The week between Christmas and New Year's usually isn't a busy one for me. I spend it catching up on paperwork and year-end details, so I was surprised when the phone rang and a new client pleaded for an emergency appointment.

Lara was a twenty-six-year-old, pretty, petite blond who had been teaching at an exclusive private school for the past year. She had no friends in New York. Her family lived in New England; she was the fourth of six children. Her father was alcoholic and her mother was sick much of the time and frequently hospitalized (in retrospect, Lara felt that her hospitalizations were probably due to depression).

"I realize that I have a big case of social phobia," Lara said. "I always knew that I was shy. I never spoke up in class, I always arranged to give my oral reports in private because I couldn't bear to stand in front of my classmates and talk, but this is ridiculous!"

Lara had been desperately lonely and just before the Christmas holiday a fellow teacher, whom she hardly knew, had invited her to a New Year's Eve party. "It'll be great," her colleague said. "There will be lots of interesting guys, and good food, booze, and music." Lara had accepted, but now, three days before the party she was panic-stricken.

"What will I do? I won't know anyone. I won't know what to say. Everyone will look at me. I can't deal with parties. Help me, I need to be able to do things like this."

For a socially phobic person, encountering a sea of unfamiliar faces is a nightmare. Another phobic nightmare is having to stay at a party where everyone knows everyone else and ignores you. Unfortunately, I don't have any quick fixes for either of these nightmares, but I could offer Lara a stopgap solution. I suggested that she call the hostess and say that she couldn't stay for the party but she would love to stop by and have a drink and share good wishes for the New Year. This tactic made the event more of a personal exchange than a party with hordes of strange people and also allowed for an early escape.

Three days after New Year's Day I heard from Lara again. "It worked, it really worked!" she said. "I was able to go to the party, and I even stayed for about two hours. I talked to a couple of people I didn't know, and it was OK."

One of the problems of working in vivo with socially phobic people is that, in most cases, I can't accompany them into the situation, so I'm dependent on their ability to go into the situation alone and report back to me. Lara was so thrilled with her success at the New Year's party she could hardly wait for another assignment.

Lara couldn't do a Hierarchy Chart because she said that everything was equally impossible, but among the impossible things were: speaking up at faculty meetings; talking with colleagues in the lounge; talking with parents of her students; making telephone calls; eating with other people present; signing her name in front of someone.

Her thoughts were, "They'll think I'm stupid, or that there's something wrong with me, and hate me."

Lara said that she didn't want to live alone and in fear any longer, and she was willing to try anything to get rid of her problem. So I started with a multifocused approach by taking several of the impossible tasks and breaking them down to the smallest possible pieces. I gave her three assignments for the week:

1. At the weekly faculty meeting after a colleague has said something that she agrees with, she should respond, "Yes, I agree with that."
2. In the faculty lounge she was to start a conversation by commenting on the weather.
3. She was to go into the cafeteria with a spoon and a container of yogurt and eat at least two spoonfuls.

At our next appointment Lara reported complete success with all three assignments. At the faculty meeting when she said, "Yes, I agree with that," several people looked approvingly at her. When she said, "Some weather, huh?" in the faculty lounge, fellow teachers engaged her in a rousing conversation. In the cafeteria, although she was sitting alone, she ate the entire container of yogurt.

The first thing we learned was that her impossible tasks weren't impossible. The second thing we learned was that no one thought she was stupid, that something was wrong with her, or hated her—she was treated pretty much like a regular person.

"But this is the easy stuff," she said. I reminded her that a week ago it was impossible.

"Yeah, it was," she said. "But this is so impossible I didn't even bother to mention it—there's this guy who teaches literature who is so cool, I really want to be able to talk with him."

"OK, but first let's take last week's assignments a little further. At the faculty meeting say, 'I agree with that, and in addition . . .' or 'but . . .' In the faculty lounge talk with one of the other teachers about a difficult student, and in the cafeteria stand in line and get something to eat. Remember, we are testing whether or not people will really think that you are stupid or that there is something wrong with you. Before you risk all on a cool guy let's get better information."

Lara arrived at our next appointment flushed with success. "I've been talking to everyone! I spoke up at the faculty meeting, I talked to other teachers in the lounge, I even had lunch with two other people. I'm ready to talk to Tom (the literature teacher), I know it!"

"OK. What do you want to say? 'Tom, I think you're a cool guy'?"

"No, it's got to be something smart, clever."

"What about talking about a student you might have in common?"

"No. It's gotta be something really sharp."

"Like what?"

"I don't know."

Lara arrived for our next appointment looking really beaten. "What happened?" I asked.

"This isn't working. I'll never get better. There's something really wrong with me—I think I need drugs or something."

"But what do you think changed?" I asked. "You had been doing so well."

"He's engaged."

"What?"

"Tom's engaged."

"Are you telling me that because Tom is engaged you need drugs?"

I watched Lara struggle with that for a while, then I said, "OK. I'll get my reference book and look for an appropriate drug for you. But tell me, shall I look under 'Tom' or under 'Engaged'?"

First Lara gave me a baleful look, then she started laughing. "This is serious," she said.

"Of course it's serious," I said. "You wanted this guy to be as interested in you as you were in him, but he wasn't—no medication will change that. Now what do you want to do? You've discovered that you can speak up at faculty meetings; you can talk to your colleagues; you can eat with other people. Do you want to erase all that because Tom is engaged?"

"Why do you put things like that? Don't you realize that my whole purpose in this was not to be alone any more?"

"Well, no. I knew that it was an important part of your purpose, but I didn't know that it was your whole purpose. Now, let's be specific—was Tom your whole purpose, or just not being alone for the rest of your life?"

LARA and I worked together for six months. During that time she did not find the perfect partner, but she enjoyed an active dating life, spoke up at faculty meetings, ate in the cafeteria, and developed several good relationships that belied her theory that people would think she was stupid, that there was something wrong with her, or would hate her.

AL: FEAR OF ELEVATORS

Al was fifty-seven years old, married with three grown children. He was referred to me by his general practitioner, who recognized that his bouts of chest pain and shortness of breath were caused by anxiety.

Al's problem began about six months prior to our first appointment, when the other three partners in his firm overrode his objection and decided to move from the ground-floor space that they had occupied for twenty years to new offices on the eighteenth floor of the Empire State Building. Although the firm desperately needed additional space, Al objected furiously to the move. The other partners were in agreement that the move was not only necessary, but that they would have more space for less money.

Al and his partners got into heated arguments about the move, and bad feelings began to develop. His brother-in-law took him out for a drink and said, "Al, please, just give me one good reason why we shouldn't sign this new lease, and I'll take your side."

"It's a bad idea, that's why."

"But why is it a bad idea?"

"It just is."

What Al wasn't willing to tell even his brother-in-law was that he was phobic of elevators. He had always been uncomfortable in elevators, but living in New York all his life, he had to use them. He took an elevator to his apartment on the eighth floor. He used elevators in department stores; he used elevators when he called on clients—but he would never go above the fifteenth floor.

"Why can't you take the elevator to the sixteenth floor?" I asked.

"I just can't trust it."

"What will happen at the sixteenth floor that doesn't happen at the fifteenth?"

"I just can't trust it," he repeated.

I could see why his partners got frustrated with him.

Al and I started our in vivo work in a building near my office that had sixteen floors. Together we went to the tenth floor several times because Al wanted to get familiar with the elevators. Then I went to the fifteenth floor and waited for him to come up alone in the elevator. When he arrived I said, "Great! Now we've got just one more floor—shall we go to-gether?"

"No."

"Could you expand on that a little and tell me why you can't go to the sixteenth floor? What do you think will happen? Would it be easier if we walk up the stairs and see what the sixteenth floor looks like?"

"No. I just can't—that's all."

"Well, if you just can't, then I guess we're wasting our time—let's go."

"Wait a minute, you're supposed to be helping me with this."

"What can I do to help you?"

"Push me into the elevator and make me go."

"Against your will?"

"Yeah."

When the elevator doors opened on the fifteenth floor I grabbed Al's hand and said, "Come on, we're going—like it or not." He followed me with no resistance. When we got off on the sixteenth floor I asked, "How was it?"

"It was OK."

"But what was so scary about it while we were on the fif-teenth floor?"

"I don't know, it just was."

For the next couple of weeks Al and I continued to work in the building near my office, going up and down in the eleva-tor to the sixteenth floor until he was able to manage it com-fortably alone. While we were working we talked of many things, but I never got any better insight about what was so scary above the fifteenth floor. When I explained the concepts of magic thinking, or inner scenes, Al said that he didn't have any magic thoughts or inner scenes. He did talk about how angry he was with his partners. He felt that they had betrayed him and were trying to force him out of the partnership by moving the offices to the eighteenth floor.

"Do they know that you couldn't go above the fifteenth floor?"

"No, of course not, I'd never tell them that."

"Then how would they figure out that moving to the eighteenth floor would force you out?"

"I don't know—they just did."

It didn't take me long to figure out that insight was not Al's strong point. After he was able to manage the top floor of the building near my office, we moved on to the Empire State Building. "Let's start with the sixteenth floor," I suggested. "Then we only have two more floors to work on."

"No, we can't do that," he said. "This building is so much higher."

"But the sixteenth floor is the same height."

"We just can't."

We started on the tenth floor. Al continued to talk about how angry he was with his partners—how they ganged up against him in an effort to get him out of the firm.

"Why did they want you out of the firm?" I asked.

"I don't know, they just did."

"Are there any advantages to this new space?"

"Not that I know of."

"I thought that you were getting more space for less money."

"Well, yes, there is that."

"Maybe that had something to do with their decision," I suggested as we were in the elevator on our way up to the eighteenth floor.

"Maybe," Al said, doubtfully.

AL and I spent an hour a week for two months in the elevators in the Empire State Building. By the end of that time he was able to go up to the twentieth floor alone. The renovation of the new offices was complete, and we took a tour of them (he introduced me as his wife's cousin—he didn't want anyone to know that he was working with a therapist).

"The offices are really nice, aren't they," Al said.

"Yeah, they really are."

"My new office is a lot nicer than my old one."

"Yeah, it is."

"Maybe I was wrong about them trying to force me out of the firm."

"Yeah, I think you might be right about that," I said.

JOHANNA, Frank, Lara, and Al are good examples of the majority of the people I work with. I see them for two to six months, and in that period of time they pick up enough understanding to manage their problem—and sometimes even to recognize the thinking that creates the problem.

I've found that the most promising clients are high on motivation and possess a willingness to really commit themselves to the program and work hard. The next most important attribute is having a supportive person in their life—this can make their work much easier, but the fact is that it is not always available.

Magic thinking infects people from all walks of life, but the bottom line for magic thinkers is always the same. They must learn to clarify what they fear will happen and assess the facts that support that thought in order to be free of unrealistic fears.

PART III

HOW TO CHANGE YOUR OWN MAGIC THINKING

INTRODUCTION

I SUSPECT that the biggest question on your mind right now is whether or not a self-help book can really make a difference in your life. Before you began reading this book you may have felt, like Jerry, that you were the only person in the world obsessed with litter; or, like Gracie, who was so afraid of contamination that she never left her room, you may have thought that your problem was an indication of insanity, that it was only a matter of time before you were packed off to a loony bin. Now you know that your phobia or OCD is a fairly common problem; that other intelligent, competent people suffer with it; and, most important, that it is manageable. Knowing about other people who have had similar problems (although many of these cases are probably far more severe than yours) should make a significant difference in understanding your own problem.

Information changes us; it changes the way we think about things and the way we react to them. If someone were to bump into us, mumble irritatably at us and keep going, we'd get furious. "What a nasty, rude boor that guy is!" we'd think. But if we happened to know that he had a splitting headache, that he just had lost a major account, and that his wife was threatening to leave him, we would be likely to think, "Ah, the poor guy." It was the information that changed our response. The information allowed us to reassess his behavior as troubled, not rude, and our response became one of sympathy and understanding rather than anger. Being armed with accurate information about your own problem will allow you to reassess your thinking and facilitate alternative behavior.

If you or someone you love is suffering from a malady of magic thinking, this may be the most important book you ever read.

Throughout this book, for want of a better term, I have used the word "treatment." That is not really accurate. As a therapist what I really do is provide information. I help troubled people to study their own story from another point of view, and to find alternatives to the behavior that is keeping them from leading a fully functioning life. Together we develop procedures to safely test faulty belief systems and to establish appropriate behavior. This is done through education.

It often seems as though there's a conspiracy afoot that is trying to convince us that we are much too complex and our inner workings are too mysterious for us to be able to understand ourselves without the intervention of a professional healer; that the problem solving we've been doing throughout life isn't good enough to help us with anything really serious. But the very people who lead us to believe that our ability to assess our own problems and find solutions is totally inadequate are often doing battle among themselves regarding how best to manage our problems. Unfortunately, many of the people I see in therapy have accepted the view that a healing professional will mag-

ically fix them. Some feel cheated when I give them an assignment, ask them to keep a diary, and plan exposure sessions.
"You mean we can't just talk about it?" they ask. "Yes," I say,
"we can talk about it forever and ever and ever. . . . "

Anyone who has ever tried to lose weight knows that there
are diet pills, weight-loss organizations, and books galore with
sensible diet plans, and that all of them work if you *do* what's
required. And none of them works if you don't! The trick, of
course, is to do what is directed and to stay with it even when
it's boring, difficult, and agonizingly slow. Most people don't
go on a diet when they're one or two pounds overweight; they
wait until the condition creates more discomfort (tight waist-
bands, the expense of a new wardrobe, embarrassment) than
a diet. The same is true with the malady of magic thinking. Unless the emotional discomfort and disruption of life are creating more pain than the fear of change and the struggle required to make it, it is unlikely that anyone will spend the effort
and energy required to get better.

The process of change is always easier if you have understanding and supportive people to help you with it. They can
help you keep your eye on your goal, remind you of the
progress you've already made, encourage you when things look
bleak, and help you get back on track after a setback. If you
are lucky enough to have access to a self-help group, a knowledgeable therapist, a friend or family member who can help
you, by all means, solicit their aid. If you don't have a supportive person in your life your task will be harder but not impossible.

Understanding the importance of and rejoicing in the small
victories over your malady of magic thinking are critical elements in staying with the program of getting better. If a month
of hard work is required for you to be able to walk comfort-
ably half a block from your home, you may get disheartened

and think, "What's the use? I'll never get downtown at this rate." Or, "Big deal! I've reduced my showering time from four hours to three and a half hours, but I still have to get up at 4:00 A.M. to get to work on time." When you find yourself getting bogged down with these kinds of thoughts, remind yourself that the essence of this work is to change the thinking. Time or distance is only important as an indication of how the thinking is expressed. Originally you may have thought that it was unsafe to leave the house but now, by being able to walk half a block, you've proven that belief to be faulty. It's possible for you to see, then, that other beliefs about the dangers of being away from home are just as faulty. The job of getting better requires the constant testing of beliefs.

Accepting the small steps of progress is also important, because this program requires that you expose yourself to the very thing that you fear and have been avoiding. If the task you set for yourself is too ambitious, the thought of doing it may create so much anxiety that somehow it never quite gets done, and you just quietly drop the program. No step is too small—a series of small steps will finally add up to a big step. The most important thing is to keep moving.

Whether I work with you in person or through this book, all I can do for you is give you information and direction—the rest is up to you.

CHAPTER FIFTEEN

How to Get Better

THE GOOD NEWS is that you can get better. You are not alone with the problem of magic thinking; thousands of people have had a similar (or worse) problem and conquered it. The bad news is that getting better requires hard work and commitment. If you've read through Part II, Case Examples, you probably noticed that there are no miracle cures. In fact, you may have noticed that some of the cases involved years of frustration and hard work, with unpredictable ups and downs. That is the way with the maladies of magic thinking. Anyone who has had a problem with magic thinking for five, ten, or twenty years knows that more than a minor adjustment needs to be made.

In this world of fast foods and twenty-four-hour loans, we have come to think in terms of quick fixes. Effective therapy changes the way you think, the way you feel, and the way you behave. Therapy will require time and patience. While working on getting better, remember one of the most helpful tech-

niques: think in small steps. For instance, if because of the understanding acquired by reading this book you were to gain
only a 5 percent improvement in your life, you are already, at
this point, 5 percent ahead of where you were before you
opened it. Now, if you were to follow the self-help program
outlined in this book, and each week you gained a 5 percent
improvement—imagine where you'd be in a year.

Of course, real life doesn't work quite that way. Progress is
usually irregular. At first you may make frustratingly small
steps—both forward and backward—followed by surprising
quantum leaps. Don't be dismayed by what appears to be neg-
ligible improvement in the beginning, because over time the
cumulative effect will be gratifying and decidedly worth the
struggle. The more effort you put into this program, the more
successful you will be in ridding yourself of negative behavior
caused by magic thinking.

Magic thinkers are usually great intellectualizers. But you
can't just think your way out of a magic thinking malady. You
must be willing to do the tasks, expose yourself to the
frightening stimuli, resist performing the ritual, and allow
the anxiety. I know this is hard; that is exactly why you have
to start with small, manageable tasks. If the initial goal is too
high and the tasks are too ambitious for your capacity to deal
with the distress, you will only be setting yourself up for failure.

Some of the following information will seem to have more
relevance to obsessive-compulsive disorders than to phobias;
as both are maladies of magic thinking, the line dividing the
two is often blurred. Generally speaking, phobics are more
prone to avoidance, while obsessive-compulsives are more
likely to ritualize; but people who depend on magic borrow
solutions from both categories without concern for the
labels.

TREATMENT OBJECTIVES

The treatment objectives for a magic thinker consist of helping her to learn to view reality and assess the danger potential in common situations the way a person free of the malady would. This is done through the following means:

IDENTIFY THE THOUGHT

Those terrible feelings and the overwhelming urge to flee, avoid, perform the ritual, or repeat a litany come from a thought of impending disaster. The thought may be, "I've touched the kitchen counter where a can of insecticide stood. Now I'm contaminated with poison and if I touch someone I will cause that person's death." In actual fact thoughts pop into our heads in a type of "thought shorthand," so the above thought might actually have been recorded as follows: "Counter-insecticide-death." Certainly the possibility of causing someone's death is disastrous and would cause anguish to most people, and the immediate response would be to do whatever would be necessary to avert the disaster. In this case it would be to decontaminate oneself. The "thought shorthand" becomes an urgent demand, "Counter-insecticide-death-decontaminate!" without any reasoning taking place in the magic thinker's mind. The performance of the ritual or the saying of a litany relieves the physical sensations and banishes the thought—for the time being. Our first step is to identify that thought which sets off the phobic or obsessive-compulsive response. Use the Thought/Consequence Chart on page 301 to help you identify the thought.

TEST REALITY

Because avoidance is so much a part of a magic thinker's life and he finds only confirming negative proof in his belief systems ("I haven't died or gone crazy driving over a bridge because I've always managed to get off just in the nick of time"), he may have no experience of staying in an anxiety-producing situation until the discomfort abates, and therefore no personal reality on which to test his theory. Reality testing can seem very dangerous when the apparent risk is death to oneself or another. Learn how to look at the rest of the world for confirmation of risk factors. Have you ever seen supermarket checkout clerks handling cans of insecticide while at the same time touching food, money, and people? How many people do you know who regularly drive over bridges without going crazy or dying? Observe other people doing the things you fear and make a note of what happens to them. You might have a friend or family member model for you by touching the floor or touching an insecticide container and then putting her hands to her face. If other people do these things and don't die or go crazy, why will you? Use the Thought/Consequence Chart to help you reality test.

EXPOSE FAULTY "CAUSE-AND-EFFECT" THINKING

One client I worked with was convinced that if she threw out her pantyhose in Manhattan it would cause a murder. Another, Jerry, from Chapter 6, had to go up and down the subway stairs picking up the most minute pieces of litter because if he didn't he believed that someone would fall on the stairs and be killed, and he would be responsible. Another could walk three blocks from her home on the north side of the street but was sure that something terrible would happen if she walked an equal distance on the south side. Like the farmer who snapped his fingers to keep his house safe from tigers, these magic thinkers use faulty cause-and-effect reasoning.

Describe in detail the series of events that would cause the feared result to happen. How could discarded pantyhose be responsible for a murder? Try to picture the sequence of acts. You throw your pantyhose into the trash. Then what? They slowly creep out of the trash and slither across the floor, out the door, and down the street. Then some innocent passerby comes along, and the pantyhose fly into the air and attack by wrapping their legs around the person's neck and squeezing until the poor hapless victim drops dead on the sidewalk, never knowing what evil lurked in the pantyhose. Imagine a newspaper headline about your dreaded event: "DISCARDED PANTYHOSE MURDER MOTHER OF SIX." Would you believe this headline if you saw it on the newsstand?

ASSESS THE PROBABILITIES

Magic thinkers feel they need 100 percent certainty, while the rest of us fumble along on faith and hope. If a can of furniture polish has the word "poison" on it, a magic thinker will act as though the can itself is poisonous; and because of the "contagion" phenomenon, everything that comes into contact with the can becomes "poisonous." Poisoning then becomes an all-encompassing probability because the magic thinker doesn't differentiate between drinking the contents of the can and the properties of the can itself. People do die of accidents, disease, and poisoning, but let us examine the causes and the probabilities. If thousands of people eat food purchased from the local supermarket, what are the chances that this particular container of cottage cheese is contaminated? If millions of people regularly travel up and down every day in elevators without mishap, what is the probability that the elevator you are on will plunge twenty floors to the ground or get stuck and hold you prisoner for an eternity? Use the Thought/Consequence Chart to help you reality test the probability of the dreaded consequence.

REDUCE YOUR NEED FOR REASSURANCE

The magic thinker's constant need for reassurance can alienate friends and family. Many therapists have a firm rule against any reassurance. I limit reassurance to one request. In limiting the requests for reassurance, I am very specific that the sufferer must phrase the request in twenty-five words or less, and he cannot repeat it even though he feels sure that he left out important details. If you don't limit the demands for reassurance you won't really be doing your own work on reality testing and cause-and-effecting. You can't be free of the maladies of magic thinking until you are able to trust your own sense of reality. By seeking reassurance from others you undermine your own reality.

EXPOSURE AND RESPONSE PREVENTION

IN VIVO EXPOSURE IS ABSOLUTELY NECESSARY! Be prepared to leave your home and visit supermarkets, shopping malls, tall buildings, elevators, bridges, and public restrooms, wherever your phobia lurks. The exposure tasks should be planned carefully in advance, and always start with small steps and work gradually through the more distressing situations. After you have exposed yourself to the feared situation (leaving your safe area, looking at a picture of a snake, etc.) you must resist the performance of your ritual. This will be difficult, because even when you can effectively reality test you may still experience high levels of anxiety along with distressing physical sensations. Remind yourself that every time you avoid a situation, flee, perform the ritual, or say the litany to free yourself of the uncomfortable feelings, you are strengthening the stranglehold of magic thinking.

KEEP AN EXPOSURE DIARY

Use the Exposure Diary on page 300 to make note of how long the anxiety lasts so you have a factual record of the anxiety abating without having to leave the situation or perform the ritual. Most people remember only the discomfort and forget that it didn't last forever. Follow the directions for using the Task Sheet (page 298) to establish a hierarchy of problems to work on for exposure exercises. Once established, start with the last item on your list and use the Exposure Diary to record your experiences.

GRADUALLY LIMIT RITUALS

It isn't realistic to think that people who have been "keeping themselves safe" by washing their hands eighty times a day or repeating litanies seven times will be able to stop all obsessive-compulsive behavior overnight. Unless you are in an inpatient treatment setting where your activities can be strictly monitored and controlled, it will be more effective to plan a program of limited rituals. If you are currently washing your hands sixty times a day, can you reduce it to fifty-five times for the next week? Then, if nothing terrible has happened, can you reduce it to fifty times, then to forty-five times the week after that? Continue with the reduction of hand-washing until you are washing your hands only after using the bathroom (or gardening, working on the car, etc.) and before handling food.

If you are spending ten minutes washing your hands, go into the washroom with a friend or family member and have her demonstrate how to wash the hands in fifteen seconds. Then repeat the action while counting to fifteen.

TASK ASSIGNMENTS

Tasks should be manageable. Always start at the bottom of your Task Sheet (see page 298) and work up. Repeat the task until it no longer causes distress before you move up the chart to a more difficult task. It is usually a good idea to repeat the tasks performed the previous day before moving on. If there are items in your home or workplace that are too "contaminated," or bridges too high, or elevators too difficult to deal with alone, either find a way to break the problem into smaller steps or have a friend or relative help you work on it by modeling. Magic thinkers are very often reluctant to do their tasks because of their fears. A technique you may find helpful in approaching these difficult tasks is to leave a message on an answering machine of a supporting person when you are about to start the assignment, describing what you will be doing, what your fears are, and asking him to call you if he feels that there is any real danger. Keep a log of your phone calls and the results of the exposure task.

FAMILY INVOLVEMENT

The families of magic thinkers are usually worn out by the anxiety, the constant need for reassurance, and the involvement in rituals. They get trapped into the rituals and reassurance because it is easier to comply than to deal with the person's panic. (I had a client who insisted that her mother, father, and husband take off all their "outside" clothes—which included everything except underwear—in the vestibule and change to "inside" clothes before coming into the house.) It is much more expedient for supporting people to take off all their clothes before entering the house or to not insist on going away for a vacation or to do all the shopping and driving. But that expedient is a disservice to everyone involved because it continues the dependency and doesn't help the sufferer develop the skills that will lead to freedom from the malady of magic thinking.

The family or supporting person must join forces with the treatment program and insist on a "real world" conformation of facts, where contamination is not contagious and most events have a reasonably understandable series of steps that lead from an initial cause to the final effect. Instead of the family agreeing to take off all their clothes before entering the house, they might start by taking off only their shoes and coats for a week or so and monitoring what happens. Or, if you are fearful of supermarkets, a family member might accompany you to the store while you shop. Then, when it has been confirmed that nothing terrible has occurred, agree to take another small step toward recovery. When possible, sit down with your family and discuss treatment procedures and have family members help you with the task assignments and reassurance limitations. (See Chapter 17 on how to be an effective supporting person.)

Keep a Daily Diary

Diary keeping is essential (see page 296). It will provide a factual record to assure you that risks were taken and none of your dire expectations took place. It will also identify the anxiety-producing thoughts and demonstrate that the symptoms do abate even when you don't leave the situation or perform a ritual. I've offered several types of charts (pp. 296–301). One of them will certainly suit your situation. You may find it even more helpful to use several different types, depending on the task and the situation.

BE PREPARED FOR SETBACKS

For most of us, life is complex. When we finally get one area of our life together, unexpected difficulties may arise in another area: a loved one might get sick, or we might lose our job. Magic thinking is likely to manifest its worst qualities when you are under stress. That does not mean that you will be back at square one. Because this program is a learning experience, you will never totally lose what you've gained, but on occasion you may have to work harder to maintain your improvements. When a setback occurs, be patient. Refer to an early page in your Daily Diary to remind yourself of how much progress you've made. Go back to square one on your Task Sheets and repeat the tasks; you'll find that the things that held real terror for you six months ago have lost their fire, and you will proceed through the tasks much more rapidly than when you originally started the program. You do not get better through magic or luck. You get better through diligent efforts at learning and understanding yourself.

USING THE CHARTS

By now you probably have considerable insight into your problem. The treatment objectives and the reasoning behind them have been explained, and you are ready to plan your own treatment program; but first, look over the charts on pages 296–301. They have been designed to identify the thoughts, objects, or situations that create your anxiety and to aid you in planning your exposure tasks. Either photocopy the charts in the book or make your own copies in a notebook. Use a separate Exposure Diary sheet for each task. Also, use a separate chart for every Thought/Consequence exercise you do. Be prepared to make many copies of each of the charts.

SET SHORT-TERM GOALS

Because of your perfectionistic attitude, anything less than a 100 percent cure may be viewed as a total failure, so begin your work by limiting your immediate goal. You might start by working toward a 5 or 10 percent improvement for the first week. Study your hierarchy of situations and/or objects that create anxiety. Start to work on the least challenging items—remember, no step is too small. If you encounter a situation that seems to be impossible to approach, either break it down into smaller steps or put it aside for the time being and work on something else, but keep working! KEEP YOUR GOALS REASONABLE AND SHORT-TERM.

LEARN TO QUANTIFY YOUR ANXIETY

In order to become aware of the thoughts that create your anxiety and the need to avoid, flee, or perform a ritual, learn to quantify your anxiety or discomfort; that is, assign a number to it on a scale from 0 to 10, 10 being the most intense anxiety you have ever experienced and 0 being no anxiety at all. Learn to be sensitive to your anxiety level and catch it at the lower numbers; reality testing will be much easier when your anxiety level is lower. The anxiety scale also provides a tool for measuring and assessing the degree of discomfort, as well as a specific means of communicating your feelings to the therapist or supporting person.

OTHER HELPFUL INFORMATION ABOUT YOUR BEHAVIOR

How long have you had the problem? Did the onset of the problem coincide with difficult or unusual life events? Do other members of your family have a similar problem? Often by examining these issues people can see that the behavior made a kind of sense at a different time or under different circumstances. Or the behavior may have been learned from a relative who engaged in magic thinking.

When it can be clearly understood that the behavior is a relic from the past that no longer applies to your situation, it is easier to test the mistaken beliefs.

SCHEDULE A SPECIFIC TIME TO WORK ON YOUR PROGRAM

Set aside an hour every day for this program. I can't count the number of times I have heard people tell me that they just couldn't seem to find the time to work on their problem. Indeed, the time can't be found; it must be made. Look at this program as if you were taking a course in school. The time is scheduled for that purpose and that purpose only. If you set aside 6:30 to 7:30 as your hour to work on this program, let your family know that you won't be able to walk the dog, answer the phone, or stir the stew during this hour. An hour is the minimum amount of time you should spend on the exposure tasks. Two hours is preferable but not always possible.

Because magic thinkers can get obsessive about all kinds of things, I think a word of caution is appropriate here. If you find yourself spending hours and hours a day on your diary, or recopying your checklists to make them neater or more detailed, you are probably being too obsessive. Do not worry about doing them exactly right! The activity is more important than the accuracy.

When you fill out your charts, be as specific as possible. If bridges are your nemesis, describe the type of bridge, starting with the most "dangerous." Your list might look like this:

1. Long, high, steeply arched bridges over water
2. Long, high, flat bridges over water
3. Long, low, flat bridges over water
4. Long, high, flat bridges over a highway
5. Short, low, flat bridges over a highway

Instead of listing "dirt," indicate what kind of dirt, and what kind of contact. For instance: touching the dirt in the pot of a houseplant might create less distress for you than seeing dog feces from a distance of three feet—that's a very important distinction when it comes to doing exposure tasks.

Starting with the most upsetting, list all objects or situations that trigger anxiety or rituals, describe what you think will happen when you encounter your feared situation, and describe the extent of your commitment to the belief.

Sam's (chapter 13, the man who was phobic of snakes) Degree of Commitment chart looked like this:

Object or Situation	What Will Happen	Action or Ritual	Degree of Commitment
Seeing a snake	I'll go crazy.	wash self, disinfect area	100%
Nature magazine	will see picture of snake and go crazy	destroy book, wash self, disinfect area	100%
Rooms with dark corners or low furniture	snake may be hiding, will come out and I'll go crazy	search seven times	100%
Walking on unfamiliar street	may see snake in pet shop and go crazy	focus on side walk and say litany	100%
Hearing words: "snake, slimy, slither, slink"	think of snake and go crazy	say litany	75%
Walk somewhere a snake may have been: grass, etc.	think of snake and go crazy	say litany	75%

Sam started out being afraid of snakes. The fear quickly escalated to include pictures of snakes and words or images that would suggest snakes. Originally the fear was that being in close proximity to a snake would make him go crazy. Then the fear progressed to seeing a snake; seeing a picture of a snake; and thinking of a snake. Sam's commitment to his belief that any exposure to a snake (real or imagined) would cause him to go crazy was so vehement that I decided not to question it for the time being. In New York City snakes are not all that easy to come by. Thoughts are too difficult to tack down and make specific. Pictures of snakes abound. Although Sam claimed to be 100 percent committed to the belief that seeing a picture of a snake would make him go crazy, I felt that for the time being a picture of a snake offered the best possibilities for breaking tasks into manageable steps. I started by getting more specific. Would a picture of a toy snake make him go crazy? Would a picture of snake jewelry make him go crazy? Would a picture of a snake held eight feet away from him make him go crazy?

After considerable negotiating and my offer to sign a contract that I would not come any closer to him with a picture of a snake than he agreed to, we started our exposure tasks with a picture of a bracelet in the shape of a snake.

This is a good example of breaking a problem down to a manageable task. We started with a picture of a snake in a nature magazine; we settled with a picture of a bracelet in the form of a snake.

1. Look at picture of snake bracelet for two minutes.
2. Hold picture of snake bracelet for five minutes.
3. Touch picture of snake bracelet.

In order for him to look at the picture of the snake bracelet without holding it, I put it on a low end table with a serving tray on top of it and a heavy dictionary on top of the tray to weigh it down. When Sam practiced looking at it he was able to lift the tray off the picture without touching it.

Sam's Exposure Diary looked like this:

TASK: LOOK AT PICTURE OF SNAKE FOR TWO MINUTES

Date Time		Start Anxiety Level	End Anxiety Level
5/8			
10:00A	said litany 5 times	8	4
2:00P	said litany 7 times	8	2
3:00P	didn't say litany	8	8

On the first day Sam did the task three times. He was successful in bringing his anxiety level way down by saying his litany; but when he did the task without saying the litany, the anxiety level stayed high.

TASK: LOOK AT PICTURE OF SNAKE FOR TWO MINUTES

Date Time		Start Anxiety Level	End Anxiety Level
5/9			
9:30A	didn't say litany	8	6
5/9			
11:00A	didn't say litany	7	8

He practiced, without saying his litany, twice on the second day. My guess is that the high anxiety level discouraged him, so he didn't practice as diligently as he might have.

TASK: LOOK AT PICTURE OF SNAKE FOR TWO MINUTES

Date Time		Start Anxiety Level	End Anxiety Level
5/10 9:30A	said litany 5 times	8	5
5/10 1:00P	said litany 5 times	6	6
5/10 3:00P	said litany 3 times	6	6
5/10 5:30P	said litany 3 times	5	4
5/10 8:00P	said litany 3 times	5	3

Wisely, Sam decided to take smaller steps on the third day, and returned to saying his litany but fewer times than the usual seven. This proved to be very successful in bringing down the level of anxiety he experienced while looking at the picture. He practiced five times that day.

TASK: LOOK AT PICTURE OF SNAKE FOR TWO MINUTES

Date Time		Start Anxiety Level	End Anxiety Level
5/11 9:30A	didn't say litany	5	8
5/11 11:30A	didn't say litany	7	7
5/11 2:00P	didn't say litany	7	6
5/11 5:30P	didn't say litany	6	4
5/11 8:00P	didn't say litany	5	4

On the fourth day, flushed with the success of the previous day, he approached the picture with relatively low anxiety; he didn't say his litany while looking at the picture and experienced a rise in anxiety. He persevered through the day, practicing five times, and ended with low anxiety.

TASK: LOOK AT PICTURE OF SNAKE FOR TWO MINUTES

Date Time		Start Anxiety Level	End Anxiety Level
5/12 9:00A	didn't say litany	5	2
5/12 11:00A	didn't say litany	4	2
5/12 3:00P	didn't say litany	4	1
5/12 4:30P	didn't say litany	2	1
5/12 8:00P	didn'y say litany	2	1

The fifth day was a success! Sam approached the task with low anxiety; said no litany; and ended the day with minimal anxiety.

TASK: LOOK AT PICTURE OF SNAKE FOR TWO MINUTES

Date Time		Start Anxiety Level	End Anxiety Level
5/13 9:30A	didn't say litany	2	1
5/13 11:00A	didn't say litany	2	1
5/13 2:00	didn't say litany	2	10

Look at day six! Sam started the day with very low anxiety, and had no trouble looking at the picture of the snake bracelet until midday, when his anxiety level skyrocketed to a 10. He destroyed the picture, and spent the rest of the day scrubbing and disinfecting the entire apartment. At that point he decided that he was a failure, the treatment wasn't working, and he wouldn't continue. When I discussed the situation with him the following day it turned out that he had had a disturbing phone call just prior to doing the task. The anxiety had been displaced onto the picture of the snake bracelet, but Sam didn't understand that until we analyzed his Exposure Diary.

Use the Degree of Commitment chart to identify the thoughts and images that trigger rituals. Describe the ritual; what the ritual is designed to prevent; and degree of commitment to your belief. This exercise will help you to reality test and work on cause-and-effect thinking.

Sam's Degree of Commitment chart looked like this. This is very abbreviated; his chart actually had about twenty-five thoughts or images on it.

Thought, Object, or Situation	What Will Happen?	Ritual	Degree of Commitment
Snake	snake will appear	say litany	55%
Adam & Eve	snake will appear	say litany	30%
The color green	snake will appear	say litany	30%

Again I decided to focus on a concept that would be easy to reality test. I asked Sam to explain how thinking of the color green would cause a snake to appear. If it were possible to make something appear by thinking of it, why didn't he think of a million dollars? Do people who think about buying green curtains or a green dress or a green car make snakes appear? What is the mechanism by which this works? Are there wavelengths that carry all the thoughts of all the people in the world, and snakes somehow tune into this wavelength and appear to the people who have snake-related thoughts? I used the thought of the color green to work on because it offered so many possibilities for reality testing. I found things in varying shades of green for us to look at and think about to see how many snakes would appear. During our thinking about snakes period Sam agreed to reduce saying his litany silently from seven times, to five, then to three, one, and finally not at all. No snakes ever appeared.

Sam and I spent months working on the magic qualities of the color green, but when we came to the other items on his list (Adam and Eve, and so on) he found that they no longer had any power over him. By reality testing a small part of the theory that thoughts make things happen, and finding it to be false, we shook the validity of the entire theory.

Gracie (chapter 10) insisted that she couldn't keep a diary or use the charts. She said they wouldn't apply to her problems; that she already knew what her problems were and she wouldn't learn anything from the diary and charts; and that they were a waste of time. Besides that, she would not share her thoughts with anyone. After much coaxing and cajoling, she finally filled out a Task Sheet.

Gracie's Task Sheet looked like this:

1. Go to the bookstore.
2. Have dinner with family.
3. Clean room.
4. Let someone come into my room.
5. Reduce time spent bathing.
6. Reduce time spent washing hands.
7. Reduce time spent saying litanies.

Initially Gracie was unable to be more specific than identifying dirt as her Thought, Object, or Situation on her Degree of Commitment Chart, but eventually she produced the following chart. Many of her anxiety-producing thoughts were so scary she was afraid to write them down. She numbered her scary thoughts (but wouldn't tell me what the numbers referred to). Her chart read:

THOUGHT, OBJECT, OR SITUATION	WHAT WILL HAPPEN?	RITUAL	DEGREE OF COMMITMENT
#3 & #6	contamination by dirt & death	washed hands for 30 minutes	100%
#14	contamination by dirt & death	said litany 7 times	65%
#9	contamination by dirt & death	said litany 7 times	83%
#2	contamination by dirt & death	washed hands for 45 minutes	100%

This helped me tremendously because I could clearly see that Gracie was deeply committed to the lower numbers, so I thought it best to start by chipping away at the less scary items. We started with thoughts numbered 10 and over. Each time she had a thought in that category she was to reduce saying her litany from seven times to three times. Then, if nothing terrible happened, not say a litany at all (in her magic system, one was worse than none). After Gracie was able to significantly reduce her litany reciting she was willing to do a series of Degree of Commitment charts that enabled us to establish a hierarchy and work on doorknobs and eventually get to the bookstore.

Janet's OC behavior (chapter 7) was limited to driving, her only task was to "To be able to drive like a normal person." We combined her Exposure Diary with on-the-spot reality testing.

A very abbreviated version of Janet's diary looked like
this:

TASK: IN CAR, TRYING TO DRIVE LIKE A NORMAL PERSON

Date/Time	Thought	Anxiety Level	Ritual or Response	Reality
Wed 7:00	dead body	9	checked	a dead bush
Thr 7:00	dead body	8	checked	garbage bag
Fri 7:30	dead body	6	reality-tested	an empty six-pack
Sat 2:00	dead body	9	checked	unidentifiable junk
Sun 4:00	dead body	5	reality-tested	same dead bush
Mon 7:00	dead body	8	checked	very dead squirrel

Janet thought that every bump she felt while driving and
every object on the side of the road was a dead body. The first
week of her practice she checked the road four times out of
six. She reality tested without checking only twice. At higher
levels of anxiety she wasn't able to resist the compulsion to
check, but at lower levels she was able to stay inside the car
and reality test by describing to herself what she saw ("It's
about twelve inches long, red and white, and has the word
'Miller' printed on it"). Her own assessment of her thoughts
was invaluable. She asked herself, "How could I possibly think
that an empty six-pack was a dead body?" When she came
upon the same dead bush later in the week and reminded herself that she saw the bush from her dining room window every
day and knew that it is only a dead bush and then wonders
how it suddenly becomes a dead body, she is questioning the
OC belief system. Every day Janet and her husband practiced
in the car for at least an hour. For the first six months her diary
was a record of frustrating and unpredictable ups and downs.

But in time it became evident that the general level of her anxiety was gradually lowering. After six months her diary looked like this:

TASK: IN CAR, TRYING TO DRIVE LIKE A NORMAL PERSON

Date/Time	Thought	Anxiety Level	Ritual or Response	Reality
Wed. 6:30	dead body	5	reality tested	bump in road
Thr. 7:00	don't know	3	reality tested	garbage
Fri. 7:00	dead body	7	checked	old tire
Sat. 2:00	dead body	7	checked	discarded clothes
Sat. 3:30	dead body	5	reality tested	car fender
Sun. 1:00	don't know	4	reality tested	bump in road
Mon. 7:00	dead body	4	reality tested	tree stump

At this point Janet's highest level of anxiety is 7 (as opposed to 9 six months earlier), and she is reality testing more than checking. However, she is still stopping the car and studying the object or situation to do the reality testing, so she is still not "driving like a normal person." During this time she was still accumulating vast quantities of Polaroid shots of roadside junk, which were kept in a scrapbook to remind her of all the false dead body alerts.

MR. More (chapter 12) wanted to work on many issues: obsessing, inability to make decisions, social competency, and hoarding, so we used volumes of charts to describe the problems, identify the thoughts, determine the anticipated disaster, reality test, and cause-and-effect. The obsessing we handled like this:

THOUGHT	CONSEQUENCE
I should have worn my blue socks instead of the black.	People will think I'm morbid.
People will think I'm morbid.	They will reject me.
People will reject me.	I'll be alone all my life.
I'll be alone all my life.	I won't be able to survive.

Prior to the filling out the Thought/Consequence chart, Mr. More had thoughts like a broken record: "I should have worn my blue socks instead of the black—I should have worn my blue socks instead of the black—I should have worn my blue socks instead of the black. . . . " The undeclared disaster was that he would not be able to survive as result of having worn the black socks instead of the blue. Mr. More's "thought shorthand" was "black socks-rejection-death by loneliness." Once we had identified the anticipated disaster, we were able to examine the cause-and-effect sequences and reality test the premise.

"Do people necessarily conclude that anyone who wears black socks is morbid?"
"Do people spend a lot of time even thinking about other people's socks?"
"If I am judged morbid because I wore black socks on Tuesday does that mean that I'll be rejected by everyone forever?"
"If I am rejected by people who observed my black socks on Tuesday does it necessarily follow that I'll be alone forever? I could choose to wear blue or even red socks for the rest of my life; why does one day of black socks mean 'alone forever' "?
"If, because of my heinous crime of wearing black socks, I am rejected by everyone and will be alone forever, why won't I be able to survive? I've already been basically alone

for twenty years and survived reasonably well; what will suddenly happen to affect my ability to survive alone?

By writing down the thoughts and reality testing them, Mr.
More was instantly able to see that none of the consequences
was inevitable or even realistic.

Please note: For reasons I don't know, you cannot effectively
reality test in your head. You must put pen to paper and write
it down, one step at a time. Shortcuts don't work!

Another prolonged period of obsessing concerned Mr.
More's concluding a conversation with his boss by saying "Have
a nice day." His "thought shorthand" was "I'm a twit–I'll be
fired–I'll be a street person." His Thought/Consequence chart
looked like this:

THOUGHT	CONSEQUENCE
I shouldn't have said "Have a nice day."	He'll think I'm a twit.
He'll think I'm a twit.	He'll fire me.
He'll fire me.	I'll never find another job.
I'll never find another job.	I'll go broke.
I'll go broke.	I'll end up in the street

He reality tested: "Maybe some people think 'Have a nice
day' is a twitty thing to say, but others consider it an innocuous social pleasantry.

"Even if the boss thinks it's twitty, is it grounds for firing me?
I'm a pretty good accountant, and a real good employee. I
don't goof off, I come in on time, I don't take a lot of time off;
it's not likely that I'd be fired for saying, 'Have a nice day.'

"If the boss was a total jerk (which he's not) and he were to
fire me, I could get another job without too much trouble. Before I took this job I had three other offers. So I could certainly
find another job now with all my experience.

"In the very unlikely event that I couldn't find a job, I certainly wouldn't go broke. Between unemployment compensation and my savings I could live without working for about eighteen months.

"If, for some unfathomable reason I couldn't find a job in eighteen months, I wouldn't have to live on the street because I could move in with my mother. I would hate that, but I know I'd never really end up on the streets."

When Mr. More wrote down his thoughts and the fearful consequences and reality tested, he could see that none of it was very realistic. When the terror was removed from the thoughts, he no longer felt an urge to obsess.

In a relatively short period of time Mr. More made good progress, but his obsessive hoarding also demanded our urgent attention, so we shifted our focus. The first in vivo exposure task we did together was to throw out paper bags. His assignment for the week was to continue to prepare the remainder of the bags to be thrown out by tearing them open and flattening them.

His Exposure Diary looked like this:

TASK: COLLECT, TEAR OPEN, INSPECT, & FLATTEN WRINKLED BAGS

Date Time	Thought	Start Anxiety Level	End Anxiety Level
Fri. 9:00	I can't handle this.	9	9
Sat. 2:00	I can't handle this.	9	8
Sun. 4:00	I can't handle this.	9	8
Mon. 8:30	I can't handle this.	9	9

The diary stopped on Monday. I was surprised at the very high levels of anxiety Mr. More experienced while doing the assigned task. I suggested that we do a Thought/Consequence chart together. He refused, saying he couldn't handle it.

"You can't handle what?" I asked.

"I know that this is all leading up to throwing everything out, and I just can't handle it," he answered.

"Can you handle tearing open and flattening the wrinkled bags?"

"Yes, I can handle that, but that's just the beginning—it won't stop there."

"Why not?"

"What?"

"Why won't it stop there?" I asked. "You can tear open and flatten all the wrinkled bags and then fire me. It can stop right there if you want it to."

Mr. More was way ahead of himself. He really couldn't handle throwing everything out at that stage of treatment. But worrying about what might come much later affected his ability to do an exposure task that he could, in fact, handle. Bringing him back to the task at hand and pointing out his option (firing me) made it possible for him to continue working on the task. Keep reminding yourself to take one step at a time. If you get to the point where you feel you can't handle a situation, you can always back up a bit and repeat an easier task or change directions and work on a different aspect of your problem for a while.

When Mr. More started throwing out the bags, he did a Thought/Consequence chart that looked like this:

THOUGHT	CONSEQUENCE
Something important might be in a bag.	I'll lose something important.
I'll lose something important.	It will cost me a lot of money or time and effort.
It will cost me a lot of money or time and effort.	I won't be able to handle it.
I won't be able to handle it.	I'll go crazy.

Prior to doing the Thought/Consequence chart Mr. More didn't really know why he had to hold onto everything; he just knew that the thought of throwing anything out caused so much distress that he wasn't able to do it. When he identified the underlying fear (going crazy because of the difficulty of replacing something valuable), we were able to reality test and see that there was no validity to the fear. Even though he successfully reality tested and found the dreaded consequence unlikely, his anxiety level remained quite high. It was difficult for him to resist the compulsion to rush out and retrieve the bags, because that would give him instant relief from the anxiety symptoms. I reminded him that performing the ritual would strengthen the grip of the OCD.

We changed focus again when Mr. More decided that he wanted to develop social skills. After writing scripts and role-playing social encounters, we agreed upon an exposure task of a two-minute conversation at the water cooler in his office. His starting anxiety level often preceded the actual doing of the task by as much as an hour. When he thought about the task, his anxiety would elevate, so he would work at bringing it down with a Thought/Consequence chart like this:

Thought	Consequence
I'll sound like a jerk.	He/she will reject me.
He/she will reject me.	So what?! I'll try with someone else.

I think it only fair to point out that Mr. More was able to be so cavalier about a possible rejection because he was choosing to practice his social skills on people in the office who he didn't particularly like or whom he deemed "insignificant" in the office hierarchy.

His Exposure Diary looked like this:

TASK: TALK TO VARIOUS PEOPLE FOR 2 MINUTES

Date Time		Start Anxiety Level	End Anxiety Level
Mon 10:00	Talk to Alan for 2 minutes	9	6
Mon 3:30	Talk to Sue for 2 minutes	9	9
Tue 10:30	Talk to Alan for 2 minutes	9	4
Tue. 2:00	Talk to Alan for 2 minutes	6	3
Tue. 4:30	Talk to Sue for 2 minutes	9	6
Wed. 9:30	Talk to Sue for 2 minutes	7	4
Wed. 11:00	Talk to Alan for 2 minutes	4	2
Wed. 2:00	Talk to Marge for 2 minutes	9	9

No more entries for the week. Mr. More had felt that he was a failure and therapy wasn't working because he was getting worse instead of better. His two-minute conversation with Marge was a disaster because his anxiety started high and stayed high. He thought that because he had become relatively comfortable talking with Alan (a young man who distributed mail to the offices) and Sue (a motherly type of woman who worked in the message center), he had mastered social skills. But Marge didn't fit his target group of people whom he didn't care for or were "insignificant." She was an attractive, newly hired attorney who was on the firm's fast track. He viewed a rejection by Marge as more of a liability. I coaxed him into doing a Thought/Consequence chart so that he could see that a talk at the water cooler isn't always just a chat.

THOUGHT	CONSEQUENCE
Marge is a bright, attractive woman. She has an in with the boss.	She'll probably be a partner in the firm.
She'll be a partner in the firm.	She'll be able to fire me.
She'll be able to fire me.	If she thinks I'm a jerk she will fire me.

By doing the chart Mr. More could see the difference between talking to Alan and Sue and talking to Marge. With Alan and Sue he was just practicing his social skills; with Marge he felt that he was putting his job on the line. With this information we were able to reassess his Exposure Diary and appreciate just how successful he was. To make his exposure tasks more manageable we did a hierarchy of people in his office so that he could gradually work his way through the degrees of "significance."

Whenever you start to feel as though you are experiencing a setback, do what Mr. More and I did and take a little time to review. Have you set unrealistic exposure tasks for yourself? Are other things in your life particularly stressful? Be willing to slow down or change directions until you are feeling more settled. Remember, this isn't a "quick fix" program. You are doing long-term learning that will enable you to change the way you think, the way you feel, and the way you behave.

TREATMENT SUMMARY

The techniques offered in this book have evolved over many years of my experience and observations on what didn't seem to work, what did work, and what worked best. The program requires diligent effort on your part. A friend or family member helping you will make it easier. Consider it as you would a course of study that requires a serious commitment of time and energy. The more you put into the program, the more you will get out of it. These are the techniques that worked the best for the most people:

IDENTIFY THE THOUGHT

Those terrible feelings that create the need to perform rituals are caused by a thought.

REALITY TEST

The thought is usually not based on reality. Learn how to observe the world around you for confirmation of safety.

EXPOSE FAULTY "CAUSE-AND-EFFECT" THINKING

Stepping on cracks does not break mothers' backs. Most things happen as result of an understandable series of events.

ASSESS THE PROBABILITIES

People suffering from OCD and phobias turn even the most remote possibility into an overwhelming probability.

REDUCE YOUR NEED FOR REASSURANCE

Asking for reassurance undermines your trust in your own reality.

EXPOSURE AND RESPONSE PREVENTION

You must resist that urge to avoid anxiety-producing stimuli or to perform a ritual. Every time you avoid situations or perform the ritual to relieve the feelings, you intensify the grip of magic thinking.

TASK ASSIGNMENTS

Plan manageable tasks and do them every day.

FAMILY INVOLVEMENT

Working with another person will make it easier to reality test, face your anxiety-producing situations, and resist the rituals.

KEEP A DIARY

Use the charts and keep a daily diary; this will help you to see how much you've accomplished.

BE PREPARED FOR SETBACKS

Reassess; the tasks may be too hard, or you may be under stress. You'll never lose what you gained.

Get to work; you too can be free of the malady of magic thinking!

YOU must allow the distress and resist urge to flee from the situation or performing the ritual in order to get better.

CHAPTER SIXTEEN

How to Be an Effective Supporting Person for the Magic Thinker in Your Life

BECAUSE the maladies of magic thinking are so common, millions of people suffer from them; by extension we can assume that there must be between 6 and 10 million people whose lives are affected by magic thinking through association. It has only been recently that information, understanding, effective therapies, and support groups have been available to the phobic and obsessive-compulsive person; but the families, friends, and loved ones still have very little information to guide them.

This chapter is intended for the parent, spouse, friend, or roommate of the magic thinker. It will help you understand the confusing and sometimes infuriating behavior of the troubled person in your life. It also offers specific information on how to be a valuable support person—how to encourage a new way of thinking and independent action and how to aid in the struggle for freedom.

On the one hand, you know that your magic thinker is intelligent, talented, and competent; on the other, there are times when he makes absolutely no sense, lies, manipulates or is hysterical, seemingly over nothing. The family of a magic thinker is often worn out by and resentful of the additional household duties imposed upon them because their magic thinker is too fearful to do common tasks or spends many hours every day performing rituals. They get drawn into bizarre routines because it seems easier to accommodate the person than to resist. The magic thinker may tyrannize the family with his fears and constant need for reassurance.

Because your magic thinker fears losing control of herself, she may try to control everything around her (including you). Because her fears limit the things she can do, extra demands may be made on the people sharing her life. Because she often lies to hide the extent of her problem, she will frequently try to manipulate people and situations in order to get her needs met rather than make direct requests or demands.

To understand why a magic thinker is sometimes so difficult to live with, it's necessary to know what she is thinking and feeling.

THE first time Barbara was to meet her in-laws-to-be she was no more than ten feet inside the door when she saw the cat. She screamed, ran out to the car, and sat there sobbing hysterically. "For God's sake, it's only a cat," Mark said. "She doesn't even have any claws!"

Mark was seeing the family's five-year-old cat, who spent most of her life sitting on laps purring. But Barbara was seeing an inner scene of the cat leaping to her face and chewing and clawing her eyes out. Along with this scene came the feeling of terror—rapid heartbeat, wobbly legs, dry mouth, dizziness—and an urgent need to escape from the source of the terror.

Barbara had been phobic of cats for as long as she could re-

member. Mark came from the kind of family that picked up
and cared for stray cats and dogs and caught mice in humane
traps so they could release them unharmed in fields or woods.
When Barbara heard that Mark's parents had three cats in per-
manent residence, she flatly refused to visit. She claimed that
cats were creepy, dirty, and dangerous. Mark, who grew up
hugging and sleeping with cats the way other little kids do
teddy bears, was confused and angry with Barbara's irrationality.

THE first thing that an effective supporting person must understand is that the magic thinker really believes that the object or situation is dangerous. Barbara had heard of diseases carried in cat feces, of cat scratches getting terribly infected; this
was incontrovertible proof to her that any contact with a cat
was dangerous. A magic thinker needs 100 percent assurance;
to them, even the tiniest percent of a chance of disaster means
that disaster is inevitable. Barbara didn't think she was being
irrational; she thought that she was being sensible in avoiding
a dangerous situation. The woman who makes her family re-
move all their clothes before they come into the house really
believes that she is keeping them safe from dangerous contamination.

The supporting person needs to help the magic thinker reality test. Mark pointed out to Barbara that he and his family
regularly got ill from other people but never contracted a cat-
generated disease. Although the cats might scratch if their play
got too spirited, they never intentionally scratched or bit.

Barbara was better able to assess reality when she was well
removed from cats, but because she was "sensitized," encountering a real live cat instantly created the disturbing physical
sensations of terror and the overwhelming sense of doom or

disaster. She felt that she had to rid herself of the sensations because the sensations themselves seemed to be dangerous. Mark had to help Barbara reality test not just the actual danger potential of the cats but also the thought that the sensations brought on by the fear were dangerous.

Mark was an effective supporting person, because although his initial response was "It's only a cat," he made the effort to find out how Barbara was viewing the situation and to discover her inner scene of disaster, then patiently helped her to reality test and gradually to expose herself to the cats.

THE second important objective for an effective supporting person is to help plan exposure tasks with the magic thinker. The tasks should be agreed upon by both the supporting person and the magic thinker. The purposes of the exposure practice are to create enough anxiety to stimulate the catastrophic thinking, thereby providing an opportunity to reality test, and to desensitize the magic thinker to the physical sensations of anxiety.

For the exposure tasks Mark enlisted the aid of his family. The family put all but the most placid of the cats in the basement. First Mark's mother and then Mark would hold the cat while Barbara got used to having the cat in the same room. Eventually she was able to pet it while it sat on their laps. Then they let another cat into the room, and Barbara became accustomed to having the cats rub against her or jump into her lap. During this time when Barbara felt the anxiety sensations, she would tell Mark that her heart was beating fast and that she felt dizzy or light-headed, and he would remind her that they were normal sensations of anxiety, they weren't dangerous, and they would abate as soon as she shifted attention away from them.

By the time Mark and Barbara were married several months

later, none of the cats had to be banished to the basement when Barbara visited. On their six-month anniversary Barbara surprised Mark with a kitten of their own.

Mark was an unusually effective support person. He understood how inner scenes of disaster can make even the most benign situations terrifying, because about a year prior to his meeting Barbara I had worked with him on his phobia of tunnels. He knew how important it was to be patient and gently insistent that Barbara continue with the graduated exposure tasks. He recognized that Barbara's irrational behavior came from her fear and wasn't an attempt to manipulate or control him.

HOW TO HELP YOUR MAGIC THINKER

Here are some general techniques for being an effective supporting person.

Establish a Sound Working Relationship

An effective supporting person understands the problem from the magic thinker's point of view and demonstrates that understanding to him. A sound working relationship between the supporting person and the magic thinker is the pivotal factor affecting the pace and extent to which the magic thinker will be willing to subject himself to the feared situation.

The effective supporting person always demonstrates respect and understanding for the magic thinker's thoughts and feelings. Settings viewed as innocuous by the supporting person may be seen as fraught with danger by the magic thinker. Unless the magic thinker feels secure with the supporting person—feels that the supporting person understands his feelings, knows what she is doing and will be able to help control the anticipated panic, and, above all, is dependable—the magic thinker will resist exposure to the feared situation.

The magic thinker may be uncomfortable sharing all of his fearful imagining. He may be worried about incurring ridicule, disapproval, or rejection by the supporting person. Often the magic thinker is too anxious or frightened to discuss the problem because discussing it seems to make it more real; he may give only partial information until trust is established.

The magic thinker may fear that he is weird, crazy (or about to become so), or out of control. It is important for the supporting person to know that magic thinkers who suffer from anxiety disorders often have such thoughts or feelings. It may appear that your magic thinker is being difficult or uncooperative, but keep in mind how formidable discussing one's worst imaginings can be.

Assume nothing! We often think we know how people feel—and we are often wrong. Learn to communicate using the anxiety scale so that when your magic thinker tells you that she is nervous, you know exactly how nervous on a scale from 0 to 10. Together write up a "fear survey" of possible anxiety-producing situations to which your magic thinker can respond by quantifying, on a scale of 0 to 10, the amount of anxiety that each situation might produce.

Educate Yourself and Your Magic Thinker about the Problem

A recent study by the National Institutes of Mental Health has found that anxiety disorders (including phobias and obsessive-compulsive disorders) are the most common groups of psychiatric disorders in the United States. The person who suffers from them has millions of fellow sufferers who experience the same distress.

Anxiety is the response of the safety-alert system built into us (and all other animals). The Neanderthal person who unexpectedly encountered a saber-toothed tiger in the forest recognized danger. Her safety-alert system instantly made her heart beat faster, her eyes dilate, her hands and legs quiver with excitement. These effects increased her normal strength and stamina so that she would be able to deal with the tiger—either to fight or to run like crazy (the "fight or flight" response). It is an appropriate response to a threatening situation. The physical sensations—rapid heartbeat, dry mouth, light-headedness—are all a normal, healthy response to a possible danger. *They are not dangerous!*

A problem arises when a realistic assessment of the situation is not made and the magic thinker anticipates danger where in actuality there is none. The anticipation or sense of danger comes from thoughts or images. When a person thinks she is in danger, the physical sensations instantly follow. When the thoughts or images are changed, the physical sensations abate.

Get facts that relate to your magic thinker's problem. Know how elevators work. Know that if a product says "poison" on the label, that means it's poisonous to drink; it doesn't mean that it exudes poisonous ether that contaminates everything around it. Know how many minutes it takes to drive through a particular tunnel or over a bridge. If you will be working on public transportation, know the bus routes and how long it takes to get from point to point. Know the probability of dying in a plane crash or of encountering a poisonous snake. Obviously this will require a lot of research on your part, but it will be of enormous importance in working with your magic thinker.

To help your magic thinker become aware of the thought/feeling connection, teach him to quantify the anxiety on a scale of 0 to 10, with 10 being the worst panic he has ever experienced and 0 being no anxiety at all. By monitoring the anxiety level, being aware of the changes, and recalling the thinking or images just prior to an increase, your magic thinker can identify the source of the anxiety and reality test the thinking. The anxiety scale also provides a tool for measuring and assessing the degree of discomfort as well as a specific means of communicating his feelings.

Although there is a difference of opinion as to the effect of diet and exercise on anxiety, it is clear that some things make most people feel bad. I always recommend that people eat nutritious food, get regular exercise, and learn a relaxing breathing technique. Overdoing nicotine, caffeine, alcohol, and sugar will probably cause feelings of shakiness, dry mouth, and rapid heartbeat—all those sensations that are so disturbing to a magic thinker. It is well known that regular exercise relieves depression and enhances a sense of well-being.

When anxious, most people either hyperventilate (take short, rapid breaths) or hold their breath. In either case changes in body chemistry occur that may cause a sense of breathlessness, rapid heartbeat, dizziness, blurred vision, numbness, and tingling in the hands and feet. A breathing exercise will help to counteract these sensations. Probably the easiest to do and to remember is to breathe out to the count of six, breathe in to the count of four.

This is effective because when anxious, most people inhale more than they exhale, which leaves the person feeling as though they can't get a satisfying breath—and indeed, they're not, because the lungs are never completely emptied and the exchange of air is minimal. Just be sure not to count so fast that the exercise becomes another form of hyperventilation.

COLLABORATE ON A PROGRAM FOR THE *IN VIVO* PRACTICE SESSION

By establishing a hierarchy of feared objects and/or situations, you will be able to clarify which situations lend themselves to immediate in vivo tasks and which are so anxiety-producing that they will have to be approached gradually. Remember, you may not have complete or accurate information at this time. Often a magic thinker initially will give only as much information as she thinks other people (or herself) can handle. She will divulge more information as trust and confidence develop.

List all situations that your magic thinker finds anxiety-producing on a scale from 0 to 10, with 10 being the most difficult. If there are many situations (bridges, tunnels, public transportation, elevators, snakes, dirt, wide streets, and so on), choose just one on which to start work immediately.

Examine the list of anxiety-producing situations. If the supermarket rates a 4 and an elevator an 8, normally you would start with the supermarket—unless your magic thinker lives on the twenty-sixth floor. In that case you have to start with the elevator. The magic thinker may want to start with public transportation so that she can get to work, but if she can't cross the street to get to the bus, that would not be the best starting point.

Once you have agreed upon a starting point with your magic thinker, develop a hierarchy of difficulty with that situation. For example, a person who fears crossing wide streets may have this hierarchy:

> four lanes, with two-way traffic, no stop light
> and so forth
> four lanes, with two-way traffic, and stop lights
> four lanes, with one-way traffic, no stop light

four lanes, with one-way traffic and stop lights
three lanes, with one-way traffic, no stop light
three lanes, with one-way traffic and stop lights

Start with the one that seems easiest to your magic thinker. Remember, a magic thinker is convinced that encountering the feared situation will cause irreparable harm to his physical or psychic well-being. The supporting person's function is to help the magic thinker question and test this conviction by reality testing:

1. Elicit specific thoughts or images of the anticipated catastrophe.
2. Help your magic thinker assess whether her view of the "danger" is accurate or probable.
3. Help her assess whether her reaction to the danger is appropriate.
4. Help the magic thinker examine assumptions, rules, or beliefs that may be self-defeating.
5. Help her assess her abilities to cope with the danger.

Develop Distraction Techniques

Distraction techniques will not "cure" magic thinking, but they will effectively bring down the level of anxiety and demonstrate the effect that thoughts have on anxiety. A good distraction technique will contradict the cognitive distortion as well as change the focus of attention.

In order to contradict loss of mental function (the feeling of going crazy):

Count backward from 100 by 3s or 7s.
Do multiplication problems.

Do anagrams or other word puzzles.
Tell a joke.
Play electronic hand games.

Contradict loss of physical function (the feeling of being about to faint or collapse):

Do breathing exercises, sing, hum.
Do knee bends.
Do isometric exercises.
Tap feet on the ground.

Contradict loss of physical presence (the feeling of unreality or not existing):

Thump umbrella, cane, or bag on the ground.
Ask passerby the time or for directions.
Focus on a single point and walk toward it.

When people are feeling very high levels of anxiety, it is hard for them not to get caught up in catastrophic thinking. Help your magic thinker make a series of realistic statements on three-x-five index cards based on his own experiences. The cards may read something like this:

"I have often felt this way, but I have never lost control."

"My legs have often felt very wobbly, but I have never fallen."

"My heart has frequently pounded like this, but I have never had a heart attack."

"I have felt dizzy and disoriented before, but I have never fainted."

Suggest that the magic thinker carry these cards when he practices on his own and, if he gets to that point when the mind seems to go blank and he can't remember what it is he is supposed to think, he can pull the cards out of his pocket and read them.

A "safety kit" can also be helpful. It may contain the "safety cards," a can of fruit juice or soda, a radio, a word puzzle book, a relaxation tape, medication, name and address, and the name and phone number of his doctor.

COMMITTING YOURSELF

Many excellent helping intentions have been dashed because a realistic appraisal of the problem wasn't made and reasonable limitations weren't established in the beginning. Before you decide to commit yourself to this mission, recognize that it may be a long-term project. Assess your own position: will you really be able to put aside at least one hour a week for maybe a year or more to work with your magic thinker? The time you schedule to be a supporting person must be devoted to your magic thinker—it can't be used to also walk the dog or run errands.

Are you free enough from fears and obsessions that you will be able to confidently work in vivo with your magic thinker? If you do magic thinking of your own about pervasive contamination and elevator dangers, it is not likely that you will be an effective reality tester.

Setting limitations can be difficult, but it's absolutely necessary. Your magic thinker must agree to a limited amount of time to devote to her problem. That means that although you are a supporting person, your magic thinker doesn't have the right to demand that her problems take precedence over your shared activities or that she has the right to call you any hour of the day or night when anxiety strikes. Nothing can sour a helping relationship faster than unceasing demands made upon the helper.

Remember that your job as a supporting person is to help your magic thinker stay grounded in reality and to assess physical sensations accurately. In order to do this, it is vitally important for you to be honest, dependable, and knowledgeable about the anxiety-producing situations.

Once you have come to an agreement on how to work, stick to it unless your magic thinker wants to change it. Never use trickery! If you have agreed to keep all the cats in the basement, don't suddenly tell your magic thinker that one of the cats is actually sitting on the windowsill.

Here are a few hints I think you will find helpful in your role of supporting person:

1. *Assume Nothing.* Ask questions. Your magic thinker is the only source for facts about what he is thinking and feeling.

2. *Stay Calm.* A panic attack can be very dramatic. If you respond with anxiety, your magic thinker will accept that as confirmation that something really is wrong.

3. *Acknowledge Facts.* "Yes, this elevator is small." "Yes, the bridge is very high." If you underplay the reality, your magic thinker may feel that either you are out of touch with reality yourself or that you are being manipulative.

4. *Be Specific.* Know your facts, use neutral descriptions, and don't use metaphors. ("The elevator is about four feet by six feet with wood-paneled walls, a stainless steel rail all around, a tan rug, and medium-bright lighting.")

5. *Be Creative.* Think of original ways to approach the problem. If your magic thinker has difficulty walking away from the house, is it easier if he walks backward keeping the house in view?

6. *Be Flexible.* Expect the unexpected with in vivo work, and be prepared to use it to advantage. ("Who would have thought that there would be a robbery at the bank while we were standing across the street? But notice how your anxiety level dropped with all the excitement.")

There are many correct ways to help people. An experienced therapist will see several possible approaches in addition to the ones I have illustrated. When working in vivo with magic thinkers, I try to stay right in the moment and repeat her own words for reassessment. Because it is difficult for most people to concentrate while they are very anxious, I am as parsimonious with words as possible, and I review and assign homework and give information (how many minutes between subway stops, and so on) in non-anxiety-producing locations. Always communicate important information about the situation before going into it, and recap the experience after you have retreated to a "safe place."

In the beginning it will be very difficult for your magic thinker to make the connection between thoughts and feelings. It will be even harder for him to accept the fact that the sensations aren't dangerous. As the work progresses and he has more control over his panic, the initiating thoughts will be easier to identify and the sensations will become less frightening. Setbacks will occur. By reminding your magic thinker that progress is the result of learning and that learning isn't lost, you will help your magic thinker weather setbacks.

Being a supporting person can be physically and emotionally draining, but I believe that you will find that understanding your magic thinker and helping her to attain a life free of crippling fears will be one of the most rewarding experiences of your life.

CHAPTER SEVENTEEN

WHAT ABOUT MEDICATION?

IN the early 1980s there were regular shoot-outs between the promedication and the antimedication contingents at the annual conferences of the Phobia Society of America (now the Anxiety Disorders Association of America). Over the past several years the two contingents have stopped shooting and recently have actually been known to cooperate with one another. Current thinking is that the combination of medication and cognitive/behavioral therapy is the most successful treatment for OCD and anxiety disorders. One reason for this development is the relatively recent availability of drugs that effectively treat these conditions with few negative side effects.

Still, attitudes about medication vary wildly. Some people just want to take a pill and have all the bad feelings go away. Others resist medication, thinking that pills are just a crutch. To those people I say yes, they are a crutch, but if you had a broken leg, you'd be foolish not to use a crutch, and when you don't need the crutch any longer, you throw the crutch away.

Many of the people I work with have been referred to me by doctors or psychiatrists who are treating them with medication and also want them to have the benefits of cognitive/behavioral therapy. Other clients are phobic of medication and have refused to take it, even though they have been advised to. Still others have been on the fence about medication and have decided to explore it as an adjunct to the cognitive/behavioral work they do with me.

Even the person who is all too willing to use pills to make bad feelings go away should give careful thought (and get good advice) before using an antianxiety agent ("tranquilizer" is an obsolete term; the newer antianxiety agents don't really tranquilize; they keep a cap on anxiety). All medications can have negative side effects. Which medications to take and when and how to take them should be thoroughly explored with a doctor knowledgeable in psychiatric medication.

WHEN TO CONSIDER MEDICATION

Generally speaking, if a person has been in a cognitive/behavioral treatment program for a couple of months and seriously doing the work (keeping a diary and doing the homework assignments) but not experiencing any improvement or possibly feeling worse, it is time to think about medication. Or if the anxiety levels are so high that the person is not able to concentrate clearly, she will be more successful if she starts a medication program before she begins to do the cognitive/behavioral work.

Often people feel more secure doing the in vivo work just knowing that they have an antianxiety agent in their bag or pocket, even though they may never use it. One woman I worked with carried Valium with her for years, and when she got too anxious on the subway she dug around in her bag until she found it, struggled to get the cap off, shook a pill out onto her hand, then licked it, put it back in her bag, and felt instantly better, even though the medication could not possibly have had time to work.

WHAT MEDICATION TO TAKE

This section is intended only as a general overview of available medication. All medication must be taken under the direction of a medical doctor who has a through knowledge of psychiatric drugs.

BENZODIAZEPINES

Benzodiazepines are the most commonly prescribed psychiatric medication. Currently the most popular of the benzodiazepines is Xanax, which has replaced Valium in popularity. Other frequently prescribed benzodiazepines are Klonopin, Tranxene, Ativan, Serax, Centrax, and Paxipam. These medications can be taken on an "as needed" basis. The antianxiety effects can be felt within minutes, although extremely anxious people may have to take a medication regularly over a period of time before experiencing relief from anxiety. However, 30 to 35 percent of those who try it will not experience any benefit, and there is no way of predicting who will and who will not benefit from the medication. Often people will take a benzodiazepine only occasionally to reduce discomfort before entering situations they expect to be anxiety-producing.

The benzodiazepines should not be used over a long period of time (more than four or six weeks), since a dependency may develop. Terminating the use of a benzodiazepine should always be done by gradually reducing the dosage. Withdrawal symptoms may include all those unpleasant feelings and sensations that led to the use of the medication in the first place.

Possible side effects of benzodiazepines may include:

Drowsiness—usually noticeable during the first few days of taking the medication. If the symptoms persist, consider lowering the dosage or switching to a different medication.

Impaired coordination—driving or operating heavy equipment could be hazardous; it can be doubly dangerous because people who experience this side effect don't always realize that their coordination is impaired and fail to use proper caution.

Impaired memory and concentration—it appears that benzodiazepines negatively affect short-term memory. Some people even experience a type of amnesia in which they completely forget spans of time.

Muscular weakness—people complain of their legs feeling so heavy they can hardly walk up hills or steps, or an inability to lift things or to participate in normal activities like dancing or hiking.

Many of these problems completely disappear when the medication is stopped. Most of these side effects can be reduced by lowering the dose or switching to a different member of the benzodiazepine family. A few people have had extremely negative responses to a benzodiazepine. If you suddenly experience intense feelings of anger, rage, hostility, depression, anxiety, irritability, or severe insomnia, contact your doctor immediately.

There are two main drawbacks to the use of benzodiazepines: one is the possibility for dependency; the other is the potentially dangerous interaction with alcohol and certain other drugs.

BUSPIRONE (BUSPAR)

For people who find the side effects of the benzodiazepines un-acceptable or are not good candidates for the medication be-cause of a history of substance abuse or medical contraindica-tions, BuSpar may be a good alternative. BuSpar doesn't impair coordination, cause short-term memory loss, or interact dan-gerously with alcohol. There is little potential for overdose or dependency, and therefore it may be used over a longer period of time. However, the antianxiety effects may not be felt for one to three weeks after one begins taking BuSpar, so it can't be taken on an "as needed" basis. Also, it isn't possible to switch from a benzodiazepine to BuSpar; the benzodiazepine must first be discontinued through gradual tapering off before tak-ing BuSpar.

BETA-BLOCKERS

These drugs are most effective for social phobias and perfor-mance anxiety. They tend to lessen the physical sensations of anxiety (the rapid heartbeat, dry mouth, shaky hands and legs, nausea, etc.) that are so formidable for a performer. Again, there is a dangerous interaction between alcohol and beta blockers, and they are contraindicated for people who suffer from cer-tain medical problems. The most popular beta-blocker is pro-pranolol (Inderal).

TRICYCLIC ANTIDEPRESSANTS

For many years the medications most prescribed for anxi-ety and panic disorder were the tricyclic antidepressants (Elavil, Triavil, Tofranil, and since 1990, Clomipramine). Clomipramine (Anafranil) was one of the first drugs to show real promise in controlling the severe symptoms of obsessive-compulsive disorder. However, not everyone benefited, and many people found the side effects of the medications too distressing. Immediately upon the heels of Clomipramine came a whole new development in medications for panic and obsessive-compulsive disorders—selective serotonin reuptake inhibitors (see below).

MONOAMINE OXIDASE INHIBITORS (MAO INHIBITORS)

MAO inhibitors (Nardil, Parnate, and Marplan) were introduced in the early 60s and found to be effective in controlling the symptoms of depression and panic disorder, but because of potentially dangerous interactions with some foods and other medications they were used less often than the tricyclics. In recent years the MAO inhibitors have been pretty much supplanted by the serotonin reuptake inhibitors, described below. However, they may still be prescribed for people who find these medications either ineffective or who find the side effects to be intolerable.

SELECTIVE SEROTONIN REUPTAKE INHIBITORS

These are unrelated the tricyclic and tetracyclic medications previously used for depression, anxiety, and obsessive-compulsive disorders, and most people find that they are more effective and have fewer side effects. Researchers have found a correlation between low levels of the neurotransmitter, serotonin, and depression and anxiety in some people. The selective serotonin reuptake inhibitors work by not allowing the serotonin to flow into the nerve endings thereby maintaining higher levels of it in the spaces around the nerve endings in the brain. Currently the serotonin reuptake inhibitors are the medications most frequently prescribed for obsessive-compulsive behavior and panic disorder. They are Prozac, Zoloft, and Paxil.

   Prozac was the first of this group to become available, and
it was greeted with a great deal of publicity. In 1993 *Listening
to Prozac* made the best-seller list, and its author, Peter Kramer,
was heard on talk shows across the country extolling the virtues
of Prozac. In the book Kramer described the transformation of
a dull, shy, unattractive woman into an outgoing, interesting,
attractive person. The message was, "Prozac can fix whatever
is wrong with you." As result, Prozac was prescribed for depression, anxiety, phobias, obsessive-compulsive disorders,
panic disorder, eating disorders, addictive behavior, low self-
esteem, PMS, and other difficulties.
   Zoloft and Paxil followed shortly after the introduction of
Prozac. The newest addition to the selective serotonin reuptake
inhibitors is Luvox. Each of these drugs varies slightly in its
makeup, and if one doesn't alleviate the symptoms or pro-
duces intolerable side effects, taking another may be more successful. Currently it appears that Luvox is the most effective in
relieving the symptoms of OCD without quite as many side effects as Clomipramine.
   Do medications really work? Yes, for many people they do,
but many others find that they can't tolerate the side effects, or
the symptoms still occur. All of the serotonin reuptake inhibitors are long-acting medications and must be taken for
two to six weeks before the beneficial effects are felt. The most
common side effects include headache, anxiety, nervousness,
sleeplessness, drowsiness, tiredness, weakness, tremors, sweating, dizziness, decreased sex drive, and dry mouth. With Luvox
the major side effect is nausea. Studies have found that 15 percent of people taking serotonin reuptake inhibitors stopped because of the side effects. The relatively high dropout rate is
probably due to the fact that the benefits of the medication
aren't felt for weeks after initially taking it, but the negative side
effects are felt almost immediately.
   Medication may make your recovery faster and/or easier, but

all medications can have serious side effects. If you are considering medication, be sure to see a doctor who is knowledgeable about psychiatric drugs, and have a complete physical (people with medical problems have to be especially
careful). And give your doctor complete information about the
following:

If you are under the care of any other doctor, and why
All medication taken on a regular basis
All nonprescription medications regularly used
Any allergic reactions you've had to food or drugs
If you are on a special diet or taking vitamin or mineral sup-
plements
Your tobacco, alcohol, and recreational drug use
If you are nursing, pregnant, or planning to get pregnant

Discuss with your doctor the medication he or she is pre-
scribing for you. Ask questions, including these:

What is its name? (Write it down.)
Why this particular medication—what are its pluses and mi-
nuses?
What are the possible side effects?
How should it be taken—before meals, after meals, morn-
ing or night?
What should you do if you forget to take it on time?
Should you avoid any foods or beverages? (alcohol is always
contraindicated with these medications)
Can the prescription be refilled without seeing the doctor?

Medication can make your progress a lot easier, but you
must be an informed and discriminating consumer.

APPENDIXES

APPENDIX 1

GLOSSARY

Anxiety Level Anxiety is quantified on a scale from 0 to 10 with 10 being the worst anxiety you've ever experienced and 0 being no anxiety. Anxious people tend to think that their anxiety has no end, that it will spiral up and up to infinity, but it doesn't; it has a peak, and the peak is number 10.

Automatic Reaction This is a reaction that occurs without any conscious effort on your part. It is the physical response (rapid heartbeat, wobbly legs, difficulty in breathing, dizziness, dry mouth, etc.) that results from a threat of danger. Because the danger threat isn't immediately obvious, the phobic person thinks the physical symptoms come "out of the blue."

Automatic Thoughts These are thoughts that pop into the mind without conscious effort, thoughts such as "I'm in danger!"

Belief System This is a person's personal theory of who she or he is and how the world works. It is so deep and innate that the person assumes that it is a universal truth and can't conceive of questioning it.

Catastrophic Thinking Thinking that leads a person to immediately fear the worst possible scenario without any factual indication that a catastrophe is likely.

Cause-and-Effect Reasoning Turning the switch on the lamp closes the electric circuit, which sends electricity into the bulb, heating the element and thereby creating light. Turning the switch is the cause; illumination is the effect. Faulty cause-and-effect reasoning says that knocking on wood will keep something bad from happening.

Cognitive Distortion Cognition means "to know," or the act or process of knowing. In this book the word is used interchangeably with "thoughts." Cognitive distortions are false assessments of reality, such as "I can't function anymore," when in fact the person is functioning but maybe at a slightly reduced level.

Compulsion An irresistible need to perform an act (such as washing hands, checking, counting). The compulsion follows an obsession and is performed to relieve the anxiety caused by the obsession. (See Obsession.)

Desensitize To make less sensitive by gradual exposure to the feared object or situation.

Exposure Encountering the feared object or situation.

Hyperventilate Breathing by taking very short, very rapid breaths. Hyperventilating is the cause of many of the disturbing physical sensations experienced during a panic attack.

Imaginal Exposure This is a method of desensitizing by relaxing very deeply and imagining yourself in the phobic situation.

Inner Scene Many people think by seeing pictures or whole scenes in their mind. These are quick visual flashes of imagined or actual past occurrences that are experienced too quickly to be accompanied by words.

In Vivo In vivo means "in life." Working in vivo (or in vivo exposure) means going into the feared situation (a public bathroom, the bus, or supermarket) or encountering the contaminated object (a can of insecticide or a cat).

Magic Thinking The abandonment of rational thinking and cause-and-effect reasoning in favor of superstitions, hunches, and misleading beliefs.

Obsession A thought or idea that forces itself into consciousness. It is usually a frightening or forbidden thought that repeats itself again and again seemingly against the will of the person experiencing it.

Obsessive-Compulsive Disorder (OCD) A condition manifesting itself as a combination of disturbing, repetitious thoughts that create intolerable anxiety and can only be relieved by performing an act such as washing the hands, repeatedly opening and closing a door, ritualistically repeating a litany, and so on.

Panic Attack An episode of overwhelming anxiety characterized by a rapid heartbeat, shortness of breath, sweating, trembling dizziness, and/or fear of dying or going crazy.

Phobia An exaggerated and often disabling fear of an object or situation unrelated to any realistic danger. The fear often leads to avoidance and panic attacks.

Reality Test OCD and phobic fears are based on cognitive distortions (thoughts make things happen, contamination is contagious, etc.) Examining the distortion and questioning the accuracy of it is reality testing.

Rituals Repetitive acts that must be continued until the person feels that they've been done exactly right or is exhausted. Performed as a part of an obsessive-compulsive disorder.

APPENDIX 2

SELF-HELP WORKSHEETS

YOU NEED to do more than just think about getting better; you must do the work. These worksheets serve several purposes: They guide your work, clarify your thoughts, and provide an invaluable history of your progress.

You'll need more of some sheets than others. Copy as many of them as you need. Some people find it easier to work with a single sheet at a time, but others prefer to keep them in a three-ring binder. Be sure to date them so you have an accurate record.

See Chapter 15 for examples of worksheets and how they can help you.

DAILY DIARY

Make an entry into the Daily Diary every time you experience an increase in your anxiety level.

People have a tendency to remember the worst and will report that they were anxious all day, but when they keep an actual account of their anxiety levels, they often discover that they really had only two or three episodes of anxiety. The Daily Diary will also help you to recognize your anxiety-producing thoughts.

For the first week or two you may have a hard time filling in an actually rational "Rational Response." Don't worry about it; it will come with practice.

Make many of these, and keep the diary throughout the work.

DATE

TIME DATE	ANXIETY LEVEL	ACTIVITY	THOUGHTS	RATIONAL RESPONSE

HIERARCHY CHART

The Hierarchy Chart will help you get started. The first item on the list should be the most difficult thing you can imagine. If your fear is cats, it might be petting a cat. Then reduce the difficulty so that your list looks like this:

1. Petting a cat
2. Having a cat sit near me
3. A cat walking around the room
4. Someone else holding a cat
5. Knowing a cat is in the house
6. Knowing a cat is in the basement with the door closed

You may need only one Hierarchy Chart, but if there are several objects or situations that create anxiety, make a chart for each one.

DATE

1.

2.

3.

4.

5.

6.

7.

8.

9.

10.

TASK SHEET

If you have only one object or situation that creates anxiety, you won't need a Task Sheet. However, if you have filled out several Hierarchy Charts, you will need a Task Sheet to know where to start your exposure excercises.

List the least anxiety-producing items from your Hierarchy Charts. You may be able to work on several simultaneously.

DATE

1.

2.

3.

4.

5.

6.

7.

8.

9.

10.

DEGREE OF COMMITMENT

If you find that you are having a hard time getting yourself into the exposure exercises, it may be because you haven't assessed the items on the Hierarchy Charts accurately.

The "What Will Happen?" is the anticipation of what will happen if the action or ritual is not done.

Start with items on your Hierarchy Chart where the commitment to the anticipated dire outcome is lower than 50 percent, and you'll find that the exposure excercises will be much easier.

DATE ....

THOUGHT, OBJECT, OR SITUATION	WHAT WILL HAPPEN?	RITUAL OR ACTION	DEGREE OF COMMITMENT

EXPOSURE DIARY

You'll need many of these; they are the log of your in vivo work.

Most people find that the anticipation of doing the task creates more anxiety than the actual task itself. It may be necessary to repeat the task many times in order to convince yourself that you have mastered it.

DATE ....

TASK ....

DATE/ TIME	START ANXIETY LEVEL	END ANXIETY LEVEL

THOUGHT/CONSEQUENCE CHART

The purpose of this chart is to help you assess the reality of your anxiety-producing thoughts. As strange as it may seem, we often don't know why we feel the way we do.

Enter the initial anxiety-producing thought first, then the consequence of that thought. Enter the consequence of the thought on the next line and the consequence of that until you reach the "bottom line."

DATE

THOUGHT   CONSEQUENCE

RESOURCE GUIDE

BOOKS

Baer, L. *Getting Control: Overcoming Your Obsessions and Compulsions.* Boston, Mass.: Little, Brown, 1991.

Beck, Aaron, G. Emery, and Ruth Greenberg. *Anxiety Disorders and Phobias: A Cognitive Perspective.* New York: Basic Books, 1985.

Foa, E.B., and R. Wilson. *Stop Obsessing!* New York: Bantam Books, 1991.

Kernodle, W.D. *Panic Disorder: The Medical Point of View.* Rev. Ed. Richmond, Virginia: Cadmus Publishing, 1995.

McCullough, C., and R. Mann. *Managing Your Anxiety.* Los Angeles: Jeremy P. Tarcher, 1985.

Neziroglu, F., and J. Yaryura-Tobias. *Over and Over Again: Understanding Obsessive-Compulsive Disorder.* Lexington, Massachusetts: Lexington Books, 1991.

Rapoport, J. L. *The Boy Who Couldn't Stop Washing.* New York: E.P. Dutton, 1989.

Ross, J. *Triumph Over Fear.* New York: Bantam Books, 1994.

Steketee, G., and K. White. *When Once is Not Enough: Help for Obsessive Compulsives.* Oakland, California: New Harbinger Press, 1990.

Weekes, Claire. *Simple, Effective Treatment of Agoraphobia.* New York: Bantam Books, 1979.

Wilson, R. Reid. *Don't Panic—Taking Control of Anxiety Attacks.* New York: Harper & Row, 1986.

Young, J. E., and J. Klosko. *Reinventing Your Life: How to Break Free from Negative Life Patterns.* New York: E.P. Dutton, 1993.

Zal, H. M. *Panic Disorder: The Great Pretender.* New York: Insight Books, 1990.

NEWSLETTERS

ABIL Incorporated
1418 Lorraine Avenue
Richmond, VA 23227

Council On Anxiety Disorders
P.O. Box 17011
Winston-Salem, NC 27116

Encourage Newsletter
13610 North Scottsdale Road
Suite 10-126
Scottsdale, AZ 85245

NPAD News
1718 Burgundy Place
Suite B-S
Santa Rosa, CA 95403

P.M. News
White Plains Hospital Center Phobia Clinic
Davis Avenue at East Post Road
White Plains, NY 10601

WHERE TO FIND A THERAPIST

The following organizations maintain an up-to-date listing of therapists and support groups that treat anxiety and/or obsessive-compulsive disorders.

The Anxiety Disorders Association of America
6000 Executive Boulevard
Rockville, MD 20852

OC Foundation, Inc.
P.O. Box 70
Milford, CT 06460-0070

National Institutes of Mental Health
Call: 1-800-64-PANIC
FAX: 301-443-5158

When choosing a health-care professional to help you, be sure to ask if he or she will accompany you into anxiety-producing situations or will come to your house. The NIMH suggests asking these additional questions:

How many patients with panic disorder have you treated?
Do you have any special training in panic disorder treatment?
What is your basic approach to treatment—cognitive behavioral therapy, medication, or both? If you provide only one type of treatment, how do I get the other if I need it?
How long is a typical course of treatment?
How frequent are treatment sessions? How long does each session last?
What are your fees?
Can you help me determine whether my health insurance will cover this?

Self-help support groups are an important source of aid. To find a support group near you, contact:

American Self-help Clearinghouse
St. Clares-Riverside Medical Center
Denville, NJ 07834

(201) 625-7101

INDEX

adrenaline, 164, 166
agoraphobia, 19–21, 79
  anticipation of anxiety as cause
    of anxiety, 67
  avoidance behavior, 65–66
  development of agoraphobic
    condition, 63–66
  home, refusal to leave, 62–63,
    66–67
  information processing and,
    60–61
  isolation, sense of, 65
  magic thinking, 75
  mild and extreme forms, 60
  panic attacks, 58–60, 61–62,
    64–65, 69
  reality testing, 69
  relationships and, 74–76
  safe or unsafe qualities credited
    to people and places, 60

  secrets and, 71–73
  sensations, fear of, 65
  therapy for, 66–81
  vulnerability, sense of, 60,
    64–65
  women as victims, 74
Al case study, 221–25
alcohol abuse, 29, 80–81
  bridge phobia, 116, 130–31
  driving phobia, 98, 103,
    104–5
Anafranil, 284–85
analytic therapy, 211
anger:
  bathing compulsion and, 146
  bridge phobia and, 120
  driving phobia and, 105
anorexia nervosa, 133
antianxiety agents, *see*
  medication

anxiety, 10
  anticipation of anxiety as cause
    of, 67
  diet and exercise, effect of, 273
  quantification of (scale of anxi-
    ety), 23, 57, 243–44,
    245–46, 272–73
  worksheet for, 297
  as safety-alert system, 56–57,
    272
  see also panic attacks; thoughts
    accompanying anxiety
Anxiety Disorders Association of
  America, 211, 280
Ativan, 282
avoidance behavior, 234
  agoraphobia, 65–66
  bridge phobia, 117–18
  magic thinking and, 47–48

bad thoughts, *see* secrets
Barbara and Mark case study,
  267–70
bathing compulsion, 139, 140
  anger and, 146
  childhood experiences and,
    144–45
  days and times, magical qualities
    of, 147–48
  diary keeping, 153
  goal setting, 158
  personal space and, 156–57
  rituals and litanies, 151, 153
  schoolwork and, 145–46
  therapy for, 147–60, 252–53
  time spent bathing, 146, 157,
    159
bathroom use, 144–45
Beck, Aaron T., 27
belief systems, 15, 41–44

benzodiazepines, 282–83
beta-blockers, 284
Boy Who Couldn't Stop Washing, The
  (Rapoport), 14–15
breathing exercises, 273
bridge phobia, 29
  alcohol abuse, 116, 130–31
  anger and, 120
  avoidance behavior, 117–18
  control, sense of loss of, 123–24,
    125–26
  diary keeping, 118–20, 129
  goal setting, 127–28
  management techniques, 121,
    127, 128–30
  origins of, 117, 118
  panic attacks, 114–16, 121–22,
    125–26
  supporting person and, 124–27,
    131
  therapy for, 116–31
  thoughts accompanying anxiety,
    122–24, 129–30
BuSpar, 284

case studies, 55–57
  see also specific cases
catastrophizing, 45
cat phobia, 267–70
cause-and-effect thinking, 15, 32,
  40, 42, 43, 209
  exposure of faulty thinking,
    236–37
Center for Cognitive Therapy, 10
Centrax, 282
certainty, need for, 46, 51, 182–83
change, process of, 231
cleaning compulsion, 21–22
  causes of anxiety, 92–93
  expectation of disaster, 89–91

magic thinking, 91–92
panic attacks, 85–86, 89, 92
reality testing, 86–88
responsibility, exaggerated sense
    of, 84, 85, 89, 91, 93–94
rituals, 94, 96
secrets, 92, 93, 96
therapy for, 82–91, 95–97
Clomipramine, 284–85
cognitive/behavioral therapy, 9, 10
medication and, 15, 280, 281
structure of, 150
see also in vivo therapy
cognitive distortions, 45
*Cognitive Therapy and the Emotional
    Disorders* (Beck), 27
collecting compulsion, 177–79
accumulation of possessions,
    179–80
anxiety accompanying disposal
    of items, 182–83, 184–88,
    190, 195
diary keeping, 188
Dumont's childhood experience
    with, 176–77
Exposure Diary, 258–59
goal setting, 190–91, 194
"housecleaning" efforts, 180
reality testing, 186–88, 256–58,
    260
"rejection by therapist" issue,
    193–94
rituals, 185
social phobia and, 180–81,
    188–90, 192–93, 195,
    260–63
therapy for, 181–95, 255–60
Commitment Chart, 246, 251,
    253
sample worksheet, 299

commitment to the belief, assess-
    ment of, 246–47, 251–52,
    253
compulsions, 50–51
see also obsessive-compulsive
    disorders
contamination concerns, *see*
    bathing compulsion; eating
    phobia
Contextual Therapy, *see* in vivo
    therapy
control, sense of loss of, 44
bridge phobia, 123–24, 125–26
eating phobia, 139
public-speaking phobia, 163–64
snake phobia, 208
couple therapy, 73–81
crisis situations, 95
cure issue, 56–57

daily diary, *see* diary keeping
David case study, 161–75
days and times, magical qualities
    of, 147–48
dead bodies, concern about, 98,
    102–3, 104, 106, 108,
    111–13
Diagnostic and Statistical Manual-IV
    (DSM Four), 28
diary keeping:
bathing compulsion, 153
bridge phobia, 118–20, 129
collecting compulsion, 188
driving phobia, 107–8, 254–55
public-speaking phobia, 170
risks of, 188
sample worksheet, 296
therapeutic role of, 241–42
see also Exposure Diary
diet, 273

Dirty Donnie, 33
distraction techniques, 275–77
driving phobia:
  alcohol abuse, 98, 103, 104–5
  anger and, 105
  dead bodies, concern about, 98,
    102–3, 104, 106, 108,
    111–13
  diary keeping, 107–8, 254–55
  hitting animals and people,
    concern about, 98–102,
    109–10
  photo scrapbook technique,
    108–9, 110, 113
  powerlessness, sense of, 110
  reality testing, 254–55
  therapy for, 103–13, 253–55
  two people, sense of being,
    110–11, 113
drug treatment, *see* medication
Dumont, Raeann, 9–10
  collecting compulsion, adoles-
    cent experience with,
    176–77
  hand-washing compulsion,
    31–34, 35
  impetigo in childhood, 31–32
  "inner scene" experience, 26–27
  in vivo therapy, training in, 23
dust phobia, 34–35

eating phobia:
  control, sense of loss of, 139
  eating crusade to overcome,
    137–39, 141–42
  family issues and, 139–40,
    142–43
  panic attacks, 138–39
  poisoning, fear of, 133, 134,
    136–37, 139, 140

  reality testing, 136, 140–42
  responsibility, exaggerated sense
    of, 141
  therapy for, 132–43
  thoughts accompanying anxiety,
    136, 137
Einstein, Albert, 41
either/or thinking, 45, 153, 171
Elavil, 284
elevator phobia, 221–25
embarrassment concerns, 167–69,
  170–71
emotional reasoning, 45
Epictetus, 29
exercise, 273
Exposure Diary, 239
  collecting compulsion, 258–59
  sample worksheet, 300
  snake phobia, 248–51
  social phobia, 261–62

family involvement in therapy,
  240–41
fears, 52
"fight or flight" response, 166,
  272
food phobia, *see* eating phobia
Frank case study, 214–17

genetic basis of obsessive-compulsive disorders, 143
goal setting:
  bathing compulsion, 158
  bridge phobia, 127–28
  collecting compulsion, 190–91,
    194
  short-term goals, focus on,
    231–32, 233–34, 243,
    259
Gracie case study, 144–60, 252–53

hand-washing compulsion, 31–34, 35
healing professionals, 230–31
Henny Penny story, 13–14
Hierarchy Chart, 297
hitting animals and people, concern about, 98–102, 109–10
hoarding compulsion, *see* collecting compulsion
Hughes, Howard, 38
hyperventilation, 273

ignoring the positive, 45
impetigo, 31–32
implosion therapy, 197
Inderal, 284
information about phobias and OCD, therapeutic importance of, 229–30
information processing, 27–28
    agoraphobia and, 60–61
inner scenes, 25–27, 123
inpatient therapy, 151
intellectualization, 154
in vivo therapy, 9, 22–23
    challenges of, 23–24, 183–84
    exposure of phobic object or situation, 36–37, 238–39, 269–70
    hierarchy of anxiety-producing situations, use of, 23
    information processing, focus on, 28
    training in, 23
isolation, sense of, 65

Janet case study, 98–113, 253–55
Jerry case study, 21–22, 82–97
Johanna case study, 212–14

Klonopin, 282
Kramer, Peter, 286

Lara case study, 217–21
Listening to Prozac (Kramer), 286
litanies, *see* rituals and litanies
Luvox, 286

magic thinking, 15, 39–40, 49–50
    agoraphobia and, 75
    avoidance behavior and, 47–48
    certainty, need for, 46
    cleaning compulsion and, 91–92
    cognitive distortions, 45
    contagion of harmful properties, 46
    control through, 44
    counter-magic strategies, 40–41
    defining characteristics, 14
    Henny Penny story, 13–14
    malady status, 14, 50, 52
    personal belief systems and, 41–44
    reality, doubts about, 44–45
    responsibility, exaggerated sense of, 47
    superstition and, 40, 41
    thoughts, belief in power of, 45–46
maladaptive behavior, 22
MAO inhibitors, 285
Marplan, 285
"mating game," misconceptions about, 192–93, 220–21
medication, 15, 151, 280–81
    benzodiazepines, 282–83
    beta-blockers, 284
    BuSpar, 284
    cognitive/behavioral therapy and, 15, 280, 281

medication (*continued*)
   MAO inhibitors, 285
   physician consultation about,
      287
   selective serotonin reuptake in-
      hibitors, 285–87
   side effects, 283, 286
   tricyclic antidepressants, 284–85
   when to consider medication,
      281–82
Melody, 39–41
memory retrieval, 43
Mr. More case study, 177–95,
   255–63
mysophobia, 34–35

Nardil, 285
National Institutes of Health, 14
National Institutes of Mental
      Health, 271
nervous breakdowns, 197, 199,
   203
Nora case study, 58–81
Norm case study, 29, 114–31

obsessions, 50
obsessive-compulsive disorders, 9
   common features of, 51–52, 234
   cycle of OC behavior, 185–86
   debilitating nature of, 36
   defining characteristics, 50–51
   erroneous premises of, 38
   hand-washing compulsion,
      31–34, 35
   as information processing prob-
      lem, 27–28
   as inherited condition, 143
   inner scenes, 25–27
   "label" perspective on, 22
   origins question, 55–56

phobia-OCD overlap, 28–29
possibility viewed as probability,
   206
prevalence of, 14
reality, questioning of, 182–83
thoughts accompanying anxiety,
   35–36
treatment for, *see* medication;
   therapy
uncertainty problem, 182–83
writings about, 14–15, 27
see also bathing compulsion;
   cleaning compulsion; collecting compulsion; magic
   thinking; rituals and litanies
OC Foundation, 211
origins question, 55–56
overgeneralizing, 45

panic attacks, 23, 76, 78, 79
   agoraphobia, 58–60, 61–62,
      64–65, 69
   bridge phobia, 114–16, 121–22,
      125–26
   cleaning compulsion, 85–86, 89,
      92
   eating phobia, 138–39
   physical sensations of, 52, 64–65
   public-speaking phobia, 164–67,
      171
   subway phobia, 212–13
pantyhose phobia, 236, 237
Parnate, 285
partners of phobic and obsessive-
      compulsive people, *see* sup-
      porting persons
Patty case study, 19–21
Paxil, 285, 286
Paxipam, 282
perfectionism, 161, 171–72, 175

performance anxiety, *see* public-speaking phobia
personal belief systems, 15, 41–44
phobias, 9
    cat phobia, 267–70
    common features of, 51–52, 234
    defining characteristics, 50
    development of a phobia, 63–66
    dust phobia, 34–35
    elevator phobia, 221–25
    erroneous premises of, 38
    as information processing problem, 27–28
    inner scenes, 25–27
    "label" perspective on, 22
    origins question, 55–56
    pantyhose phobia, 236, 237
    phobia-OCD overlap, 28–29
    prevalence of, 14
    smoke phobia, 134–35, 140
    street-crossing phobia, 214–17
    subway phobia, 212–14
    treatment for, *see* medication; therapy
    see also agoraphobia; bridge phobia; driving phobia; eating phobia; magic thinking; public-speaking phobia; snake phobia; social phobia
Phobia Society of America, 280
photographs used in therapy, 68, 108–9, 110, 113
poisoning, fear of, 133, 134, 136–37, 139, 140
polio, 32
possibility viewed as probability, 206, 237–38
powerlessness, sense of, 110
progress in therapy, 111, 234
propranolol, 284

Prozac, 285, 286
public-speaking phobia:
    causes of anxiety, 161
    control, sense of loss of, 163–64
    diary keeping, 170
    embarrassment concerns, 167–69, 170–71
    panic attacks, 164–67, 171
    perfectionism concerns, 161, 171–72, 175
    self-defeating assumptions, rules, and beliefs, 174–75
    speaking experience, 162–63
    tape recording used in therapy, 173–74
    therapy for, 162–75
    thoughts accompanying anxiety, 162

Rapoport, Judith L., 15
reality, 15, 42, 43
    questioning one's own reality, 44–45, 182–83
reality testing, 37
    agoraphobia, 69
    cleaning compulsion, 86–88
    collecting compulsion, 186–88, 256–58, 260
    driving phobia, 254–55
    eating phobia, 136, 140–42
    snake phobia, 207–9, 251–52
    street-crossing phobia, 215–17
    supporting persons and, 268–69, 275
    techniques for, 236
    writing down thoughts as essential to, 257
    see also diary keeping
reassurance, need for, 200–202, 209–10, 238

responsibility, exaggerated sense of, 47
  cleaning compulsion, 84, 85, 89, 91, 93–94
  eating phobia, 141
reward systems, 157
rituals and litanies, 36, 51, 52, 234
  anxiety-relief through, 48
  bathing compulsion, 151, 153
  cleaning compulsion, 94, 96
  collecting compulsion, 185
  as counter-magic strategy, 40–41
  cycle of OC behavior and, 185–86
  defining characteristics, 41
  gradual limitation of, 239–40
  snake phobia, 196–97, 203, 207–8

safety kits, 277
Sam case study, 196–210, 246–52
scheduling time to work on therapy program, 244–45
"secondary gain" philosophy, 30
secrets:
  agoraphobia and, 71–73
  cleaning compulsion, 92, 93, 96
selective serotonin reuptake inhibitors, 285–87
sensations, fear of, 65
Serax, 282
serotonin reuptake inhibitors, 285–87
setbacks in therapy, 242
smoke phobia, 134–35, 140
snake phobia, 126
  childhood experiences and, 199
  control, sense of loss of, 208
  Exposure Diary, 248–51

  hierarchy of fearful objects and situations, 206
  onset of, 202–3
  pictures and images of snakes, fear of, 203–5
  reality testing, 207–9, 251–52
  reassurance, need for, 200–202, 209–10
  rituals, 196–97, 203, 207–8
  social life and, 200, 209–10
  therapy for, 197–210, 246–52
  work life and, 199–200, 205, 209
social phobia:
  Lara's case, 217–21
  Mr. More's case, 180–81, 188–90, 192–93, 195, 260–63
  see also public-speaking phobia
"step on a crack and break your mother's back," 39–40
Stevie case study, 132–43
street-crossing phobia, 214–17
subway-cleaning compulsion, see cleaning compulsion
subway phobia, 212–14
superstition, 40, 41
supporting persons, 154–55, 231, 266–67
  Barbara and Mark case study, 267–70
  collaboration with magic thinker on in vivo program, 274–75
  commitment by, 277–79
  distraction techniques, 275–77
  education for, 271–73
  exposure tasks with magic thinker, 269–70
  family members as, 240–41
  helpful hints for, 278–79

ideal support person, 113
reality testing and, 268–69, 275
setting limitations, 277–78
task assignments and, 240
understanding of phobic/OC
    disorder, 124–27, 131
working relationship, establish-
    ment of, 270–71

tape recording used in therapy,
    173–74
task assignments, 240
    sample worksheet, 298
Temple University, 151
therapy:
    for agoraphobia, 66–81
    analytic therapy, 211
    anxiety, quantification of,
        243–44, 245–46
    for bathing compulsion, 147–60,
        252–53
    behavior, assessment of, 244
    for bridge phobia, 116–31
    cause-and-effect thinking and,
        236–37
    for cleaning compulsion, 82–91,
        95–97
    for collecting compulsion,
        181–95, 255–60
    commitment to the belief,
        assessment of, 246–47,
        251–52, 253
    couple therapy, 73–81
    cure issue, 56–57
    disregarding of advice by
        patient, 184
    for driving phobia, 103–13,
        253–55
    duration of, 56, 217
    for eating phobia, 132–43

for elevator phobia, 222–25
exposure and response preven-
    tion, 238–39
family involvement, 240–41
implosion therapy, 197
information about phobias and
    OCD, importance of,
    229–30
inpatient programs, 151
miracle cures, fallacy of, 233
objectives of treatment, 235–42
obsession with therapy tasks,
    avoidance of, 245
origins question, 55–56
photographs used in, 68, 108–9,
    110, 113
probabilities, assessment of,
    237–38
progress, concept of, 111, 234
for public-speaking phobia,
    162–75
reassurance, reducing need for,
    238
rituals, limitation of, 239–40
scheduling time to work on ther-
    apy program, 244–45
setbacks, dealing with, 242
short-term goals, focus on,
    231–32, 233–34, 243, 259
for snake phobia, 197–210,
    246–52
for social phobia, 217–21,
    260–63
staying with the program,
    231–32
for street-crossing phobia,
    214–17
for subway phobia, 212–14
successful therapy, elements of,
    225

therapy (*continued*)
  summary of techniques, 263–65
  tape recording used in, 173–74
  task assignments, 240, 298
  thought of impending disaster,
    identification of, 235,
    256–58, 259–61, 262, 301
  video taping used in, 159–60
  worksheets, self-help, 242–43,
    295–301
  see also cognitive/behavioral
    therapy; diary keeping; in
    vivo therapy; medication;
    reality testing
Thought/Consequence Chart, 235,
    236, 238
  collecting compulsion, 256–58,
    259–60
  sample worksheet, 301
  social phobia, 260–61, 262
thoughts:
  belief in power of, 45–46
  uncontrolled thoughts, 51
thoughts accompanying anxiety,
    35–36
  bridge phobia, 122–24, 129–30
  eating phobia, 136, 137
  identification of, 235, 256–58,
    259–61, 262, 301
  public-speaking phobia, 162
  subway phobia, 213

Tofranil, 284
tranquilizers, 61, 103, 116,
    165–66, 203, 281
Tranxene, 282
trauma, 43
Triavil, 284
tricyclic antidepressants, 284–85
two people, sense of being,
    110–11, 113
Tylenol poisonings, 140

uncertainty problem, 46, 51,
    182–83

Valium, 281, 282
video taping used in therapy,
    159–60
vulnerability, sense of, 60,
    64–65

washing compulsion, *see* bathing
    compulsion; hand-washing
    compulsion
White Plains Phobia Clinic, 22
worksheets, self-help, 242–43,
    295–301

Xanax, 282

Zane, Manuel, 22, 23, 25, 35
Zoloft, 285, 286